Searching ...

For Healing After Reunion

Carol Schaefer

Searching ...

ISBN 9781497394261

Cover design by Carol Schaefer

Searching …

For all who have crossed my path
over these many years …
your stories forever fine gold threads
woven within my healing journey.

.

Searching …

BOOKS BY CAROL SCHAEFER

*The Other Mother: A Woman's Love for the
Child She Gave Up for Adoption*

An Ancient Tear

*Grandmothers Counsel the World:
Women Elders Offer Their Vision for Our Planet*

Mary Queen of Scots

John's Book of Everyday Transformation

Searching ...

*"Somewhere in Virginia, at this moment,
a lonely young woman is facing
the heartache, the soul-searching,
the disgrace of being an unwed mother."*

Richmond Times-Dispatch
(May 6, 1963)

Searching …

Chapter One

It was strange when the memories began returning - shattered fragments of myself long forgotten, yet now so essential. How had I lived without them? Who had I become instead?

For months, I had been curled up practically in a fetal position, often wrapped in a comforter, healing candles lit even during the day, as tears, frozen for so long began to flow, writing by hand from a need to own the truth of my story.

"You should write a book!"

The table lamp had cast a cozy glow that enveloped the three of us: me, my son Jack, whom I had met for the first time three days before, and his adoptive mother, Rosemary. We were marveling at all the strange synchronicities in our lives when Jack made the suggestion.

Immediately, all the fears and taboos that prevented my keeping my firstborn nineteen years before flooded in. How would my mother handle such a public revelation of my secret child? How could I reveal to those closest to me my deepest feelings about all I had been through, when I had protected everyone from them for so long? What would they think of me? How could my son ever forgive me? Would he? How could I ever forgive myself? And, as it would turn out, every emotional aspect of all that I had lived through giving him up would prove to play out and have to be confronted in the writing and the extraordinary aftermath, and as I attempted to heal and integrate Jack and his other family with my own.

When I was sequestered in Seton House, a Catholic home for unwed mothers in Richmond, Virginia, now a pariah, the message from society was clear: from the sin of a broken condom I had become the wrong mother for my own child. Like from some dark fairy tale, I had to surrender my firstborn son to strangers, so that the neighbors would never find out about my unwed pregnancy and so I could return to a "normal" life, finish college, marry and have children of *my own* some day. "Go on with your life and pretend "it" never happened. This is God's Will," was the litany of advice. After returning home, having left my baby behind to an unknown fate, no one ever spoke about it again. The year was 1966.

As I looked into my son's eyes again nineteen years later, I was suddenly nineteen again, isolated from friends and family in my hospital bed and holding him as he opened his eyes for the first time. I was unprepared for their power. It was as if I had known his soul for eons. Yet, as I unwrapped his hospital blanket and took in the heady fragrance of a newborn, I felt like a criminal and feared the nurses or nuns would rush in and accuse me of contaminating my own son. Even now, sitting with him and his adoptive mother, the woman who had been there for him when I was too powerless to be, I wondered if I had a right to even be there. Still, I knew he was far too beautiful a person to ever be considered a secret. Somehow, I had to release us both from our exile as mother and child. And, what about all the other banished mothers? If I couldn't write the book for myself, I would do it for them.

Facing my fears about writing a book about my traumatic past turned the clock back and gave me a second chance to confront all the obstacles that were still obviously a part of me - a mirror into my wounded soul – and do things differently. This time I would keep the "baby," I would write the book. No way could I have known then what my sudden passion was about to set into motion, and that I was about to embark on an extraordinary creative and healing journey. The year was 1985.

To free up enough money to have time to write, I decided to sell my home and buy another. My writing experience was as a journalist and an advertising copywriter. Never had I imagined I could write a book. But, for some as yet unknown reason, the stakes seemed too high not to at least try.

In the aftermath of the trauma of giving up a child, memory shuts down to protect the soul from pain. During the search for my son, I learned millions of women and their children shared our story. Hearing the stories of the women in my support group was helping me remember my own. We were all tiptoeing out of the woods asking each other, incredulous, "Did that happen to you, too?" As I began to think about how to write the book, I found I didn't want to just tell my story, I wanted my book to validate women too isolated to find support, be one they could give to a loved one to help them understand what we were all just beginning to comprehend ourselves.

We had been sent away to the over 600 homes for unwed mothers that existed in the United States at the time. Or we were sequestered with distant friends, relatives or strangers. If we did stay at home, we were hidden in closets when guests came and ducked below the car window on the way to the doctor's office so as not to be seen by the neighbors. We were given over to the care of doctors, social workers and nuns who, we were to learn, saw us as sexual deviants in need of reform, strangers who often treated us in a punishing manner. If we had stayed in our communities and kept our babies, we would have been expelled from school, few of us would have been hired, and many families would not have welcomed us back if we brought our children home. We submitted to these atrocities to protect our families from the shame of our unwed motherhood and to protect our children from the stigma of being born illegitimate. Our only redemption was to surrender our children.

Twenty years later, the world had changed so much. Would anyone even be interested in our story? Was selling my home in order to write the book worth the risk?

I'd bought the house after Ron and I divorced and I became a single mother rearing two sons, Brett and Kip – living out the taboo that had caused me to lose my firstborn. Built in 1905, the year before the Great San Francisco Earthquake, the house was beautiful and charming, and I loved it. How was I going to let it go? I was only now learning to let go of things after finding Jack again, a typical reaction of mothers who'd lost their children to adoption.

I chose my next-door neighbor, Britt, to be my real estate agent because it felt like destiny had had a hand in our meeting. The day after she and her husband had moved in next door, I was outside on the patio steps calling out to Brett and Kip for the third time to come in for lunch.

"Breeeeeeeett! Kiiiiip! Hurry up!"

Suddenly, from next door I heard a perfect imitation of my voice ringing out with all its impatience. Britt's mynah bird had mimicked my tone perfectly, revealing how awful I sounded. When I laughed at how silly I sounded, the bird mimicked my laugh. By then, I was in tears laughing so hard, the bird laughing along with me, I didn't care how long the boys took coming home. I vowed never to speak like that again.

A few days later Britt and I met. When she told me she was from Shaker Heights, Ohio, I told her that my father had moved there after my parents divorced and had a gift shop in town. As it turned out, Britt had become good friends with my father and would often stop by his shop to talk with him during her lunch breaks. It took us both a little time to get over such an incredible coincidence.

As wonderful as the house was, it had a difficult time selling. Several deals fell through. As I tried to peer into my future, fear kept me from seeing anything but the worst. The house would never sell, and I wouldn't be free to write the book. So, I called my friend and psychic John Norman, whom I had first met when searching for Jack. John's revelations of Jack's life, when I hadn't even known my son's name, had astonished me with their accuracy and changed my life. The fact that he could only get the information by "reading" me had to mean that on some level I already knew where Jack was and how his life had been, which was a great comfort and an even greater mystery. So now I had a huge stack of books on metaphysics and spirituality, trying to figure everything out. Nothing I had read yet, however, prepared me for what John was about to tell me.

I was sitting on the edge of my bed, looking out through the upstairs bay window at the gorgeous fuchsia bougainvillea clinging to the pink slate wall of the back patio as I dialed John's number. John patiently listened as I told him about my plight. Then I asked him what he thought of the two couples that had recently expressed interest in the house. One couple seemed to be ideal buyers, but the other couple to me felt like the right ones, even though the deal might be more complicated with them. What did he think?

"Well, I believe you're right about that couple," he chuckled. "But it's not really the couple who's choosing the house, it's their baby. Do they have a child?"

"No." I was beginning to think I'd made a mistake asking John.

"Is she pregnant?"

"No. They aren't even married, yet, though they plan to be in a few months." How was I going to get off the phone?

"Well, if she's not pregnant now, she soon will be. That's the couple that will buy the house. It's not the house, it's your connection with the three of them that he's making."

I found myself sitting on the edge of the bed long after I'd hung up the phone, trying to take in what John had just revealed. How could any child, let alone one that hadn't yet been conceived, choose the house where they wanted to live? That was just impossible to believe. But, as I contemplated the possibility, I felt I was in some altered state that made the idea easier to accept.

When Britt called the next day to tell me that the couple wanted to come by to make an offer, I told her John's story.

"Tell Cindy. She'll love it!"

"No way," I said. That seemed like a horribly manipulative way to sell a house. I couldn't believe she was even suggesting it.

Two days later I was sitting with Britt, Cindy and Jim around our antique parson's dining room table, sunshine flooding through the French windows lining two of the walls. We were all laughing and enjoying each other's company as if we were old friends. At one point, Britt took me aside and suggested I tell Cindy what John had said. I told her no way, but she insisted. So, finally I asked Cindy to come upstairs with me, that I wanted to show her something. I felt that if I told the story in front of Jim I'd blow the whole deal.

Cindy and I sat facing each other on the pillows on the ledge of the bay window in my bedroom while I told her all that John had "seen."

"I'm not at all surprised," Cindy remarked, after I told her everything. "When I was eighteen, a psychic told me I would have one son, and he would be quite special. So, I'm not surprised he's choosing the house."

I found myself afraid of the whole idea, yet fascinated at the same time.

Three weeks went by, and I hadn't heard anything from them. Another deal had fallen through I was certain. Then one morning Cindy called.

"Carol, I'm so sorry I've taken so long to get back to you. I haven't been feeling well, and I began to sense my intuition was telling me not to buy the house."

My heart sank to the pit of my stomach.

"But I went to the doctor and he told me I'm pregnant!"

"Congratulations!" I squeaked out.

"John was right. But now how am I going to fit into my wedding dress?" she laughed. "By the way, Jim and I want you to come to the wedding."

Another month went by and the required inspections weren't taking place. I was beginning to feel uneasy and told myself writing the book was not meant to be. So, I created an advertising portfolio, hoping to get a copywriter job. But my years of not working were proving to be a huge obstacle. One day, I met with a friend from the tennis club who headed the largest agency in San Francisco and begged him to let me work for free so that I could prove myself. His refusal was a shock. What was I going to do?

Then Cindy called with devastating news. She'd suffered a miscarriage, and, on top of that, Jim's investment portfolio had lost a lot of money. How could such a thing happen when John had been so certain? I felt foolish believing in all that otherworldly stuff. But, despite everything and after much soul searching, Cindy said they were determined to buy the house anyway. They wanted to wait to move in until after the wedding. That was fine with me.

The thought of moving from a house I loved so much was now wrenching. How could I ever find another one I loved as much? One Sunday, with my friend Yvonne, I set off to look at open houses I'd selected from the newspaper. On the way to one, we passed by an open house sign I hadn't listed. The house for sale wasn't visible, and as I gazed down the road I thought no way. An office building was across the street and an apartment building and a mish mash of eclectic but rundown looking houses faced the Corte Madera Creek on the other side of the road. Not the sort of neighborhood I was used to. But Yvonne insisted we check it out, and I remembered how lately I had been involuntarily looking down that street every time I passed by it. So I made a last minute turn onto Lucky Drive.

Like the others, the house faced the Corte Madera Creek, a waterway that connected directly to the San Francisco Bay. But, unlike the others, it was brand new and very modern and interesting looking. As we got out of the car, I found myself feeling excited, though the lack of any landscaping reminded me of all the homes we had moved to when I was a child of the fifties, where all trees and anything alive had been leveled to make houses for the booming post war generation of families.

The view when we walked in took my breath away. A short hall opened up to one big room with a cathedral ceiling two stories high and windows all around that revealed an expansive view of the creek and sky. I looked up at the peak of the ceiling and thought I saw a golden angel and felt a peace and certainty come over me.

From the deck was a gorgeous view of Mt. Tamalpais, the beloved and many, including the Dalai Lama, believed sacred mountain of Marin County. Snowy egrets, geese and ducks mucked along the low tide, looking for lunch. We followed the builder up the stairs to the master bedroom, with its own deck and windows high enough to lie down on a bed and look up at the stars.

On the other side of the large master bathroom was a small room with an angular ceiling that created the illusion of a Parisian garret. It was meant to be a walk-in closet.

"So, you would like to use this as a sewing room instead?" the builder had responded when I told him the room was too cool to be a closet.

I looked at him like he had two heads. "Sewing room? No, this is where I would be writing my book."

I'd fallen in love with the house. Outside in the car, I knew I wasn't risking my sanity when I told Yvonne about the angel, since we both were open to such ideas, though I'd never had that experience before. Still, I was shocked when she said she'd seen the angel, too.

The move had been stressful and exciting at the same time. The new house was the opposite in every way from the last one and felt like a necessary new beginning. Even so, I felt guilty uprooting Brett and Kip, though they weren't complaining, and promised we would get a boat. I don't know what I was thinking.

As soon as we moved in, I had the deck expanded, to take advantage of the great view, and a pier built out to the creek. One day, I was watching a Chinese man, a Buddhist monk, sink the supports for the new pier into the mud the old fashioned way, by jumping up and down on a cross bar, and felt transported back to some ancient time. Our dog, Buffy, lay in the mud, oblivious to the ducks, watching a tennis ball floating in front of her nose.

Long walks in the redwoods and eucalyptus trees of my former neighborhood had seen me through my search for Jack. Their magnificence had absorbed the pain and frustration of having to feel like I was committing a crime by circumventing the laws that forbade my knowing him. Now I knew, as I stood out on the deck of my new home, that it would be the sky and the water that would nurture me as I wrote the book.

As I prepared to write, I decided I needed to make my writing space the most beautiful room in the house, so it would be a place where I couldn't wait to be, a sanctuary and not a desk shared with piles of bills, unread mail and misplaced to do lists. I filled it with crystals, candles and flowers, and the comforter.

It took me a little while to be disciplined to write, especially since each day's writing I knew would throw me back into emotional turmoil. But I approached it as a job and sat down to write every morning at ten. In order to lure myself back the next day, I always stopped at a point in the story that I couldn't wait to write about the following morning. The one difficult thing was turning off my mind when I finished the day's writing. In the beginning, I found that Brett and Kip were asking me a question two and three times when they got home from school before what they'd said registered. So, I would walk out to the end of the pier or go for a hike to let that day's writing go before they came home, and that worked.

Instead of chronicling the story, I allowed my deepest feelings to dictate what I wrote about. Much like watching a black and white photographic image emerge in the developing tray, when the image is faint at first and then the blacks appear stronger and the grey tones begin to fill in, memories like pictures began to form from the feelings. Sometimes I would find myself staring at the words written by my own hand, hardly believing what I had lived through. I was beginning to feel like a character in a Charles Dickens novel.

In the beginning, I doubted everything I was writing about. But then magic happened, as if I was cosmically linked with my future readers and somehow they were writing with me, helping me to heal, too. Whenever I began to question my memory (the nuns weren't really that bad!), the phone rang within minutes. On the line was a woman making the very point I had doubted. This happened countless times.

I had come to understand by working with my therapist, Toni, that when we commit to search and reunion we commit to transformation, that we are not simply in the process of searching for and reuniting with a lost child or family, we are also searching within ourselves and reuniting with a long denied part of our identities. The paradox is that we are shattered and we are also whole; we need to find each other but the answers to our healing are all within. Taking this inner journey will create a richer, more fulfilling life, whether or not the search and reunion is successful, was the promise. At that point, I could only hope that was true.

Chapter Two

Unexpectedly, the first thing to heal, as I began writing, was my relationship with my mother. For years, a subliminal anger toward her ran like a hidden stream and caused a permanent strain in our relationship that I could not seem to change. I'd find that searching for a Mother's Day card always triggered an unexplainable feeling of rage toward her, as sweet as she really was. The source of my anger had been deeply buried.

The first time I made the connection was when we talked after she read my letter informing her I was searching for my child. Where I had been comfortable telling my Dad over the phone, my fear of my mother's reaction, that maybe she would be furious and tell me not to, maybe not even speak to me after, made me believe writing a letter was preferable to hearing her rejection. But I was about to realize just how much the past colors our perceptions of the present.

As soon as she read the letter, Mom called, thrilled that I was searching for my son. In fact, she said, she had thought strongly about searching for him herself three years before. I was shocked.

"Didn't you ever notice the little red stocking ornament hanging on the tree every year, the one you brought back from the home?" she asked, surprised. "I hung it on the tree in honor of my first grandchild. I always hoped you'd notice and talk about it, but you never did. Would you like me to send it to you?"

No, I told her. I wasn't ready for that. I didn't even remember the ornament and the thought of having something from the home for unwed mothers unnerved me. She might as well have been talking about a bomb. As I hung up the phone from our conversation, I felt a fury like I'd never experienced. I had tried many times after returning from the home for unwed mothers to talk about all that had happened, but she had refused. Little did I know at the time the huge role that little ornament would play in the future.

My mother's mother had died when my mother was five. Soon after her death, my mother was diagnosed with St.Vitas Dance, a diagnosis back then that covered any sort of nervous disorder. She and her younger sister had been passed around to relatives and then into the care of a woman who had been a family friend, whom he later married. When my Grandfather married my mother's mother, a Catholic, his wealthy Protestant family had disowned him. On her deathbed, my Grandmother had requested that he continue to bring their daughters up in the Catholic faith, which he did, and throughout her life my mother practiced her religion without questioning any of the teachings.

So, she had been quite vulnerable as we sat before Sister Dominic, the stern social worker who seemed to tower over us even from her chair, as she declared we were doing the right thing by giving the baby up for adoption. "In fact, it is God's will," she proclaimed.

Faced with the prospect of her daughter's life being derailed down a path so foreign to her middle class values, what choice did my mother have but to defer to the authoritative advice of her priest and this nun? How would she have known, as I had later learned, that priests and nuns had often been trained to respond to a confession of an unwed pregnancy with adoption as the only

19

option suggested. After all, the church only wanted good Catholic families as part of their flock. Never would Mom have dreamed of encountering the woman I'd recently spoken with at a conference, who told me of meeting with her parish priest to get help for the pain and grief of losing her baby, and instead being raped by him just days after giving birth. She hadn't told a soul for years after, her shame was so great.

We all seemed to have the same mother – one unable to imagine what was being asked of their daughters, despite being mothers themselves. Fearful, conforming, somewhere along the way stripped of their own authentic power, they were unable to discuss even the most rudimentary feelings, except perhaps their anger.

My mother had been especially controlling, always dictating what I wore and how my hair should look, to conform with the rest of the world, as she knew it. Six weeks of grounding was punishment for talking back. If she felt she couldn't own her own life, how could she allow me to have mine? How would I know to?

My mother would spend half the time at Mass watching all the babies. Why didn't she have a change of heart, as she wrote to me every day while I was in the home? She was losing her first grandchild. Not until we talked, after I told her I was searching, did she reveal that Catholic Social Services had told her that once I entered the home there would be no choice but to give up my baby. Had the nuns explained away such a blatantly unlawful declaration as a "necessary lie"?

I had never been told that such an insidious bargain had been made. All the time in the home, I had hoped to find a way to keep my baby, not knowing such a possibility would never have been permitted.

Sitting on the small white couch in my writing room, knees tucked up and notebook on my lap, I stared for the longest time out the window up at the passing puffs of clouds in the pale blue sky, as the realization took hold that my mother had been a victim, too. And I began to forgive her.

A few days later, our birth mothers' support group met, and I was able to offer my newfound insight about the role her mother plays to an unwed pregnant woman. In those days, we squeamishly called ourselves birth mothers, for lack of a better term - other than mother. By then, I was facilitating the group, a part of a Bay Area wide adoption organization called P.A.C.E.R (the Post Adoption Center for Education and Research).

The tiny musty library of Mission San Rafael, where we met, was unnerving for many of us, with books about the lives of the saints surrounding us as we sat around the metal table in the middle of the room. But the room was free and did evoke memories of brainwashing by stern nuns and the ensuing guilt that we could finally laugh at and let go of.

A new person to our group, Miranda, in her late twenties and eight months pregnant, was in great distress. As she described how just the other day she'd waded out into the ocean with the hope of killing her baby, we all listened in shock, way over our heads about how to respond. She would have none of our comforting remarks that, compared to her rage, sounded shallow and gratuitous. The boyfriend had abandoned her and she would never have the life she hoped for, if she had to take care of a baby as a single mother. If only this baby would die!

Something struck me about the vehemence of her stance. Despite all appearances, my instincts told me she actually loved this baby and I took a big chance.

"How did your mother like being a mother?" I asked, terrified of upsetting her more but trusting my gut. At that point, she clearly could have been considered psychotic.

"She hated being a mother," Miranda replied. "She'd always wanted to be an opera singer and blamed us kids for killing her dream."

There it was. "Do you think it's possible you've taken on your mother's attitudes as your own?" I asked.

We were all tense as we awaited Miranda's reply. She didn't say anything for a long time, but her face began to relax and light came into her eyes. "I never thought of it that way before. Those *are* my mother's thoughts, not mine."

Though Miranda had taken up the whole meeting and none of the other mothers had a chance to speak, we all were helped as we offered Miranda the support that had never been given to us.

Out of the blue, Jack called, asking if it would be all right if he and his girlfriend, Anna, could come up for the weekend. I was thrilled. Jack had met Anna a month after we had our reunion. I could see from the moment they walked in that she was good for him – outgoing, fun, honest and direct. Already I had observed that Jack was a lot like me in the way we would make certain everyone was happy at the expense of being our real selves. But Anna felt free to ask questions that neither Jack nor I had the nerve to, but still wanted answers for.

Even though we were naturally people pleasers, I understood that the proverbial "walking on eggshells" was something real that we were both dealing with as well – afraid to be real with each other for fear of losing each other again. But I soon came to understand that there was another unconscious agenda going on, that we were also tiptoeing around ourselves, hoping that by keeping everything nice we wouldn't have to face the real trauma we'd been through.

During the early stages of developing a relationship after reunion, everything feels tenuous, including our selves. The more we look to the developing relationship to make us feel better so that we can avoid our own issues, the more we risk pushing the other away. No one can fix what is only ours to fix. Both mother and child had become unreal to themselves, from the secrecy and lies, and so how could we be real to each other? Intellectually I knew all this, but still had to live it out.

Anna sat down next to Jack on the couch. As I stood talking with them, I stared at the space next to Jack, hesitant to sit by him. He was obviously happy to be with us, but his muscle spasms and eye twitch betrayed him, revealing his underlying stress.

In our first conversation, Rosemary explained that Jack developed muscle twitches during a cross-country drive when he was six. Her first husband, whom Jack was named after, had died in Viet Nam when Jack was twenty-two months old. After his death, she had been afraid that I would find out and reclaim Jack, now that she didn't have a husband and the adoption had yet to be finalized. He was all she had to live for then and was terrified of losing him. She didn't know that I would be the last person the agency would call under any circumstances.

She'd returned home to live with her parents in Queens, New York, and eventually met her second husband. Soon after she moved back to Queens, I also moved to New York City, one of the coincidences we'd discovered. After they married, they moved to California, which was the reason for their cross-country trip.

Rosemary's second husband didn't have any children, she'd explained, and didn't understand Jack's need to have frequent stops along the way to release his pent up energy. By the time they reached Northern California, they had to take Jack to the emergency room his muscles were twitching so badly. I had to wonder, too, if the sudden loss of his cousins and Grandmother wasn't also the cause, compounding the loss of his original family. It had been so difficult hearing how my son had been in such distress, but the fact that I had married and moved to San Francisco within two months of their arrival and that we'd lived only forty minutes away from each other overshadowed the reason for the emergency room visit, until seeing him suffer now.

Sometimes I just had to override my strange emotional reactions, instead of giving them any weight, and so I took a deep breath and sat down next to my son. The couch was small, so we sat right up next to each other, and I could feel his body relax as we talked, until finally all the muscle twitching subsided. Not only did they not return during the visit, Jack said later he never suffered from them so severely again.

The writing had been going well, memories were flooding in. So, when I'd sat for three days, purple felt-tipped pen poised and ready and nothing came to me, I panicked. Was this writer's block or something else? I'd reached the part in my story where I was in labor at the home, trying to convince the nun that I was indeed about to deliver, though the pains were all in my lower back and my belly a powder puff. I was remembering my dismay at being told that I would be taken to the hospital in an ambulance and that no one in the home was going with me. From the scanty medical records I'd obtained, I'd learned the name of the ambulance company – Lakeside Volunteer Rescue Squad. I remembered the icy nighttime January air that hit me when the doors to the home opened and I was put into the ambulance. But that's when all became blank.

Finally, desperate, I called my friend Rob, with whom I'd already done some hypnotherapy to unblock memories. The first time we met, Rob explained that a part of my mind was going to try to control what I was seeing by negating everything, but that I just had to put that part aside and let it observe what was unfolding. He was right. I was resistant to opening up. But then, to my amazement, I popped into a past life that I would never have dreamed of but that made complete sense. The last time we'd met for a session was months before, when he guided me to discover my essence. Again I was resistant. What was he talking about? But then I saw my spirit and knew it to be true. "How would you describe it," he'd asked. "Playful and childlike," I'd answered, still amazed. "Good," he'd said.

Now sitting before him I was far from being playful and childlike. I was miserable. His efforts at getting me into trance were not working, despite the fact that I knew to feel safe with him and the process. I'd experienced how the trance state actually makes the mind sharper and able to recall everything, so no longer feared it. Why now?

Then, suddenly I was inside the ambulance and in the middle of a contraction, being strapped down by two men who were strangers. One man then hopped into the driver's seat and we took off speeding. The other, who sat by my side, looked down at me kindly, the first kind expression I'd seen in a long time, and then reached up and turned on the siren. After months of secrecy, of my mother running to be the first at the mailbox to intercept my letters, the lies that had been told to everyone, this man was announcing my situation to the world. I saw myself pleading with him to turn the siren off. "Sit back and enjoy the ride," he'd joked, to my horror.

"What a perfect metaphor for writer's block," Rob remarked. "There you were so full of life, about to bring life into this world - as creative as it gets - and you were being strapped down. On top of that, you were sent to have your baby alone, as punishment for the life you created and were about to give birth to."

In self-protection, I closed my eyes and shut down emotionally to avoid completely taking in the truth of his words. My writing never became blocked again.

The idea of being creative always swam around me but never took hold until I found my son.

One of my first vivid childhood memories was of sitting at a long wooden table with all the other children in my kindergarten class, our small fingers clutching tightly to fat crayons, trying to draw a house, which was our assignment. When I finally looked up from my efforts, I was humiliated. Everyone had drawn practically the same house – a peaked roof, one window, a door. Some had added a tree, and some the sun in the upper right corner of the paper. I looked down at my paper where I had drawn one primitive orange house in the center and an orange house in each of the corners. How could I have done something so different from the others? When the teacher hung all our artwork up on the wall, I was mortified and didn't want to go to school until I was sure the pictures had all been taken down.

Still, art was always my favorite subject in school, but so was recess and I equated the two in my mind, not knowing to value such an inner urge.

Against my wishes, I had to go to an all girls' Catholic school, St. Joseph's Academy, in ninth grade. We were living in Cleveland, Ohio at the time. Lights were turned off between classes, and we were required to pray as we walked down the dark halls to our next class, all dressed in the same ugly navy plaid uniform we would hike above our knees as soon as we got out of school. The rules were rigid, but I found I could not get myself to comply with one that required us to carry our school bag of books down by our side. Instead, I would fling it over my shoulder and was constantly reprimanded, to the point that one day my mother was called into the principle's office about it. With something so simple considered a crime, what hope did I have if I ever broke a far more serious rule?

Part of the curriculum was taking an art class, a whole hour devoted to art, which I was excited about. But the class might as well have been a math class, the way the teacher made us draw endless color wheels and never allowed us to freely express our

26

selves. Only years later, when I read about the master Zen artists, some of whom were required to study a tree for ten years before putting pen to paper, did I appreciate the patience she was teaching.

Out of the blue that year, my Dad was transferred and we moved in April to Greensboro, North Carolina. My prayers walking through those darkened halls had been answered! I was going to attend a coed public school. And, maybe I would attend a more interesting art class.

But the first day of school, which was a shock by itself after being so cloistered, I found myself disappointed again, when it was clear that the art teacher only rewarded the students drawing from scale. Still, I didn't understand what it was I wanted to do or even was looking for, and so I let go of pursuing art. The next time I gave it a try was when I went to college. But walking through the Art Department I didn't see any art that I liked and decided to try Drama instead.

Freshman year I was in a play and believed I'd found my calling. But that spring I became pregnant and, when I returned to school after being in the home and surrendering my baby, I felt I had caused enough heartache for my parents. I couldn't tell them I wanted to pursue the theater. My decision had come from an assumption, not from any conversations I'd ever had with them. My assumption was founded on the way the culture viewed actors as people way out of the mainstream, and I had already violated the rules once by becoming an unwed mother. In my mind, I had to find my way back into society, instead of being a perpetual pariah.

During a trip home just before graduation, my sister Janice discovered a beautiful colored pencil drawing of a geisha on yellowed faded paper, fragile with age. When we asked her where it came from, to our amazement Mom said she'd drawn it when she was in high school. But it's so good, we exclaimed, why didn't

27

she do more drawings? Always a private person, Mom hesitated then revealed that she had wanted to go to art school after high school, but that her father had said it was impossible, that there was only enough money to further the education of one of the children, and it had to be her only brother, my uncle Jack, because he would have to be the breadwinner for a family some day. Brokenhearted, my mother studied to be a secretary instead.

Over the years, after discovering the geisha, I would take the drawing out and stare at it, wondering who my mother would have become instead, had she pursued her goal.

After graduation, I landed a job as a copywriter in advertising and took to it like a duck to water. Being around so many creative people for the first time made me feel like I'd finally come home. My first success happened right away, when I came up with the line "Makes a girl feel pretty" for Skinny Dip Cologne. How could I have imagined, at the time, that exactly thirty years later I would walk into a bookstore and discover a memoir, *Waiting to Forget: A Motherhood Lost and Found* by Margaret Moorman, that analyzed, after she'd read *The Other Mother,* the irony of my writing that line after losing my son for adoption. Moorman was right, but at the time I didn't have a clue about how completely cut off from myself I was. Being analyzed so accurately by a stranger in a book as a result of her reading my book felt bizarre.

After two years in advertising, I gave up a promising career to marry and move to San Francisco. Over the years, as Brett and Kip were going through school, I would be the one called on to do the decorations or paint scenery for a play. Others saw in me what I never could validate for myself. But my love of photography began to call out to me too strongly to ignore.

Still, it was not until that first week when I was getting to know Jack that I had no choice but to take the creative side of my self seriously. During our second day together at their house, Rosemary insisted with great pride that Jack show me his paintings, and I was amazed at his talent. He could duplicate any of the masters. I realized right then that I had not only found my son but also a disowned part of myself. If I had a son with such talent, maybe I really did, too.

Over the years afterward, I evolved a theory that seems true, that the surrendered child might represent something essential that either the mother or the entire birth family had rejected about themselves and that reunion could be of even greater importance with such an opportunity to heal what had not before been acknowledged. Many adoptees I offered this idea to felt in their bones this was true.

But, as I looked at Jack's paintings that day, I saw that he had not done anything that was original. Instinctively, I felt that through discovering what was inside him to paint he would be able to discover who he was separate from his adoptive family *and* his family of origin. So, I suggested that someday he sit in front of a blank canvas to see what it was he wanted to paint. However, when making that proposal to him, I realized I was clueless myself about what I would do with a blank canvas before me.

My therapist, Toni, was Jungian. When I told her about my resistance to owning my creative side, she suggested I have a few sessions with a woman who was a Jungian art therapist, that this might be what Carl Jung called an ancestral task, something that needs to be healed that has been carried through a family for generations. In fact, Jung believed, like many Native American tribes also do, that when a family member heals the healing reverberates back through generations and into future generations as well. With such high stakes, I figured I might as well give it a try.

As I drove into an industrial area beyond the Bay Bridge on the way to my first art therapy class, afraid of getting lost in the unfamiliar territory, I chided myself the entire way for being too self-absorbed. With all the construction equipment everywhere, I was feeling less than inspired. By the time I found the address and pulled up to one of the many metal buildings, I was ready to turn back home. But inside Sylvia's studio, spacious and full of sunlight, the ugliness of the surrounding area melted away.

Four others were there for the therapy as it turned out, which would take five sessions. We were to paint from the opposite hand from which we wrote and were given only five minutes to finish each painting. In other words, we were not meant to ponder. This was going to get us into our unconscious minds. Okay, except that I'd already decided, in the spirit of therapy, to reproduce the painting that had mortified me in kindergarten.

When time was up, I looked at my orange houses and thought they had an oriental feel to them. We took turns discussing our process and, when it was my turn, I gave the history of the painting.

"Interesting," Sylvia commented. "You may have been tapping into an archetype. In ancient times, it was believed that four guardian spirits stood at the four corners of the earth. The guardians took different forms in different religions. It was believed fitting a divine prototype to divide a city or country in four corners with a temple, plaza or the ruler's domain in the center. For instance, ancient Ireland was the Island of the Four Kings with the 'high king' ruling from Tara at the center."

Oh, my. I hadn't expected that.

With my kindergarten painting dealt with, I finally faced an empty canvas in our next session. Paintbrush poised and ready in my left hand, I waited for Sylvia to start the five-minute clock, my mind as blank as the paper before me. What emerged had me puzzled. A black shape that resembled a Madonna was leaning over a lake. After all my Jungian therapy, I decided that must be me, and the lake was my emotions, as water symbolizes emotions, revealing how I felt about myself – all black.

But Sylvia, understanding how archetypes work in the unconscious, had a different idea. "Have you ever heard of the Black Madonna?" she asked. "Just the other day, I read about her, but I don't know too much. I suggest you do a little research."

When I next met with Toni, I asked her if she'd ever heard of the Black Madonna. Only recently, she'd said, and that was because her friend, China Galland, was writing a book on the subject. The coincidence had to have some meaning.

Even as a young girl, I would look at statues of the Virgin Mary and find it difficult to relate to her absolute purity. Yet this was the woman I was to strive to become. Mary Magdalene was far more interesting to me, far more real, but I kept that to myself. So it was with great satisfaction that my research about the Black Madonna revealed that many scholars believed there was a direct link between Mary Magdalene and the Black Madonna. Though the information was scanty, from the Church's attempts to suppress the worship around her and the mysteries of the divine feminine, statues and images of the Black Madonna survived only in pockets around the world. Her lineage some felt went back to Isis of Egypt and was kept alive by the medieval Knights Templar, but then was driven underground. She was the missing power in the Divine Feminine that the Virgin Mary had been stripped of. She was earthy, sensual, dark, mysterious – real.

My research led me to facets of history I'd never been exposed to, that put the experience of having to surrender a child to adoption in a much greater context. I learned that, beginning many thousands of years ago, our ancestors worshipped a divine and supremely powerful Mother Goddess, who was honored as Mother and Creation at once, the womb for all that lives. From Her all becoming arose.

In those matriarchal times, women bore the power because, like the Mother Goddess, they also brought forth and sustained life. A year had thirteen months based on a lunar calendar, because women's cycles were in synch with the moon and the creative powers of nature. The world was at peace. Then, beginning around 5,000 B.C., all changed as the patriarchal culture began to take over the inherent balance of male and female energies, co-opting and distorting the ancient teachings in order to gain power.

The power of the Mother Goddess could only be known from silence, but from that silence all true acts of creation arose: poetry and music, love, sex and giving birth. In this context, taking an infant from its mother was the same as taking her power, which was how most of us who'd had a child taken away described the experience. Ancient women's temples had become homes for unwed mothers. Hopefully, that would be as far as the pendulum would swing.

As wonderful as it was to have Jack back in our lives, there was so much to reconcile and we were still in the tentative stages of getting to know each other, which on some level felt schizophrenic. He wasn't a stranger I was coming to know, he was my son and I felt the bond strongly and felt I knew him. I could see many things about him that reminded me of my family. At the same time, having grown up in a different family, he was somewhat of a stranger, having acquired some of their attributes. Since he had never known anyone from his original family, I wondered if he even sensed a familial bond. After all, his adoptive family was all he'd ever known. Still, the feelings of a mother knowing her child had to be continually squashed in order not to negate his truth, that he'd had another life, and to be able to stay in it. I could control my behavior but not my hurting heart.

Holidays in particular were difficult. I had to tell myself over and over that he couldn't be with us, feelings I kept to myself since I didn't want to alarm him or his adoptive family. We had had that one Christmas together in the home, just before his birth, where he had been the only family I had with me that year.

So I was thrilled when Jack called to see if he and Anna could come for a visit just before Christmas the second year after our reunion. They would be there during the Winter Solstice. So maybe that could be our special time during the holidays, I told myself.

Brett and Kip were excited he was coming. When they first learned about their older brother, they'd hoped he would come to their games, help them with their homework, be their brother. On the other hand, I'd learned that the two younger brothers that Jack had been brought up with, that Rosemary had given birth to, were terribly afraid we would take their brother back. Neither Mark nor David remembered being told that Jack was adopted, so they were shocked when we showed up.

As I showed Jack and Anna all the ornaments on our tree, some from the mobiles that used to hang over Brett and Kip's crib, snapshots of our Christmas in the home kept popping in my head. Would the intrusive memories ever go away?

Then Jack handed me my Christmas gift. Paper flew as I eagerly unwrapped it - a painting of him and Anna. With just a few lines, he had captured the essence of each of them perfectly.

"I took your advice about seeing what I would do with a blank canvas," he said, smiling. "I want you to have my first attempt."

He couldn't have given me a better gift.

Chapter Three

The sight of the beautiful old pink stucco spire of Mission San Rafael in the distance, home of our dreary little library, was comforting as I turned my white Toyota Celica onto the off ramp to Rob's office, Jack and Anna in the car with me. Without realizing it, I'd become an adoption missionary, eager to help Jack correct any problems my giving him up would have caused – and the sooner the better.

In the same vein as asking Jack to discover what it was that he would paint, I wanted to bring him to Rob to see what his unconscious would uncover. Of all the natural problems I'd learned many adoptees face, being torn between both families and unable to be or even know who they were for themselves still felt to me the worst. Jack was willing.

Anna and I ate lunch at a nearby restaurant during the session, both a little nervous for Jack. When we returned to Rob's office, we saw they were both smiling and we let out a simultaneous sigh of relief. Naturally, I was curious about what Jack uncovered, except I didn't want to invade his privacy. But Jack was happy to talk about his experience. When Rob had asked him to go back to his birth, Jack couldn't but he'd suddenly remembered me holding him and smiling down at him, and he described the room and situation perfectly. He remembered!

Being able to see the baby at all was a new option offered at the home for unwed mothers and not advised. It would be too risky, the nuns had said. In the recent past, extreme measures had been taken to keep the unwed mother from any contact with the baby after the birth. Strong drugs like "Twilight" that were supposed to erase memory, blindfolds and even earplugs were used to prevent any bonding from occurring that would cause a change of heart about the adoption. Arms were strapped down to prevent us from reaching out and touching our babies. From the mothers I had talked with, who'd been prevented from seeing their babies, such harsh treatment didn't diminish the bond but only served to intensify their trauma.

Not knowing whether or not I was going to find a way to keep him, I'd fought hard to be able to hold him in the hospital. Rob said Jack had unconsciously carried that memory with him his whole life, and that it must have given him strength.

Jack's second memory was a mystery. He saw himself standing in a crib looking at a strange woman with long black hair to her waist. I suggested that perhaps he was seeing his first adoptive mother, the one that had given him back to the adoption agency after her divorce when Jack was eight months old. But that question would not be resolved for many years. During our first conversation, I had turned cold as ice and white as a sheet when Rosemary told me the story of Jack being given back to the nuns. She knew it would be a shock and kept reassuring me that Jack was just fine and had not suffered.

But I knew he must have suffered. As his mother I knew. While doing research for the book, I'd discovered Thomas Verny's groundbreaking book, *The Secret Life of the Unborn Child* (1982), that proved babies in the womb were already fully conscious humans - able to remember, smile, cry and react with appropriate human emotions to stimulation from outside the womb, including the mother's emotions and painful procedures. Verney's research proved that intrauterine memory comes early and is complex. Still in its infancy, the study of Prenatal/Perinatal psychology was discovering that, when regressed, patients could go back to their births and remember remarkable details and their emotional reactions to them. Re-experiencing the emotions and being able to release them created extraordinary healing results.

Priscilla, an adoptee in our group who had been searching for years with no luck, had carried a sense of shame her whole life. "But I have done nothing to feel ashamed about," she'd say. Still, she was tormented by shame. In desperation, she'd gone to a hypnotherapist and been regressed back to her time in her mother's womb, where she felt all of her mother's shame about the pregnancy. "The shame was hers, not mine," Priscilla realized, "and now it's gone," she said. "I no longer feel any shame."

Over the years, since the first studies, hypnotic regression has proved that music, events, emotions and stories are known prenatally. The initial responses to such an idea ranged from skepticism to accusations of heresy. The implications required a radically new consciousness about how prenatal life and birth were viewed and treated and thus the importance of supporting the mother/child bond. And the establishment by nature is resistant to change. I was grateful to be living in California where radical ideas were welcomed.

As such ideas have become more accepted, researchers have been discovering just how wired an infant is to his/her own mother. Now we know that newborns can recognize their mother's scent, even when presented with the scent of ten other women to choose from. When listening to a selection of women's voices, a newborn will begin to suck on a pacifier only upon hearing its own mother's voice. How bewildering, how traumatic must it be for an infant when the mother is no longer there?

Separation from her has to create life-long, if not conscious feelings of anger, grief, powerlessness, shame, depression, fear and/or isolation that can run like an underground and unexplainable current through their lives, coloring their emotional reactions to present events. Reunions had to trigger the original primal emotions surrounding the birth for both child and mother.

Realizing how my baby must have felt, lying in the nursery bassinet waiting for me to return when I never did, was hard to take in. Then to be separated from a caregiver, which must have been how he experienced his first adoptive mother. Rosemary's love for Jack had made up for so much loss.

After Jack's vision of the woman with long black hair, I couldn't rest until I found out what had happened the first eight months of his life, especially knowing now that memories of that time were stored in him and operating on some level. However, even though I felt I had every right as a mother to know, I asked Jack if it was okay with him if I pursued a search. Having had all my legal rights taken away made me uneasy about overstepping my bounds, but I still had my instincts of a mother bear to deal with. Jack said he would be curious, to go ahead. Would Rosemary mind? Probably not, but she wouldn't be interested he was sure.

With not much effort, I was able to locate the mother of Jack's first adoptive father, who reassured me that "Dennis" had been greatly loved. They had named him Dennis. I had named him Phillip, and now he was Jack – three such different names.

She was happy to know that he was fine now. But, even with the extra clues the woman gave me, the adoptive mother proved impossible to find. I'd hoped to learn more details from her and maybe even get pictures of Jack's first months of life. The analogy I'd heard, that had made all my anxiety make sense, was that our feelings were the same as how parents feel when a child is missing, say in a park, even for a few minutes. Panic sets in; only our panic stays with us until we learn about our children's lives.

It was so wrong for Jack not to know about his first eight months of life, and it was wrong for me, too.

Writing the book was taking far longer than I'd expected. I was into my second year. The longer it took the more some suggested I give it up and get a full time job, instead of earning little at the part time job I had. But the writing was so emotional and so necessary that I knew I couldn't handle any more than what I was doing. What makes you think you'll even get published many asked? All I could answer was that I had a good feeling about it - not a good enough response for most. The pressure to prove everyone wrong by being successful was creating a lot of stress and taking me away from the pure act of writing. And, even though my writing the book didn't diminish their feelings for Jack, it was causing a strain in my relationship with Brett and Kip. Where they hadn't felt any jealousy about my finding him, they were upset that I was consumed with the book. All I could do was reassure them that if it had been one of them that I'd lost and found again I would do the same. Besides, the book wasn't really about Jack, but instead about my experience and one that I hoped would help others. Despite all reassurances, I could see my preoccupation was taking its toll.

One night, when Brett and Kip were with their father for the weekend, I decided to depart from my usual schedule of writing during the day. I lit a candle in a copper butter warmer my mother had given me years before, burned some incense and, with some trepidation, began writing about my trip to Sacre Coeur, the Church of the Sacred Heart at the top of Paris, which I visited the summer I was searching for my son, and about my unnerving experience at the famous statue of the Blessed Mother there. Old

Catholic education imprinting made me wonder if what I was planning to write **about** was blasphemous. I decided to go ahead; I always could take it out.

> *"As I studied the statue, I wondered what made it seem so vital, so different from her other statues. It seemed She could step down from her pedestal and lift up one of the supplicants at any moment. Some of them looked at the statue like She already had.*
>
> *I approached slowly, taking in the whole scene. At a distance of six feet, I felt like I walked into a wall of thick air. The deepest pain from the loss of my son seemed to burst from me, and I started to cry. At the same time, it seemed Her outstretched arms had parted a curtain in front of me, and, for a split second, I saw my son standing before me."*

The small flame, in the copper butter warmer, shot up four feet, and I stared at it in alarm. Was this a sign that I was wrong to write about this or was it an eternal flame? What if the flame were a Visitation – some saint or maybe Mary herself? Should I risk my home? I reached for the coffee cup and doused the flame, surprised at how deeply ingrained my Catholic upbringing still ran, despite having left the church so long ago.

The phone rang. It was my friend, Catherine, who'd also surrendered her baby son in a Catholic home.

I'd met Catherine when she came to our group, and we had an instant connection. She was an incredible watercolorist and a sweet and fun person.

With the group's support, she'd contacted her son. "I knew one of us would go crazy if we didn't find each other," her son had told her during their first conversation. After they talked, she'd sent him a big package of photos and a small watercolor she'd done. She received no response.

After a couple of years of waiting to hear anything, and with her son's first reaction to give her strength, she asked me to call the adoptive father. "Tell Catherine to go back to her group, or whatever you call yourselves," he said. "What right did Catherine think she had coming into our lives not knowing what was going on." The disdain in his voice was palpable. He then told of how, when *his* son received her package, he threw it in the trash unopened. "It takes a big man to do that," the adoptive father bragged. Catherine and I were both heartbroken. What chance did she have of ever meeting her son? How could anyone exert so much control over another human being?

"That's just your left over Catholic guilt," Catherine laughed, when I told her about the mysterious flame. "Good thing you put out the fire!"

After publication, I received hundreds of letters from women who said, "You have told my story." The many coincidences readers shared were eerie, but none shook me more than the one from a woman who had also visited Sacre Coeur and had the same experience. She found her son two months after her visit there, as I had.

Holidays were difficult after the divorce. I missed being with Brett and Kip. Ron and I had arranged that he would be with the kids for Thanksgiving and Christmas dinner, and they would be with me Christmas Eve and Christmas morning. As I faced Thanksgiving without them, I made plans to visit my sister, Elena, in New York City.

When I told Jack of my plans, he said he was going to be in New York that weekend, too, for a family Baptism and asked if I would like to come out to Queens to meet his adoptive family. Of course, I would. I wanted very much to meet the family he'd grown up with and have Jack meet Elena, who was only five and a half years older than him, closer in age than me to be her sibling, as Elena and I were fifteen and a half years apart.

When I had called to tell her about searching for my son, Elena had faked surprise at the news. Of course, Janice, the one in the family who could never keep a secret, had told her. But it was only when I told Janice about my search that she admitted she'd known all along. Janice, who was fifteen at the time of my pregnancy, had overheard my mother and I fighting about whether or not I had to wear a girdle, when I was maid of honor at my cousin Joanie's wedding, and figured everything out. Even though I was nearly five months along and still not showing, I'd lost the "Battle of the Girdles" and ended up wearing three, so high was the level of my mother's anxiety.

On the other hand, when I told my brother, Bob, about my son, he was completely surprised, but then told me he always wondered why I seemed so angry on our drives home from college. He said he'd blamed himself, thinking I must have been mad at him for some reason. To think my anger had been so obvious to others, and I'd been unaware of it.

Elena coming into our lives had been a complete surprise. I was already in high school when my mother, at forty, had informed Bob, Janice and me that "the rabbit had died." In those days, after missing a period, a woman would bring a urine sample to the doctor, which was then injected into a rabbit. If the rabbit died that meant you were "with child" or "in the family way." Like "cancer," the word "pregnant" was never spoken out loud. The poor rabbit was all I could think.

My first reaction to the news was embarrassment. How could my mother be pregnant at such an age? In those days, pregnant women were thought of as fragile and were expected to stay at home and not be seen much in public places. Just the year before, one of my favorite teachers had to quit before she began to show.

41

When she made her announcement to the class, I felt quite disturbed. What could be so wrong that she had to disappear?

Back then, maternity clothes were designed more for little girls, with frilly collars, bows, silly prints and collars up to the neck. Not at all attractive and definitely not womanly, they appeared to be an attempt at preserving a sense of innocence, as if no sex had been involved. My mother, who was always stylish, suddenly looked silly. When I had first arrived at the home for unwed mothers, I was shown a closet full of maternity clothes, handed down from the girls who had been there before me. The same thing - I felt like I'd be dressing for third grade if I wore them. Fortunately, the tent dress was in style then, so I could wear my real clothes and feel more normal.

When I was pregnant with Brett, a new and radical line of maternity clothes was introduced, called Lady Madonna, which was only available in Los Angeles. On one of Ron's business trips, I went with him so I could shop there and bought a bright orange tee-shirt with a big apple appliqué right on the belly, a low cut black top to wear going out and a low cut peach-colored bathing suit, to take advantage of the few months when I would actually have cleavage. Times were quickly changing.

My mother had been happy about the baby to come, and it was only years later that I learned my Dad had considered divorcing my mother before she'd become pregnant with Elena. As a strict Catholic, Mom would not use birth control of any kind except the rhythm method. With three small children, she couldn't imagine taking care of more, and her fears had greatly affected their intimate life. Bob and I were only fourteen months apart, and Janice was three-and-a-half years younger than me.

Although I have no memories of that time, my mother had become pregnant when I was eight-years-old, but suffered a miscarriage. She and Dad had used turpentine while painting a room, and she was sure that was what caused it. She'd felt tremendous guilt over losing the baby and for months ritually washed her hands countless times a day and lost a great deal of weight. Her fears of becoming pregnant again worsened afterward, creating an irreparable strain on their marriage. My Dad decided to stay with Mom until Elena turned thirteen, but then planned to get a divorce. In effect, the church with its rigid teachings about birth control had torn a family apart.

The plan was to meet Jack at a Catholic church near the family home for the Baptism. Elena and I took the subway from Manhattan to Queens, found the church, and quietly slid into one of the back pews. I pointed out Jack, who was sitting next to Rosemary up front with the rest of the family.

The Baptism began with the priest declaring that all babies are born pagan and must be cleansed of this original sin, in order to be a child of God. Elena and I kept turning to each other, frowns on our faces and shaking our heads, as he went on and on about sin. What should have been a celebration of new life sounded more like an attempt to further instill the fear of God in everyone present. I was a little girl when I was first taught about Limbo, the place where all babies whom were never Baptized were sent when they died, to be forever denied heaven and seeing the face of God. It was supposed to be a nice enough place, not like Hell but more like Heaven. My imagination would run wild at times, as I tried to understand why God would create such a place to punish innocent babies.

One of the books I'd recently read from the stack by my bed was about the teachings of the Hopi. For them, at birth an infant is greeted into this world by the four basic elements of our planet: water, air, fire and earth. Water was thought to be the first element to greet the baby, as the water from its mother's womb gushed forth ahead of its birth, in effect baptizing the infant into this world. The baby's first breath represented the element air; the warmth of the parents' love symbolized fire; and the element earth was integrated with the baby's first steps. Could such a beautiful and truthful idea be the origins of Baptism - now co-opted by the Church hell bent on ridding the world of Paganism?

The service over, we all spilled out of the church. Jack spotted us and came over for a quick shy, "Hello". The others had already begun walking back to the house, and we followed in the late afternoon light.

Inside, the house was filled with people. Rosemary came from a family of nine children, so it was a big Irish gathering. Sister Dominic had indeed delivered on her promise to find an Irish family for my baby, since we at least knew my mother's mother had been Irish. I flashed on how she had cocked her head heavenward, as if personally placing her order with God.

My discomfort grew, though, when it became obvious that people didn't know whom we were and we weren't being introduced. I hadn't expected that, but a good idea at the time may have suddenly felt awkward to Jack and Rosemary. I also hadn't anticipated just how terribly sad and lost I would feel seeing all the people my son had called family all of his life, and they were all strangers to me. At the same time, I was relieved to observe how much he meant to them - so many conflicting emotions to deal with.

I was about to suggest to Elena that we leave, when one of Jack's aunts came rushing up to us all excited. Apparently, the word had leaked out about who we were. She was so happy to meet me, she said. And then others in the family came up to us - all warmly greeting us and expressing their love for Jack.

Throughout the festivities, Jack's Grandmother had been sitting like a regal matriarch in a chair against the far wall from where I stood. Jack had confided that she was completely opposed to my being there. Of all her grandchildren, Jack held a special place in her heart and he had always felt a bond with her. So, when Jack came up to me and asked if I'd like to meet her, I was feeling more than a little intimidated. Her eyes were on me the whole time we crossed the room and approached her. I wanted to make a good impression, not just for my sake but also for Rosemary's, since she'd obviously stuck her neck out inviting me there against her mother's wishes.

I bent down to shake her hand as Jack introduced us, and thanked her for being so good to Jack, complimenting her, too, on her lovely family. She nodded her head and seemed to soften. "We all love Jack," she said, still sizing me up. "I'm very grateful to all of you for all you've done for Jack," I told her, pulling away. This was not going to be a long conversation. As I turned away, I felt I was walking between two worlds with no ground underneath me to rely on.

Now Elena and I both felt it was a good time to leave. Rosemary and Jack walked us to the door, and we said our goodbyes in the vestibule. The cold of the late evening air was a stark contrast to the warmth of the house, as we walked quietly to the subway.

"I didn't expect to feel so connected to him," Elena said. "He could be my brother." Elena had grown up much like an only child, given such a gap in our ages. Our parents often said they gave Elena all that they hadn't been able to afford when Bob, Janice and I were growing up.

How to explain the bonds of blood? As the subway train sped toward Manhattan, Elena sobbed the whole way. "If only I could have known him" was all she was able to say.

It had been a year and a half since I'd started the book, and I finally felt brave enough to read through the first draft, something I had yet to do. My fear of reading it ran abnormally deep, and there was a reason. Beyond the fears from the pressure I felt from those who opposed my writing and also being so public about my life, writing carried for me the specter of punishment.

I'd become aware of the problem in a therapy session I'd had alone with the therapist Ron and I had been going to in an effort to salvage our marriage. At that point we were going through a trial separation. "You should keep a journal," the therapist had suggested. "It's a great tool for getting in touch with your deeper self."

"No way I can do that," I declared. When I was growing up, I kept a personal diary, a popular thing to do at the time for young people. I had enjoyed writing down my thoughts. But, no matter how clever I was at hiding it, my mother always found my diary and I was often punished for what I had written about, mostly things I'd done that were not permitted, like going to the drive-in movie with friends when I wasn't yet allowed to be in a car with other kids. Her reading my diary felt like a violation, and I quit writing about anything personal that might expose me in any way, and then finally quit writing at all.

"You can't let that fear run your life," the therapist had responded. "You're an adult now. Your mother's no longer around to read your diary."

So, I bought a beautiful journal and began exploring my illusive unconscious.

But when Ron and I attempted to reconcile, he'd found my diary and read it, an issue under most circumstances that could have been worked through. But to me, given my past, it was impossible. But even when we finally split on friendly terms I never wrote in a journal again.

As a result, the stakes were pretty high when I decided to write the book, given my writing had always derailed my life. So it was with horror, after reading through the first draft, that I realized it was awful.

When I was a senior in high school, we were given the assignment of writing a short story. After reading mine, the teacher asked me to stay behind after class to discuss it. Proud of what I'd done, I looked forward to her comments.

"You have a great writing style, Carol," she'd said, "but you have absolutely nothing to say."

Her words stayed with me for a long time, and were with me now casting grave doubts over my efforts. So much at stake, so much to prove, so much sacrifice – and the first draft was awful. But the writing was helping to heal so much, and it had felt like some force was behind it - I couldn't give up. So I bought myself a Mac Plus, and the book finally began to take shape.

Jack and I were still in what many described as the "honeymoon" phase of our developing relationship, where everything was going well as we got to know each other and the natural, underlying issues had yet to crop up. For us, that would not happen until after publication of the book. Meanwhile, his acceptance of me in his life was changing a distorted image I'd had of myself since first becoming an unwed mother.

I was coming to understand at deeper and deeper levels, as more memories returned during my writing, how untrue to myself I had been all the years after losing him. Having to return to my old life and pretend to others I was not a mother, when I really was, and trying to fit back into an old dream, when I was now a different person, had dramatically changed the way I related to others. How can anyone fully relate to another, be completely intimate, when a very real part of one's self had been hidden from others and disowned?

Because there had never been any studies done on the impact on a mother of losing a child to adoption, all we had in the early days as a guideline for what had happened to us were the studies of Vietnam vets, who had suffered from Post Traumatic Stress Syndrome. Besides the actual trauma of the battlefield, soldiers were returning to loved ones who, without the same experience, couldn't possibly relate to the horrors left in their psyche, leaving them feeling isolated and alone and compounding their trauma.

In addition to being unable to honestly be myself, I still carried with me the feeling of being a pariah, at least subconsciously, so that, no matter how many friends I had or accomplishments I made, at some level I never again felt like a valuable member of society.

In high school, our only knowledge of life beyond our *Leave It to Beaver* lives came through *True Confessions Magazine,* which was banned by the Catholic Church. One of the girls in our group of friends was always able to get a hold of a copy, which we'd read together or pass around. Full of emotionally charged stories of romance and the consequences of lust, the young women portrayed as in trouble were always blonde, and I was blonde. What did that mean about me? The occasional stories of homes for unwed mothers held a strange, mysterious power over me, and I would look for them. One photo of a deeply sad unwed mother, blonde of course, pushing her toddler in a stroller was burned into my brain.

By the time I became an unwed mother myself, I'd forgotten all about *True Confessions.* Yet, as I anticipated entering the home for unwed mothers, I fully expected to be incarcerated with fallen women – delinquents of society. Even though I didn't consider myself one, I felt others would. To my relief, the young women in the home were no different than me, but I still couldn't shake the feeling of having violated society.

I had been one of the rare lucky ones, as Rosemary had accepted me and I soon learned to let go of the self-image of an outcast. But so many mothers coming to our group - wonderful, good women - were being humiliated and even vilified by their child's adoptive parents, who wanted nothing to do with them, in much the same way society had cast them out for their unwed mother status years before, making their healing that much more difficult, condemned forever as pariahs unless they found a way to reclaim their own personal worth.

Research was proving that at least forty percent of women who surrendered their babies to adoption never went on to have other children, a far higher number than the normal population. In my support group and at the conferences I'd attended, the number seemed more like fifty percent. The diagnosis was secondary infertility, infertility caused by underlying emotional issues, such as loyalty to their lost child and feelings of not being worthy enough to have another baby, from being told over and over another woman would be a better mother than we could be for our own child. I could have easily been one of them.

When Ron and I married, we decided to wait a couple of years to have a child. But, as I thought about the prospect, I realized I didn't want to have any more. How could I ever explain, should I meet my son again, that I had another child that I kept? But my period had always been irregular and, like with Jack, I didn't have a positive pregnancy test until I was four months along. Brett was born ten months after we married. He was such a happy baby, such a pleasure, and I came to understand that, without him and then Kip, my life would have been desolate.

As I listened to the stories of the women in the support group who'd never had other children, some of whom had given up their children to protect them from being brought up in an alcoholic family as they had been, or to give them a chance for more opportunities than they could possibly provide, I was able to validate their maternal instincts, where they couldn't for themselves, never having reared kids.

When I first began working with my therapist, Toni, I'd expressed my concern over my rights to even wonder about my son, much less search for him.

"Of course, you have a right, Carol, you're his mother," she'd responded. "You have to know he's okay. Your self-respect will come back as you take charge of your life and find your son."

I'd needed that acknowledgment from another woman, since women were primarily responsible for my losing my son in the first place. Not a single woman back then - no nurse, no nun, no social worker, nor my mother - had come forward to offer me an alternative. From that point on, I'd developed a real distrust of women, to the point of resisting seeing a woman therapist. But Toni was a wise woman, an example I'd been seeking all my life.

"You can send him your love, you know. You're connected already. He'll feel it, whether or not he knows where it comes from," Toni told me, after listening to my frustration over the length and difficulty of the search.

So, I began sending my son love on my walks in the woods, and I felt calmer myself during the frustration of the search. Once, when I reached the top of Mt. Baldy, a small mountain near my home, it came to me to visualize myself holding my son as a baby and give him all the love I couldn't then, with the hope that the pain I had caused him would begin to heal. I told him how sorry I was for not finding a way to keep him. Even after finding him, during times when we weren't talking as much as I wanted, I could be patient using this silent communication.

Despite its more bosom heaving, bra busting romance novel connotations, "Silent Love" became the working title for my book. Silently was how I'd always loved him and, if I loved him silently, no one could try to take that love away. In that state of mind and heart, I didn't need anyone's permission to love my son or their acknowledgment of who I was to him. Silent love was the wellspring of my personal power and the source of strength that got me through everything to follow, and still does.

Chapter Four

Sun was shining through the windows all around me, as I sat on my bed, surrounded by piles of papers and books, researching for the book the negative psychological consequences of surrendering a child for adoption. I was wondering how I got spared, or if I actually did get spared the worst outcome.

Over and over, the research was revealing that, at a rate far higher than the normal population, mothers who had lost their children to adoption suffered from pathological grief, grief that is unresolved and, therefore, causes chronic major depression, a loss of a sense of self and damage to the personality, from attempts at counteracting their overwhelming feelings of loss. As a result of the grief trauma, psychiatric disorders developed, including panic and anxiety disorders, and alcohol and drug dependency. Given the intensity of the stress, physical ailments developed from so much heavy emotional energy running through the system, relationships were profoundly affected, true intimacy was naturally impossible, and a lack of faith in oneself and in society and all authority figures grew worse over time.

The word "pathological" disturbed me, as it implied there was something inherently wrong with us. Wasn't our response completely normal? How can a mother grieve a child that still lives and is out there somewhere? How could a mother's natural instincts and worry over the welfare of her child ever go away? Why couldn't society see the beauty in that?

On my bed, too, was my *Abnormal Psychology* book, which had somehow survived my many moves over the years. A faded memory had caused me to search my bookshelves and find it. I flipped through the pages until I came to the chapter, "Deviant Sexual Behavior."

> *"Other types of psychopathology, such as manic reactions, may also be of etiological significance in promiscuous sexual behavior. There is a failure to either develop normal inner controls, or a lowering of these controls as a consequence of severe emotional adjustment. In a study of 54 unwed mothers ranging in age from 15 to 39, Cattell (1954) found psychopathology in every case: 30 had character disorders, 17 were schizophrenic, and 7 were neurotic."*

One hundred percent! Yet, too much sex hadn't caused all married women to suffer psychopathological disorders. Besides, most unwed mothers became pregnant soon after losing their virginity, when their inexperience left them unprotected. If we had been prepared with condoms, we would risk being seen as one of those "loose" girls. If the researcher had not formed a prior opinion, he could have looked closer and found that the psychopathology of unwed mothers sprang from being treated and punished like social outcasts, isolated from all normal support systems, and forced to surrender their babies in order to re-enter a rigid and judgmental world.

"Disassociation" was another word that kept coming up: an emotional numbing from a trauma that disconnects the person from the original event and from themselves, sometimes causing memory loss and profound feelings of sorrow or intense anger that, like a passing cloud, can seem to come from nowhere and then disappear just as inexplicably. For some, thoughts of suicide intruded for no apparent reason.

I remembered what it felt like dressing in street clothes for the first time in four and a half months, as I prepared to leave the hospital, trying to slip back into the girl I had once been when I'd last worn the dress, and feeling like my old clothes were trapping me in a lie. All I wanted was to storm the nursery, grab my son and run out of there. But then I would be putting us both in jeopardy. They might think I was crazy and, if I couldn't find a way to keep him, they might think he could be too unfit to give to a good family.

When the volunteer matron had come to pick me up, I wasn't permitted to see him one last time through the nursery window. I remembered how at that moment some great part of me split off and went to be with him. As I abandoned my baby, my soul abandoned me to be with him. How, as a mother, could I do otherwise?

As I thought about the clinical word "dissociation," I felt it didn't exactly describe the original experience. What seemed to have happened to me and to the other mothers in the group was that, out of necessity, the self we truly were had become frozen in time, as a new persona had to take over to survive. There was no choice. When we began to take charge of our lives by searching for our child, many of us felt we were regressing, finding ourselves listening to old music and having urges to ride around in a convertible with the top down – feeling like a teenager again, an unnerving experience. But we were thawing and coming back to life again, allowing that frozen part a chance to catch up, to grow up. Becoming aware of what was happening was a relief and made the whole process easier.

Ironically, our children were also required to become someone else, too, without their original family as a mirror. Many adopted persons coming to the group talked of feeling the need to become what they felt their adoptive parents had wanted them to be, either as a replacement child or from a belief, prevalent in those times when the soul was not recognized, that an infant was a tabula rosa - a blank slate.

The phone rang, knocking me out of deep thought, and I scrambled to find it under all the papers and books. It was my cousin, Joanie, calling. When I began searching for my son, I'd confessed to Joanie that I had been an unwed pregnant maid of honor at her wedding. I'd retained the feeling that I'd somehow tainted her wedding day - the shame of my predicament so deeply imprinted that, even as an adult with full understanding, I still felt guilty telling her.

Joanie was calling with a revelation of her own to make. Her youngest sister had also had to give a baby up for adoption. My uncle had been beside himself over the situation. "But it was for the best," Joanie said. "She ended up needing psychiatric help right after. She wouldn't have been a fit mother after all."

"Oh, my God, Joanie, your sister's breakdown was the result of losing her child." I couldn't believe she called at the same moment I was reading about the damaging psychological effects of relinquishing a child. As I explained what I'd come to understand, I could tell it was awfully hard for her to hear, that I was shattering a defense mechanism the family had developed over their decision to have the baby adopted. But how would they have known otherwise when the whole culture supported such treatment of daughters who'd disgraced the family? Joanie made me promise not to tell anyone, especially her sister, since Janet was finally doing okay and had made a good life for herself.

When I got off the phone, I was floored by the secrets my family kept from each other. My mother and her sister could not confide in each other about the painful situation they were both going through. Why? What fear had such power over their minds and hearts that they couldn't lean on each other for support and, instead, had to maintain a façade of the perfect family?

John Norman was sitting alone at his kitchen table with the door half-closed. Seven of us beginning students in psychic healing waited in a circle in the living room, staring at one another in apprehension and full of self doubt. My search for my son had also propelled me on a search for answers to life's mysteries, and I was there to try to experience what I had only been reading in books.

One of the catalysts for my spiritual search was an attempt to understand how it happened that Jack always lived close by me. Besides being in New York at the same time and their moving to California within weeks of my moving there, Jack had lived twenty-five miles from me when he lived with his first adoptive parents in Charlotte, North Carolina while I was back attending college at Winthrop in Rock Hill, South Carolina. My family lived in Greensboro, North Carolina and, on trips back and forth from home to school, I would find myself trembling as I drove by Charlotte, not understanding why. Perhaps that explained why I rarely felt safe off campus. If I ever left, I would find myself looking at all the passing babies and their mothers, wondering if one was my son, perhaps sensing he was so near.

Right around the time that Jack was being brought back to the agency, Catholic Social Services, his father, Ray, had had the feeling something terrible was wrong with our son and wanted to call the social worker. His fears had frightened me, because I'd lived with fantasies, since leaving our baby behind, that something would happen and the agency would call and ask if we wanted our baby back. I'd worked it out in my mind, after dismissing a car accident or a plane crash, she would get pregnant and not be able to take care of two babies at once.

When Rosemary and her husband, Jon Ryan, got Jack, he was eight months old, and they lived near Ray. But then Jon was killed in Vietnam when Jack was twenty-two months old. Later, looking back, I realized that was the same time I had been in the school's infirmary, as sick as I'd ever been, and hallucinating that something very wrong was going on with my baby.

Until I began attending support groups, I thought our experiences were unique to Ray and me. But after attending adoption support groups, I found, much like with studies of twins separated at birth, discovering remarkable coincidences and synchronicities was very much a part of the reunion experience.

Like us, some experienced remarkable serendipity in the places where they'd lived close by or vacationed or went to school, for instance. Others found timing of major life events were remarkably similar. Multiple matches in family names were common. Uncanny similarities in occupations, philosophy, education, habits, gestures were normal. When we met, Jack was planning to major in psychology, the same major both Ray and I had chosen. In fact, he seemed to have more of a choice about his own direction after meeting us, when he changed his focus to the arts. There is a belief that being brought up separate from their family of origin allows adopted people to be more their own person, but the opposite was proving true from evidence gathered after reunions. Often the adoptee was more like the original family from being unable to see their reflection and make different choices for themselves.

One of the most dramatic similarities I witnessed was that of a reunited mother and daughter, both artists, who were astonished to discover their art was strikingly similar - one painted faceless portraits, the other sculpted the same faceless images. Perhaps such similarities only seem extraordinary because we have yet to understand all that our psyches are capable of, and are why mothers and their children who are separated from each other both feel an aching emptiness that nothing can fill. The divine order of things had been disrupted, until they met again and that void begins to fill, whether or not the reunion goes well. Maybe our fears approaching and during reunion really stem from the fear of facing Life's great mysteries and losing our grip on the false reality we've constructed for ourselves.

"Okay, you can begin drawing now," John called out in his calm, reassuring voice. Even though he was out of sight, I could still see the twinkle in his eyes.

We stared at our blank papers. Our assignment was to draw whatever John was drawing, though he was hidden from view.

I found myself first drawing a tree. Of course, I thought, I always loved drawing trees as a child. What could be psychic about that? Then I drew a small house with a chimney and the sun. Making up for kindergarten again. But then I felt compelled to draw a creek and then a fish swimming in it.

"Times up!" John announced, emerging from the kitchen.

We all were too embarrassed to reveal our pitiful psychic abilities. Why did John want to put us on the spot like that? After all, this was our first class.

John had us hold our drawings up at the same time. All eyes darted around the room. A woman to my left had drawn rather angry looking scribbles, but, to our amazement, the rest of us had all drawn a tree, a house and the sun. And, four of us had added a creek.

I apologized for my fish, but John said he'd actually thought of drawing one and decided not to. Yikes!

The whole point of the exercise was to show how everyone has latent psychic abilities. Never questioning the outcome, John explained that we mask our ability with doubt and disbelief. The woman with the scribbles agreed.

Being so immersed in adoption issues at the time, I found myself constantly applying my personal experiences to a larger context, attempting to understand common, unexplainable behaviors unique to having been separated from our children. After experiencing first hand latent psychic abilities in John's class, I now could confirm why, upon simply finding out our children's names, where they lived and that they were still alive, mothers became calm, felt a long forgotten peace. More times than not, when first coming to the group and before finding their children, the mothers would be frazzled, anxious, their unconscious yet primal "psychic antennas" up, searching for any knowledge of their children and only receiving static - static that was causing erratic thoughts and behavior. Finding out anything about their children was like finally tuning into a clear channel, and the "psychic static" was gone.

As the class began disbanding, John looked over at me and said he saw a large ball of grief coming toward me, but that there didn't seem to be anything happening in the future that would cause it. I couldn't imagine what he could be talking about, and soon forgot all about his warning.

Two days later, I was suddenly flooded with a feeling of enormous grief and sorrow, and nothing had happened to warrant it. Then I began to remember times when that had happened before and intuitively knew that it was somehow some of the grief I'd had to suppress after losing my baby, the grief that I had been denied back then returning to be dealt with.

My friend, Morgan, and I had our own remarkable coincidences. Her beloved boyfriend was lying in a hospital, dying from a surfing accident, when Morgan told him she had just discovered she was pregnant. After his death, she was sent to St. Ann's Home for Unwed Mothers in Los Angeles, with no choice offered but to surrender her baby for adoption. Because she was Catholic, she was allowed to hold her baby girl one time only, while the baby was given the Sacrament of Baptism. Mothers in the home, who were not Catholic, did not get that privilege and never saw their babies. I knew from other mothers who had been there, that St. Ann's was notorious for its cruelty. One woman told me that her parents had tried desperately to be with her when she went into labor, and were turned away at the door, forbidden to see their daughter.

Morgan was my primary support, as I searched for Jack. In fact, it was her brother who found Jack's phone number in the Los Angeles Polk Directory. Morgan was already writing a book about her experiences when I began mine. Every morning, one of us would call the other to encourage the day's work. As it turned out, Morgan's daughter was attending Fresno State College at the same time as Jack.

For two years, Jack had attended Saddleback, a junior college. He had hoped to attend USC and play water polo there. In high school, Jack had been named an All American in water polo. But finances prohibited that dream. So, after Saddleback, he enrolled at Fresno State to play on their water polo team.

One weekend, Morgan and I drove down to Fresno to see Jack and Morgan's daughter, Beth. Who would have ever guessed that, after meeting while we were both searching for our children, we would be driving down together to see our children at the same college. As with Jack's mom, Beth's adoptive mother accepted Morgan into their lives. In fact, we were staying with her for the weekend.

Beth's parents had adopted her after losing a baby in a horrific accident. Her adoptive mother had been sitting in the dugout of a baseball game, when a fly ball hit the baby's head, killing him instantly. Now, just like with Rosemary, she had practically forgotten Beth was adopted. When Beth began to mature during puberty, her mother had reacted to her enlarging breasts with surprise. "How can you have large breasts?" she asked Beth. "No one in our family has large breasts."

Being a "replacement child" is one of the great challenges many adoptees have to face. Not being with their ancestral family and having to form familial bonds with strangers leaves some adopted children vulnerable, as they search for their own unique identity. Having no genetic mirroring, becoming like the child their adoptive parents lost or were never able to conceive can feel necessary to their survival in the family, whether or not that is their parents' expectation. Often the results of such adaptive behavior are not apparent to the child or the adoptive parents, they are so ingrained. Without knowing their child's genealogical family, how would an adoptive parent know what innate attributes to nurture?

Before driving up the long winding road to their mountain home, Morgan and I watched Jack play a water polo match. Jack was already in the pool when we arrived. Rosemary had told me that, when he was growing up, Jack always got awarded "Most Improved Player" on a team, because she didn't know to nurture his athletic skills and didn't always sign him up to play sports. Water polo was the big sport in their area of Mission Viejo, and was where Olympic teams trained, so that was why he chose to play that sport as opposed to any other. Watching the match, I felt that it was even rougher than football, and Jack played the hole-position, which was the hardest physically.

As Morgan, Beth, Jack and I drove up to Beth's home, Jack spoke of his frustration that the coach didn't seem to have confidence in him. "He thinks the fact that I move slowly means I don't care," he explained. I told him moving slowly was a family trait, that I'd been misunderstood for that myself. "But, think of it this way," I said. "You never see a Native American Indian chief running around!"

Beth's mom welcomed us with genuine warmth when we arrived. I was struck right away with how different she was from Morgan in many ways, and Beth and Morgan were so much alike.

During our visit, it was obvious that Jack was enjoying being the observer in the situation, instead of in the middle. He wasn't into support groups, and so hadn't had any experiences other than our own.

As always, it was hard to say goodbye, but this time I was left with the feeling that Jack wasn't happy at Fresno. He seemed lonesome. Maybe he was missing Anna, also named an All American, and going to college in Idaho on a volleyball scholarship. As we drove away, I couldn't shake the fear that always came up when leaving him that I would never see him again – another irrational response I had to learn to live with.

Our next support group was meeting just before Mothers Day. For me this would be the third Mothers Day since first contacting Jack. Support group meetings around Mothers Day were always especially sad. A few of the mothers would be acknowledged by their found children, but for the majority anticipating that day only magnified their loss. So much of our struggles involved holding on to our inner truth, that we had brought our children into this world and cared deeply about them and were their mothers, too, even though the world and most of our children couldn't acknowledge us as mothers. But the struggle was great.

The ability to access our inner truth had been systematically eroded, especially for those who had stayed in maternity homes. Whether deliberate or not, brainwashing techniques had been applied in the name of doing what was best for the mothers and their babies. Upon entering the home, most young women were immediately stripped of their identity, told they were not permitted to reveal their last names or anything of a personal nature to anyone, under the implied threat of stricter confinement. Some were actually assigned a name and were forced to go by it, whether or not they even liked the new name. One woman in our group had been told she would be known as Vera in the home, a name so opposite from her own and which she hated. The depths to which she was affected could only be imagined.

Isolation from friends and family was mandated; visits, outings, phone calls and mail were under strict control - allowed as a reward for compliant behavior and withdrawn as punishment for any act of rebellion against the strict rules. One of the mothers in the group told of being put in what was called the "crying room," when she first arrived at a Salvation Army Home. A young woman was not permitted out of the crying room until she stopped crying and adjusted. In that home, the crying room was located above the labor room, and hearing the screams of the young women in labor was especially terrifying since she had not been prepared.

Rigid daily schedules were enforced regarding wake up and bedtimes, meals, chores and time in the recreation area. Visits and outings had to be approved. Options about how to keep the baby were rarely offered, and instructions about labor and delivery were minimal and excluded any education about the care of a newborn.

In most of the homes, the new mothers were kept away from the ones who had yet to deliver, and so there was no way to gain feedback or learn what to expect. What if a new mother had warned the others waiting to deliver that they would be all alone during labor and delivery, that they would not be given pain medication as a punishment and a lesson, or would be so drugged that they could barely remember anything? What if they knew ahead of time that they would be isolated from the maternity ward, unable to see their babies? What if the new mothers told them that everything would change after the birth, that they would be overwhelmed with feelings for their baby, that they would never be able to go on with their lives and forget, as had been promised?

With our own inner knowing and power over our own lives so systematically eroded, we not only had lost our children, we also lost our ability to trust our own truth - that we were mothers and we had a right to love our children. Getting back to our innate wisdom was like peeling layers off an onion, with all the tears that came with the chore. We were so essential to each other in remembering our core truth, especially on such a fraught day.

The first two Mothers Days after meeting Jack, I'd sent a card to Rosemary, wanting to reassure her that I knew who had been Jack's Mom. Even though I'd fought with my expectations, trying to be rational about Jack's reality, I lost the battle and found myself disappointed that I didn't get a card from him. Finally I let the expectation go. Wishing was only making me miserable. But I found a gift in my struggles that I could apply to other aspects of my life. I was learning how expectations kept me from experiencing what was really happening in my life and were driven by my ego's fears and not my heart.

We were all navigating our way through establishing a relationship with our children and dealing with all the extraordinarily complicated emotions involved, without any established guidelines for support. Instinctively, we knew that we were going through all the growing up stages we missed with our children. After the initial euphoria of reconnecting, which mimicked the newborn stage, came the "terrible twos," when the child naturally pulled away to integrate his or her own identity. When this happened, panic invariably stepped in for the mothers. Was that it? Would they ever see their child again? The original loss was felt all over again, but this time magnified.

But when all was going well there was no need to face the trauma of the past, something most of us would naturally do anything to avoid. But, unless the past is confronted, necessary healing is impossible, and the unconscious anger and grief will eventually push our children away, perhaps permanently. As difficult as it is, when our children pull away in order to integrate all the reunion brings up for them, that is the time to delve into our own healing.

One of the platitudes in the New Age thinking I found most annoying, and yet challenging, promised that when you finally let go of something is when you will have it. Try telling a mother who lost her child to adoption to let go of anything!

The day after the meeting, worn out from the emotions the writing was bringing up, I found myself pacing the living room, the bright blue sky outside taunting my gloomy mood. What if I just let go of all the sorrow? But then I found I was actually frightened at the thought. Would there then be anything left of my relationship with Jack, since sorrow and longing were such an integral part of it? Facing the possibility was like taking a leap over an enormous chasm. As overly dramatic as it sounds now, I honestly didn't know at the time what was on the other side, or if I could even make it without falling into the abyss.

The image was literal in my mind, and I found myself wanting to take the chance, to find out what was real between us. And so I took the leap, made it over the abyss, and discovered so much more love on the other side. Whew!

That night, I got an unexpected call from Jack. He was coming to town that weekend for a water polo match. On Saturday, he and Kip went to my favorite store and bought a Mothers Day present. Their shopping together was gift enough for me. Wow, letting go of expectations might allow more to happen than ever expected!

After Jack left to return to college, Kip came up to me in the kitchen while I was cleaning the dishes.

"Mom, I told Jack today how happy I was to have him as my brother."

Brett was twelve, in the seventh grade, and Kip was nine, in the fourth grade, when I first told them they had a brother. I'd been advised by others in adoption reform to tell the boys early on, in case they might misunderstand my natural preoccupation and take it personally. It had taken me days to screw up my courage. As irrational as I knew I was being, I still found myself envisioning a very real hoard of social workers lined around the block, coming to take my children from me for being such a bad mother.

Quite a number of friends, on the other hand, had questioned the wisdom of my telling the kids about their brother, especially at such young ages. But I felt I would be depriving them of a chance to grow emotionally. Besides, I trusted their capacity to understand, and they had proved me right. The key I had learned from working with Toni was to try to forgive myself first, so that when I told them they wouldn't mirror my own unresolved feelings.

Brett had given me the perfect lead in when I told them I had something serious to talk with them about. "Is this about the birds and the bees?" he asked.

"Well, yes, in a way," I responded, and told them the whole story, calmly and simply, with no excuses.

"That must have been so hard for you," was Brett's first response, after the initial shock wore off.

Such depth of compassion from someone so young took me completely by surprise and filled me with pride.

Kip's eyes had grown huge as he took in the news. "Could he be John Elway?"

John Elway was their hero, a Stanford University graduate, who was being wooed by both the National Football League and major league baseball teams. They were just as vulnerable to fantasy as any mother or adoptee, until the truth is known. After I answered all their questions, they were ready to hop on a plane and go find their brother. Then Kip pointed out, with a younger brother's relish, that Brett wasn't my oldest. I saw a flash of pain in Brett's eyes, and I felt terrible about the emotional cost to them.

The next day at Show and Tell, Kip shared his news with his class. My friends are real excited," he reported.

Oh, dear. I imagined the startled parents of thirty fourth-graders sitting at dinner that night, groping for some explanation as to how Kip could suddenly have another brother.

"How did Jack respond?" I asked Kip, holding my breath.

"He seemed grateful," Kip replied. "But I don't really think he knew how to respond. I think he's comfortable here with us, but at the same time uneasy. Maybe he feels conflict about needing to be loyal to his other family."

I had noticed that Jack still felt some level of apprehension around us, because I felt it, too, and couldn't figure out the cause. We needed a beer always to help us relax. Then my reading led me to understand that it was old unacknowledged grief, stored away at a cellular level, now surfacing for both of us and causing confusion.

As I wrote, it was difficult to think of myself as a victim, though I could see I was in many ways – but not in all ways. Not that I blamed myself. It was a young woman my age I had met after graduating from college and landing a job as a social worker in Akron, Ohio, who forced me to acknowledge something was missing in me that had prevented me from fighting harder to keep my baby, and, instead, caused me to capitulate to the needs of others. We even looked alike. While writing about meeting her I felt crushed.

"I parked under the shade of an enormous elm near the porch of an old, peeling, clapboard house. Despite obvious poverty, the little street retained a dignity rare in the slums. I walked up the cracked concrete walkway. The screen door rattled when I knocked. From inside came footsteps and a small child's voice. There was a long hesitation before the door was opened. Our visits were always unannounced to catch any cheaters off guard, and it embarrassed me to have to behave in this way.

66

Searching ...

A tall woman in her early twenties, hair short and wispy, peered at me through the screen. Her little two-year-old son held onto the edge of her brown cotton uniform. She was a single mother receiving Aid to Dependent Children. I introduced myself as her social worker. She invited me in, but said she had only a few moments. She had to get to work. As I checked on her salary and rent, I knew she was over her maximum allowance. I didn't say anything, but she did.

She begged me to consider letting her stay in her house. She couldn't bear to live in a more rundown neighborhood and expose her son to dangers. She hoped in six months to have saved enough to get off welfare completely. The father of her son had abandoned her when he learned she was pregnant and her parents had rejected her. No one was helping her.

The little boy's eyes never left his mother's face as we talked. As I watched her speak, with her son draped around her knee, I knew I could have been this woman, if I had only had the courage. She had come from a family that would have enabled her to go to college, have a career, dress well. She could have had all that, if she had given her child up for adoption, she said. Instead, she worked as a waitress at the Brown Derby, lived on the edge of the slums in a strange city, and didn't have enough money to spare to go to the movies. But the love she and her son shared for each other was beautiful and plain to see. She sat on the edge of the frayed sofa, the only piece of furniture in the room, and was a whole person. I sat at the other end, only half a person.

She had to rush off to work. I told her not to worry. I would keep her secret. We left together. I watched her walk down the sun-dappled street with her son, as I sat in my brand-new gold Mercury Cougar. For the first time, I took full responsibility for not keeping my son. I wrapped my arms around the steering wheel and buried my head, letting the full force of my shame and sorrow wash down over me. I fought to shove down my self-loathing. I

67

managed to turn on the ignition, put the car into gear and get myself back to the office. I was functioning. That was the bottom line."

I remembered her whenever my resolve to finish the book stalled.

At one of our support groups early on, a woman had come to the group who had just been contacted by her son and was in a panic. She'd never told her husband and, as much as she wanted to meet her son, she couldn't because she feared what her husband would say. She was terrified of losing him. He was a wonderful man, she said.

When we asked if her family had supported her during her pregnancy, she said she had been kicked out of the house and told not to come back with a baby. We helped her to see how the past was creating a dark mirror, so that she was expecting the same treatment from her husband, perpetuating her victimhood. She came back to the next meeting glowing. Her husband was only upset that she had never told him, and couldn't wait to meet her son.

I was learning that the only way to heal our terrible wound was to face the past, return to its source and forgive ourselves and everyone involved, so that we didn't keep recreating the past in our present lives. When I first began to think about the idea of forgiving, I was afraid. If I forgave would I forget and leave myself unprotected? But, little by little, I was learning forgiveness and forgetting were two different things, and that it wasn't necessary to forget in order to forgive. Those I met who did take the journey seemed so much more alive than even people who never had to live through such a tragedy. Could there be a gift, a vein of gold to be found in our suffering?

Chapter Five

One weekend in late Fall, Jack and Anna drove up in their yellow VW Bug to look at schools in the Bay Area. After one year in Idaho, Anna had had enough and had moved in with Jack at Fresno. But Fresno State wasn't their kind of place, and they were looking to attend a more cosmopolitan school. I was afraid to hope that they might live so close by.

A one-day trip turned into four, when their VW Bug broke down. It wasn't until close to Christmas, when they came up for another visit, that I would learn the unexpected and life-altering results of their previous trip.

Anna and I were driving alone together to Morgan and Patrick's annual Christmas party. The whole family had been invited. Jack had gone in Brett's car to pick up some beer for Brett, who was not legally of age to buy some – a little brotherly bonding. The night before, we had gone to see the movie *The Last Emperor* and stopped at a local pub after, then talked until the early hours of the morning. I'd sensed something was on their minds, but nothing was said. So, on the way to the party, I asked Anna if something was wrong. I was pulling the car up to park along the side of the misty road. The pungent fragrance of eucalyptus and redwood trees mixed with the scent of burning fireplaces was transporting.

"Jack and I are pregnant."

Instead of pulling to a stop, I ran smack into the tree in front of me.

They'd been trying to find the courage to tell me, even though they knew I would be the last person to judge them. "Jack feels so ashamed," Anna said. Afraid of their reaction, they weren't planning to tell their parents for another two months. Everything was going to be fine, I reassured her, trying to stay calm in the midst of my sudden elation. Maybe times hadn't changed that much after all, for Jack and Anna to react to an unplanned pregnancy with shame.

The warmth from the house and the festive party greeted us as we walked in. With Anna in tow, I searched out Morgan and, without thinking, told her the exciting news. Anna had a horrified look on her face, but I was unstoppable. Right then, Jack and Brett walked in, and I rushed up and congratulated Jack, informing Brett he was going to be an uncle. Brett was as happy as I was, while Jack seemed startled then relieved. Soon the word spread and everyone at the party was coming up to Jack and Anna congratulating them, as I floated around on a cloud.

Going public with their news all at once was not at all what Jack and Anna were prepared to deal with, but I felt, despite their discomfort, they needed such an overwhelming blessing to give them strength. If only one person had been thrilled for Ray and me about our baby's pending birth. I hoped Jack and Anna wouldn't be too angry with me.

As it turned out, Anna's parents were pretty upset with the news when she told them two months later, but not for very long. It had taken Anna's mother, a devout Catholic, many years to become pregnant. She'd pray every day, telling God she would have as many children as he deemed fitting, if He would only give her a child. In the end, she had nine children.

Another two weeks went by before Jack could get the nerve to tell his parents, but when he did their reaction shocked him. Rosemary was just fine and her husband went immediately up to the attic to get baby things.

When they called to tell me, I jokingly thanked them for giving me the perfect ending to my book.

But, as thrilled as I was about the coming baby, I found myself becoming fearful as well. My initial euphoria – oh, am I even wise enough to be a Grandmother - turned into the fear that I would never be considered one of the Grandmothers.

On the one hand, Jack could now understand the pressures Ray and I had been under with our unplanned pregnancy. But, at the same time, he and Anna were keeping their baby. How could Jack do anything but hate me when he sees his precious child for the first time? How could he even comprehend my letting him go, when even I couldn't?

The baby was due any day, when my Mom came for a visit. We were at the de Young Museum, listening to a docent tour of the Andrew Wyeth exhibit, when suddenly I just wasn't there. No matter how hard I tried, I simply couldn't focus on the paintings, nor could I hear what the woman was saying. I'd never felt like that before and didn't know what to do with myself.

The feeling continued as we found our way down to the café. As much as I tried, I found it impossible to concentrate on a word Mom was saying, and then suddenly everything came into vibrant focus, as if I were seeing the world for the first time.

That evening, as we were all about to sit down for dinner, the phone rang.

Kip answered. "Oh wow, a boy!"

After he and Jack talked for a few minutes, Kip handed me the phone.

"Congratulations, Grandma!" Jack sounded over the moon. Dylan had been born at 2:59 that afternoon. "Even before he was completely delivered, his eyes were wide open and he was looking around at everyone," Jack said. Anna's family had been there and so had Rosemary. Jack apologized that our conversation had to be cut short, since visiting hours were almost over.

A bottle of champagne was always waiting in the refrigerator for some celebration or another. No sooner had I popped the cork and the phone rang again. This time I answered.

It was Rosemary. "How does it feel to be a Grandmother?" Oh, my God. How can it get any better?

"Great! How does it feel for you?"

"Great!" She then proceeded to tell me all the details, which I would never get from Jack, just as she had when I first contacted them. This was how it should be between two mothers who shared the same child. As I listened, a part of me felt badly for all the adoptive mothers who were too afraid to allow such a unique relationship to develop, and I felt even worse for all the mothers who would remain cut off from the major events in their children's lives as a result of the adoptive parents' fears. On my part, I knew, from the moment I met Jack again, that I would do whatever it took to make such a relationship work, because I didn't have the strength it would take to live otherwise.

At that point in our relationship, Rosemary and I had an unspoken agreement to put Jack's needs first before our own. For me that meant keeping my instincts and my grief to myself and respecting the life that Jack had had. The clock could never be turned back, so all we could do was make the best of the future. I'd made that decision after the first conversation with Rosemary, when I sat for the longest time after hanging up the phone, completely shaken from the bizarre experience of hearing about my own son's life from a stranger.

That night, as I lay in bed, I felt sadness come over me, despite all the joy. How could I explain to anyone the feeling of not being able to be there for the birth of my first grandchild, when everyone else could be, even though I'd only known my son for three years and we were still getting to know each other? Such a need was visceral and no amount of rationalizing could erase something that felt so wrong.

But then I sat straight up in the bed. I had been there for my grandson's birth! He was being born at the exact same time as when I was strangely disappearing from myself at the museum. How mind-boggling, yet how comforting to know.

As much as I wanted to hop in the car the next day and go down to see little Dylan, I had to wait. My mother's boyfriend, Gordon, was coming to town for the weekend with a friend.

After dinner one evening, my mother went out onto the deck for some fresh air, and Gordon was looking at family pictures on the bookshelf. "You have three sons?" he asked astonished. After all the years they'd known each other, Mom had never told him. He was upset that she would keep something so important from him, and so was I. I'd had it with secrets and told him that, on top of that, she'd just become a great grandmother. Gordon shook his head that Mom would keep something so wonderful a secret, but I wasn't surprised. She always kept everything to herself.

On the way down to Los Angeles on Monday, I asked Mom why she never told Gordon. "There was never an opportunity," was her reply. After knowing him eight years? At that point, I had to let go of wishing she would ever be different from who she'd always been.

But there was a crack in her armor on the drive down. "Will they accept me as a great grandmother?" she asked, "or as an acquaintance? Will Brett and Kip be considered uncles, or will we all have to hold back our love?"

She and Jack had met once, when he'd flown up for the day just to meet her. My mother, who was a good conversationalist, could barely speak the whole time we were together. Jack looked so much like me and all she could do was stare, completely unprepared emotionally for finally seeing her first grandchild.

"Is it possible," she asked, "if getting pregnant out of wedlock could run in our genes?"

"I don't think we're a mutant strain," I reassured her. "Plenty of people have sex before they marry. We may be an extremely fertile family, but we aren't defective."

"We drove up to Jack and Anna's home in Long Beach in the late afternoon. Jack met us at the bottom of the steps.

I was barely breathing as I climbed the steps. This was the greatest gift I could ever have, to see their child, my grandson.

Jack opened the door for us, and my mother went in first. Her great capacity for living in the present allowed her to be spontaneous and charming. I was mute, completely caught up in the momentousness of the occasion and rendered speechless. It was overwhelming.

He was lying in the bassinet I had given him, the one Brett and Kip had occupied. All I could see at first was a mass of dark hair. It was just like Jack's had been.

I tiptoed around to peek at his face. He looked so much like Jack had looked, like a little Indian. I was so happy. Jack would be getting an idea of what he had looked like during the eight months that we had no record of.

Dylan began to stir and my mother picked him up. She had always been crazy about babies in church. She got Dylan smiling right away. I finally said, "Enough, Mom. It's my turn."

74

As I held him, Dylan's body felt so familiar to my body. Holding him somehow filled up the place that had been left empty by Jack.

At the end of the evening, after dinner was over and Dylan had been fed again, I asked Anna if she minded my holding Dylan while he slept. We all sat peacefully together, not talking much. We were pretty tired.

I held Dylan close to my heart. I looked down at Jack, sitting on the floor. In his sleep, Dylan smiled a wise and ancient smile and I felt the circle close around us, completed."
(The ending for *The Other Mother*)

Initially, when my mother planned her visit at the same time the baby was due, I'd hoped the birth would come early, so that I could meet my first grandchild alone without her. My reasons were complicated and mostly based on residual anger from all I had gone through in giving up Jack, and perhaps from some unconscious irrational fears that remained from the role she had played in my losing him. At least I understood that now, and was not controlled completely by an eruption of unconsciously displaced emotions.

In the end, it was the best thing for both of us that she'd come with me, and I was happy to share the joy with her. Dylan's birth had brought us closer.

Before heading home, Mom and I met up with Anna and her family at Manhattan Beach. Every Thursday, whoever in the family could make it had met at the same spot on the beach for years. Anna's mother was there. Rosemary was coming to meet my Mom, and Jack would arrive later from work. It was Dylan's first outing.

Beach chairs were lined up, filled with four generations of family. The elders sat in theirs like rocks, as if they had been there forever, little children running all around them. Anna had covered Dylan with a purple cotton shawl threaded with silver that I had given her, that now somehow made me feel like I really belonged there, too. The warmth of the sun and sand and the lapping waves loosened the tension I'd been holding. All felt peaceful and right.

Rosemary greeted us as she walked down the slope of beach toward the group, carrying coolers. Mom turned to look and I felt her tense up. I felt myself shrinking inward, as I always did in the presence of Rosemary's confidence. With all her acceptance of me, I still felt like an interloper. I knew I was still projecting all my issues about authority figures from the time of losing Jack – the nuns, social workers and nurses - onto her. Would I ever get over it? Sometimes my issues seemed to become more intense over time, despite all my efforts to heal.

After taking a peak at Dylan sleeping under the shawl, Rosemary graciously introduced herself to Mom. They exchanged pleasantries. Mom was a master of pleasantries. Then we all settled back down to enjoy the day.

I watched Anna as she cared for the baby, tenderly checking on him, and felt she was a natural. I was glad that she and Jack had so much family around them to help, because they were going to need it. There would be no need for a family member to be given up for adoption, if the spirit of the child was valued over the stigma society had placed on the mother's marital status, and the family could accept their new member into the fold without judgment, which Jack and Anna's families had done.

Jack arrived earlier than expected and went straight to Dylan, who was waking up, and confidently lifted him out of the car seat like he'd been a father forever. Dylan looked up at him with his unusually penetrating gaze, which Jack had told me caused some of his friends to turn away at its power. He was like a little Buddha baby.

The sky was turning a soft pink, as the sunset approached, and everyone started packing up to go. Mom and I said our goodbyes, knowing how tired Jack and Anna must be after having so many guests during Dylan's first week of life.

That night, as we went to bed in the hotel room before leaving for home in the morning, Mom said she couldn't get to sleep, that she was feeling angry by nothing in particular. I knew she was finally feeling the full force of her own loss, but I also felt it would be useless to try to break down her defenses and talk about the enormous tragedy of our situation. We could both get lost in it.

Just before I was to leave for Dylan's Christening, Cindy called with great news. She was pregnant and this time everything was going well. After they moved into the house, she'd suffered another miscarriage. In hindsight, she said the timing of this pregnancy was perfect. Before that, she confided, she and Jim had had problems to work out in their marriage.

"Do you think it's going to be a boy?" I asked.

"Feels like it," Cindy said. "We'll know soon!"

Inside the church was dimly lit, except for the area around the Baptismal font where Jack and Anna stood with Dylan and the Godparents. Dylan looked out at everyone, his old soul gaze more wise and alive than the priest's. Anna's family was there, and so was Rosemary. Everyone seemed welcoming though surprised to see me, since I'd only recently visited and lived so far away. But how could I not be there? From their reaction, I could tell they really didn't understand, and I felt like an intruder all over again. I wanted to escape and at the same time didn't want to be anywhere else. I'd missed all these milestones with Jack.

On the way out, I passed by Anna's Mom who was talking with the priest, and overheard him make a comment about pagan babies. My back was up again, like at the Baptism Elena and I had attended together, and I was glad all over again that I was no longer a Catholic – not even a guilt ridden ex Catholic. When we first met, Jack told me he felt badly that he might be responsible for my losing my faith. I reassured him that absolutely no way should he take that on, that I had long before begun questioning the authority and the teachings of the church.

But he had been partly right. I had said countless prayers to find a way to keep him, and none had been answered. The nuns and the priests had given me no solace, only lies. How could it have possibly been God's Will that I not be with my baby, that any mother be separated from her baby?

A huge percentage of the mothers I had met had also left the church after losing their children to adoption, and almost all that did had developed a deep spirituality instead, perhaps from seeking a way to fill the great emptiness - the hole in their hearts that could never be filled, until they found their children. The only remnant of my faith was a prayer to the Blessed Mother to watch over my son and his family, just in case - my last connection to my Catholic origins. Now that last connection was severed, as I realized it was my love that had watched over my son, that the church's teachings only served to keep people from feeling their own power. Maybe Mary had watched over him, too, but so had I.

We all gathered afterwards at the home of one of Anna's siblings. Where Dylan had been perfect in the church, he was now having a meltdown. Everyone tried to hold him and console him, but to no avail. When he was passed over to me, I hoped so much he would quiet down in my arms, so I could prove I belonged there. But he didn't, so I gave him to Anna's youngest sister, Christina. She had the touch, and Dylan fell peacefully asleep on her shoulder.

It was difficult to discern whether I was being paranoid from my own insecurities or if indeed I was seen as trespassing on a family event, imposing myself where I had not earned the right to be. Rosemary seemed distant and everyone else appeared to be circling around me, avoiding much contact. Was it just Jack who wanted me there, or was he simply being polite? Long repressed messages the nuns and society had given me, that I was not a good enough mother for my own child, and my own feelings about having abandoned him suddenly overwhelmed me, causing me to feel like I had in the home and while giving birth to him – isolated, misunderstood and all alone.

When I returned home after my brief visit, it felt like I had not only lost my son but now my grandchild as well, and I was devastated. Fortunately, I had learned through my work with Toni to look at such extreme reactions as an opportunity to heal the past. A part of me *still* believed the censure about who I was as an unwed mother. Opening the old wound to my psyche allowed me to clear out those old recriminations for what they were – *not the truth*. Even if the worst case were true, that I wasn't accepted as Jack's other mother, too, that I had no right to be Dylan's Grandmother, without the old judgment from the nuns and society to color and intensify my emotional reactions to their view, I could find the strength and patience to hang in there.

Back at work on the book, I found solace in my writing, as I picked up the loose threads of my life, reweaving my understanding of it. Writing the book must be so cathartic was a comment I heard often, and which I resented deeply. I wasn't writing to purge myself of my experience. In fact, the writing was causing me to realize how bottomless my emotions were. The process was making me feel more real to myself, as I began to understand just how profoundly nearly every aspect of my life had been impacted by the maternity home experience and from being separated from my firstborn, an understanding I couldn't let myself have until I could find resolution by searching for him. Even so, I had always been well aware that great sorrow was lying in wait, running like an underground stream below the surface of my life, and I was afraid of it, despite the fact that I had a good life. But sometimes a little bit of the awful pain would seep through. Each layer of denial I was able to peel away left me with a deeper level of understanding.

I realized that I'd lived with a "phantom" family - my first that should have been had Ray and I been offered any help. My fear had been, when Ray told me in the hospital after our baby had been born that we should get married, that all his life our child would be teased that he was a "bastard." After all the indoctrination in the home, I wasn't able any longer to think through our situation with any clarity, but only through the filter of shame and fear. But that didn't mean our little family had died.

When I was writing about being in the maternity home and my son's birth, I realized that I had kept the fantasy the nuns had fed me that he'd had a better life than we could give him to console myself and go on, not wanting to face the reality that my writing was forcing on me - that I had actually left him all alone in the world to fend for himself. How did I know for sure he was better off without us? The only certainty I would have had about his future was if he were with us. Now, Jack and Anna were repeating our story but with the opposite resolution. They were waiting, until after the baby was born, to get married, not having to worry about the social backlash. They had no more financial resources than we'd had, but their families supported them.

As I wrote the second third of the book, I was seeing how the whole experience had affected so much of my life and who I was in it. The one area where I didn't seem to be affected was child rearing. Where many of the mothers reported being overly protective of their subsequent children, from an irrational yet uncontrollable fear of losing them, too, I was not like that with Brett and Kip, probably because my own mother had been such an anxious parent about us. Instead, I encouraged their independence. However, I never once took for granted the joy of raising them. Thankfully, too, I didn't allow the old judgment, that

80

I was not a good enough mother for my firstborn, to undermine my confidence as a parent to Brett and Kip.

It had been at their births and the stay in the hospital afterwards that had brought up the terror of losing them. But once they were home I felt safe, a common reaction. One mother in our group told of having a great birthing experience with her second child, surrounded by supportive nurses and doctors – the opposite of her first experience giving birth. But the birth of her third child duplicated the bleak experience of her first, and her heart had stopped on the delivery table.

Now that they had a little baby, it was difficult for Jack and Anna to get away for a visit to San Francisco, so I would make the trip down I 5 to see them at their home in Long Beach. I could sense a growing tension between us.

On one trip down there, Anna and I were home alone with Dylan, when I ventured to ask her what was wrong, knowing I would get an honest answer from her. Jack would never risk speaking up and hurting my feelings.

"Every time you come down, it takes Jack three days to get back to normal," Anna told me, obviously frustrated.

I kept feeling that if everyone would just let Jack and I have time together, to go through whatever we needed to go through, that they'd all have Jack back in an even better way. But it seemed to me everyone wanted to keep Jack like they always knew him.

At the same time, I realized that writing the book and being so involved with the issues brought up in our support groups had kept me stuck in our story, and feelings had remained raw. As much as I'd tried to keep all my emotions to myself, I must have "wreaked" with them. I was glad she made me aware of it.

But, as puzzled as I was about what she meant by Jack needing time to get back to himself, I didn't know how to ask her to clarify what exactly was going on. Jack and I were never alone together, which was disappointing for me. I kept feeling we needed that kind of time to understand and process all the emotions, and then everyone would benefit. Many of the mothers and adoptees in the support group were also in therapy and dealing with feelings was paramount. Unfortunately, over time we were seeing a trend, that the one searching became the one responsible for keeping the relationship going, as the one found was either not ready or had no desire to dive right into all the complicated issues together. As a result, the development of their relationships felt blocked.

When Jack came home, I asked him if he was feeling uncomfortable in our relationship.

"Let's just take time to have fun together," was his quiet suggestion.

Ah, ha! I suddenly remembered the advice of our therapist when Kip, Ron and I were in therapy together after the divorce. "You have to lay a solid foundation before you can expect to deal with big issues in a safe way, and so that you can be heard," he'd advised. I found myself breathing a sigh of relief at the idea of just having fun together.

After that trip, one of the mothers came to our next group quite upset. She'd been to her therapist that day and then had called her son, hoping to have a *real* talk with him. She made the call just before coming to the meeting, knowing she would find support for whatever the conversation brought up.

"All he could talk about was the fact the spoon was stuck in the garbage disposal," she complained, nearly in tears. "I don't think I can deal with this relationship anymore!"

"But the spoon was stuck in the garbage disposal," I pointed out, having gained a new perspective from Jack and Anna. "He's letting you into his real life."

"He may never deal with any of his feelings," another mother pointed out. "But, if he does, it has to be when he's ready, not when you want him to be."

We were all mapping our way through the uncharted and precarious terrain of our relationship with our children, with few guidelines to help us over the humps.

A couple of weeks after my visit, I got pictures in the mail from Jack and Anna. There I was, holding Dylan and looking like I must have when I'd last held Jack as a baby – lost and afraid, and I could see then what they'd been dealing with.

Brett, Kip and I flew down to Los Angeles for Jack and Anna's wedding in March. I wasn't going to put them through another torturous Chevy Chase-like family trip to take in the sights and learn a little history along the West Coast Highway, like I did on the way to meet their brother for the first time four years before, when all they had wanted was to see Jack and hit the beach.

We went straight from the airport to the church. The church was filled with sunshine as Jack greeted us, handed me a corsage, and led us to the family pew. By then, I hadn't even let myself hope to be so honored.

But as Rosemary's husband, Jack's stepfather, stood to let us into the pew, he mumbled loud enough for us to hear, "I don't know why you all were invited."

I felt terrible that Brett and Kip had to hear such a comment. They were there with their hearts wide open. I looked down at my corsage for strength.

Anna was radiant as she walked down the aisle on her father's arm in her white gown, and I was struck again about how much times had changed, since Jack was born. Then, it was considered taboo to wear white if you even had sex before marriage, much less a child, not that any bride would have broadcast the fact by not wearing white. But the censure was strong enough to cause some to feel guilt and actually choose an ivory gown.

We waited after the short ceremony for the traditional pictures to be taken before heading off to the reception. I knew to be grateful to have been invited, since most of the mothers I'd met in the same situation were not. This was one of the milestones adoptive parents earned the right to celebrate, after all the years of changing diapers, bandaging scraped knees, packing school lunches. I understood. But I still found myself wishing we could be included in just one wedding picture, another private emotional battle that waged within no matter what I told myself to think. Finally, I had to stop torturing myself by lingering and hoping, and the boys and I left for the reception.

Dylan was asleep in his car seat on a table at the far end of the room, when we arrived at the reception. Brett and Kip went straight over to him and sat down in the chairs on either side of him, like guardians of a little prince. I walked slowly toward them, taking in the sweet scene.

At first I thought it was my overly active imagination making me paranoid, but then Brett said he was getting the feeling that people were looking at us as if we were going to kidnap the baby. People *were* staring at us, wondering who the heck we were. Finally, as our discomfort grew, I told the boys to take the rental car and explore LA. What was I thinking to let them do that!

After giving them all kinds of instructions on being safe and when to get back to the hotel, I sat down on the chair next to Dylan, wondering what kind of mother I must be to let them go out on their own like that in a strange and crazy town. From my vantage point, sitting alone beside Dylan, I observed everything as if watching a movie. Jack and Anna were so happy, and everyone was having a good time. Someone came over and picked up Dylan when he awoke, eyeing me warily.

As the music started up, Jack and Anna had the first dance, then Jack danced with Rosemary and Anna danced with her father. Rosemary was beaming as she looked up at Jack. This was a big day for her, too. As all the parents got their turn to dance with the bride and groom, I felt like a wallflower, hoping to be asked to dance, too. But I hadn't earned that privilege I told myself.

With no car and no way to get a hold of Brett and Kip in those pre cell phone days, I asked Rosemary if she would mind taking me back to the hotel when the reception wound down. She was happy to, and I tried to keep up a cheerful conversation on the way, still not understanding why I was feeling so unbearably miserable when I should have been happy about being included at all. We said our goodbyes, and I was glad to find Brett and Kip waiting for me, safe and sound from their adventures. But they were upset with me for not realizing our being at the wedding would be so awkward.

It would be a few years before I would come to understand my intense emotional reaction to all that happened at Jack and Anna's wedding. One of the first writers on the impact of adoption was Evelyn Robinson, an author from Australia, who had also surrendered a son. Since so little was known, it was up to those affected to figure it all out, and Evelyn was particularly interested in figuring out why grief for the mothers actually increased over time, why in our case Time was not the great healer.

In her first book, *Adoption and Loss: The Hidden Grief*, Evelyn came up with the term "disenfranchised grief." For grief to heal over time, the loss needs to be openly acknowledged, publicly mourned and socially supported, she'd written. Rituals around mourning are as old as the human race, because it has always been known that grieving is essential to healing. But, when a mother was separated from her child through adoption, none of these needs were recognized. Her relationship to her child was not recognized, so her right and need to mourn her loss was not acknowledged and not socially supported. In fact, she was expected to go on with her life as if she had never given birth, never became a mother, never lost her child. Because of a sense of guilt and feeling responsible for the loss in the first place, few even felt they had a right to grieve at all. Anger, sadness, depression, hopelessness and numbness were the natural result, as grief was only buried and thus became chronic without a resolution.

Nor were we able to celebrate the birth of our child and the joy of becoming a mother. No baby showers, no happy grandparents, relatives and friends to acknowledge us and our babies, and no gifts for the newborn.

My basic human need to celebrate the birth of my son, to be acknowledged as his mother, too, and the heartbreaking denial of it had suddenly surfaced from being mirrored at the celebration of his wedding. No one was at fault. How would they know, when I didn't know myself?

Where my grief had appeared bottomless, I was now discovering it was a sacred wound that was taking me deeper into my own soul, forcing me to discover aspects of myself and the wisdom that it was trying to teach and the strength to transcend it was trying to offer. On the other side of grief was the capacity to know that what appears lost to us returns in higher ways, now with the understanding that we are all one and thus never lost from each other - a lesson I would be learning over and over.

On April twenty-seventh, Cindy called. Adam had been born, and she and Jim wanted me to come by the hospital to see him. I flew out the door. Our friendship was so natural and would have developed whether or not John had seen what little Adam had in mind for us. But knowing his intention made us cherish our connection even more.

Morning light shone through the window by the bed, where Jim sat with Cindy, who was holding the baby. Adam looked like a little golden peanut, and his wise baby eyes were the brightest blue. I sat down on the bed with them, and Cindy handed me the baby to hold.

"We want you to be Adam's Godmother," she said.

I told them I would be honored. At that moment, all was perfect in the world.

There was much to ponder, as I drove back home. If the soul survives death, how could it not be just as present during its pre-birth experience?

Morgan and I developed a workshop to facilitate healing. We wanted to help the mothers discover their memories, since the trauma of relinquishment had blocked so much. Our plan was to take the mothers through every phase, from conception through pregnancy, birth and surrender, using meditation and visualization techniques to guide them back. A friend had offered her house.

Everyone had arrived on time, and Morgan and I were still debating about whether or not to include conception in the visualization, since one of the mothers had been raped.

Betsy had only recently attended our support group, and we didn't know her well. She came because she had been contacted by her son and his adoptive mother, both of whom wanted very much to meet her - something most of us could only dream of happening. Yet, Betsy was dead set against it.

At the last minute, Morgan and I decided to trust the process. If Betsy couldn't handle going back to the violent conception of her son, her own mind would prevent her from doing so.

A surprisingly beautiful peace enveloped the group, as I guided them through the visualization. When we finished and I asked everyone to open her eyes, I observed Betsy to see how she was doing and was relieved to see she was all right.

We went around the room, each taking turns telling what insights we'd gained. Betsy was the last to speak, and I held my breath while she took a long time to gather her thoughts.

"I have to say I am in shock," she finally said. "When I went back to the rape, I saw our three spirits hovering over us – the father, my son and I – and it was as if we had always known each other. We actually loved each other. How can that be, but it felt so true. In that moment of seeing, I forgave my son's father. Now I can't wait to meet my son!" That night, Betsy called her son and his adoptive mother, and two days later they had a wonderful reunion.

The workshop was a success for everyone. Besides being able to reclaim their own stories, the women were able to experience the part of them selves that was beyond their painful stories. Until then, many had believed they *were* their stories.

Chapter Six

Three years had passed since I'd first started the book. I'd been doing temp work in an effort to create time to write and still earn money, but it wasn't enough to keep going and the pressure was hurting the writing. So, in the summer, I decided it was time to see if I could get a publisher interested and began researching how to write a query letter and book proposal.

Now I was going to have to face reality. With the exception of Jack and Anna and the mothers in our group, most people I knew thought I had made a big mistake thinking I could get published and felt I had been wasting my time. Even though I knew the writing had been essential to my own healing, their criticism, even though mostly offered from a caring place, fueled my doubts and I'd find myself wandering through bookstores and wondering why the world needed another book. At the same time, I felt I had to prove everyone wrong. I was still seeing myself through others' eyes and not my own.

Lives did, out of necessity, get derailed when embarking on a search. False selves created false lives that had to be unraveled to find the truth and transform. Being with others struggling with the same issues and remembering my original passion and how far I had come gave me my strength back, as I wrote the proposal and researched possible publishers.

As I poured over the *Writer's Digest*, seeking out the best publishers to approach, I decided to try the big ones first, those who published memoirs and self-help books. But I didn't really know what I was doing. When I first explored the idea of writing a book, I had attended a literary luncheon, thinking I would learn about the publishing industry. But the speakers were so discouraging: agents never call back; royalty checks have to be chased down; finding a publisher is nearly impossible, and on and on. All I learned was to never return to a literary luncheon.

I kept going back to the list of publishers under the "Literary" category in the *Writer's Digest*. I would have given anything to be considered literary, so I put my book proposal in a violet-colored envelope and sent it off to the one publisher on the list, Soho Press, that seemed the most interesting and author friendly. Maybe, as it lay in their pile of unsolicited manuscripts, a little literary energy would rub off. And then I forgot about it.

As straight and monotonous as Highway 15 was, I loved driving down to Los Angeles, stereo blasting Enya and all the time in the world to think. This trip was for Dylan's first birthday party, and I would be staying with Jack and Anna. By now, everyone was used to my presence, and I began to feel a part of Anna's big family. Dylan was already aware that he had more grandmothers than most, and all Anna had to do to discipline him was to threaten to call all his grandmothers.

That evening, after the party, Jack and Anna had some big news. Anna was pregnant again. The baby was due the end of March. But that wasn't all. They were planning to move to Virginia and live near Ray. Jack had always felt the East Coast was more like home to him, and they both wanted to get away from the hectic life in LA. Although I understood their reasons completely, their news completely blind-sided me.

My trip back home was full of somber thoughts. Only two years before, I had thought Jack and Anna might be moving near me – a dream come true - and now they were going to be so far away, and Ray was going to have all I had hoped for. Resentments I didn't realize I had began to surface. Old, unacknowledged anger toward Ray flared up. I had protected myself from those feelings, even during my pregnancy, because allowing them would open me to feelings that he had abandoned me – abandoned us, and that would have made me face the fact that I had been abandoned by everyone, just as my baby had been.

Of course, it was much more complicated than that. Even though my father had forbidden my seeing Ray – if he couldn't do the right thing by me, why would I want to see him? – I had been in love with Ray and would have suffered two huge losses, if we never saw each other again. Even if their intention was the opposite, to love and protect me, I felt abandoned by my parents. I needed to know Ray was there for me or I would have fallen into a black hole and maybe never have found my way out. We were too young to know how our lives would be changed, how our child could be hurt.

So the deepest part of me, the part that I wouldn't admit to myself, that had hoped Ray would get on his white horse and ride straight to the unwed mothers home, swoop me up and carry us away like in some fairy tale, was feeling he hadn't earned the right to have everything I had been hoping for - my son back with me, even for a little while. As always, I kept those feelings to myself, understanding how distorted they were.

Issues around the father of our children were huge for most of us in the group, and sometimes derailed the reunion. One woman decided not to meet her son, when she saw that he looked and acted just like the father, until she worked through all her resentments and could see her child clearly for who he was and not through the filter of the past. Some mothers were thrown when their child exhibited traits of a family member they didn't like. We were all learning that we needed to go back to the original source of our resentments, and at least understand if not forgive, instead of projecting them onto our newly found children. If we didn't, there would be no chance of healing or of a good relationship, and we would be left only with our old resentments still festering.

Driving back home, it was hard to take in that they were going to be living so far away, and I wouldn't be making this trip again.

By the Fall, rejections began arriving in my mailbox, and I was reminded of the days I wanted to take a sledge hammer to it, while waiting for any leads in my search for my son. At least now I didn't have the fear that an FBI agent would come knocking on my door for breaking the law, as I had then.

With each rejection, I became increasingly discouraged. When a friend told me of how Jack London had papered the walls in one room with rejection letters, I found little consolation. Another friend suggested my story might be meeting with a great deal of prejudice, given the romance in the culture of adopting a stranger's child. The biggest criticism from publishers was that the manuscript didn't fit into any particular category. It wasn't exactly self-help and it wasn't exactly a memoir either. I had written the book that way intentionally, since I had always learned more about my own story by listening to others'. Not knowing the industry well, I didn't appreciate the need for specific categories in selling books.

One day in November, I was pacing the living room, feeling that everyone had been correct in their opinion that my hopes of being published were futile and I had wasted my time, when I stopped pacing, stood very still and suddenly knew from the depths of myself that it didn't matter whether I got published or not. I had nothing to prove to anyone but myself; what mattered was that I tried. I didn't give up the "baby".

Two days later, I found myself arguing with myself about what to do during my lunch break. By then, I was working full time as a temp receptionist at a non-profit agency that offered college scholarships. Go home. Check your mailbox. No, I don't want to go home. I have too many errands to run. I went home despite myself.

The sky was dreary when I pulled up the driveway and got out of the car. What was I going to do at home for an hour? I could see the mail had come, because the flag was down, and I pulled out the contents. There was a postcard. "Please call us. We've been trying to find you everywhere. You forgot to put your phone number on the proposal. Laura Hruska." It was from Soho Press.

The sound that came out of me could never be duplicated. It was guttural, laughter and tears all at once. I rushed into the house and went straight to the phone upstairs in my writing room. Laura answered the phone, delighted to hear it was me and asked me to wait while Juris Jurjevics, Soho's editor-in-chief, got on the other line. They said the violet envelope I'd sent the proposal in kept calling to them from the slush pile of unsolicited manuscripts, until they finally couldn't resist.

As it turned out, Juris had worked on Betty Jean Lifton's book, *Lost and Found*, when he was at Dial Press. Still, as we talked, I was feeling a certain hesitation on their part. Finally, Laura confessed that they had been debating about whether or not to tell me that she was an adoptive mother, worried that I might not feel safe enough to work with her as my editor. The fact that she was concerned was enough to dispel any worries, and I responded it was perfect, that, like with adoption, it will be two mothers sharing the same child.

I was to get half the advance for finishing the book, and the rest when it was to be published. There was a six-month deadline to finish. Laura warned me that I would most likely be more sensitive than most about the editing process, given the nature of the book. Any change might feel like my baby being taken away all over again.

As I drove back to work elated, I understood that before I could get published I had to learn the big lesson from a few days before. I couldn't live my life according to other people's ideas for me but, instead, had to always trust that following my heart's desire would never let me down.

In the beginning, Jack and Anna were happy about their move, but then their expectations were soon dampened. One night a few months after they'd moved to Ray's house in Virginia, they called and revealed how miserable they were.

Anna missed her family, whose philosophy was so different from Ray and his wife Jean's. Where Anna's family was happy to give whatever support was needed, Ray believed strongly in self-reliance. Even though Ray and Jean had given their son, Jimmy, the best education and start in the world, they expected Jack to make it on his own, as they had when they first started their marriage. Ray had helped Jack get a job, but then Jack would have to ride a bike to work, even in the middle of a snowstorm.

When I learned that Ray and Jean had had a rough start financially, I found it ironic that they had lived out the same situation that others had advised would devastate our marriage. Ray had become quite successful over time, as he would have had we married and kept our baby. In fact, he had adopted Jean's son, Jimmy, from a previous marriage and so had struggled the same as we would have in the beginning. When we first talked, Ray said that a great part of his attraction for Jean, besides his love for her, was that she had a son a year older than Jack, so he could always feel he had a sense of how our son was growing up. I had not expected him to have such strong feelings, since we'd been apart for most of my pregnancy and he'd only gotten to see his son once in the nursery, and then only the back of his head. When we'd asked the nurse to bring our baby to the window for Ray to see, she had closed the nursery curtain on us.

I had been learning how the father was often the neglected party in adoption reunions, as the adoptee naturally was more drawn to the mother in the beginning. Even in the newly evolving adoption literature, little sympathy or understanding was given to their plight. The social culture at the time didn't hold young men responsible for getting a girl pregnant. It had been up to the girl to keep her legs crossed. In fact, when they did stick by the girl, they were thought to be weak. It was also common practice to keep them out of the picture entirely and to not put their names on the original birth certificates. So, if they had feelings at all, they most likely didn't know how to deal with them or how to ask for help.

I had to suspect that some of the problems Jack and Ray were having stemmed from Ray not dealing with all the emotional issues from the past, and instead wanting to keep everything pleasant and in the present, not knowing how to do otherwise. His parents didn't even know that he'd found Jack and that they had a great grandson. Ray just couldn't tell them.

In one phone call, Jack told me he almost felt relieved that he hadn't been raised by Ray because, according to Jimmy, Ray had been an extremely strict father. Though Ray did not want to deal with his feelings from the past, his fears that Jimmy might find himself in the same situation spoke volumes. The ripple effect from the original trauma touched so many lives. I told Jack that I doubted Ray would have been so strict had he not felt so much pain about losing him and wanted to spare Jimmy all he had gone through.

So, even though I had been jealous of Ray's opportunity to get to know Jack and our grandson in a far more natural way by living together, I felt badly for both of them that neither one was getting what they wanted from the relationship, at least not yet.

Jack and Anna didn't want to hurt Ray and Jean by leaving, and neither did they want to seem like failures by returning to Los Angeles. I felt their despair, happy they could confide in me and that I hadn't lost them after all. I didn't want to undermine their relationship with Ray and Jean, but it did seem that at least Anna needed to go back home, especially since the baby was due in a few months and she needed her family. "No one's going to judge you," I assured them. "In fact, everyone will most likely be thrilled to have you back."

Not long after, Jack and Anna returned with Dylan to Los Angeles. Ray and Jean wouldn't see Jack and Anna for another seven years.

Jack and Anna were temporarily staying with Rosemary, until they found their own place. By then, Rosemary was separated from her husband. I wondered if my finding Jack helped a little to give her the strength she needed to do what was right for herself.

As soon as they were settled, I went down for a visit.

I was sitting on the living room floor, watching Jack silently watching me as I played with Dylan, and I felt a foreboding. His expression was one I had been dreading. Maybe I was imagining things, creating fiction as my mother would have called it, but I felt he was angry as he watched me play with his son the way I should have played with him if I had kept him, as I should have.

"Carol, we don't think the kids should call you Grandma," Anna said, as she walked into the room.

I tried not to react, although I wanted to die right there on the spot. Were they seeing me in a different light after their unsuccessful attempt at living with Ray? Was Rosemary becoming insecure after all her generosity? I'd observed that it was not uncommon for adoptive mothers to need more reassurance after grandchildren arrived. Perhaps the children were at least a subliminal reminder of the lack of blood connection, and the relationship felt too tenuous suddenly. Was it too difficult for Jack to think of me as Grandma, when he didn't call me "Mom"?

"We think it will be too confusing to the kids to know the whole story about how you didn't raise Jack," Anna explained. "We want them to know you first, before they hear it."

So, that was it. Know me first. That could only mean that they felt the kids could possibly hate me for giving their father away, and they didn't want them to feel that way about me, which was sweet but at the same time troubling. I'd always found that a child's response was formed by how an idea was presented to them. I could see now that the deeper issues were finally surfacing between us.

"Do you think you could come up with another name for Grandma that the kids could call you?" Jack suggested.

"I'll try."

How could I explain that I was feeling ripped apart? Would my sentence as a birth mother ever end? I couldn't bear becoming a 'birth grandmother," too, and have this stigma continue for generations to come. But I couldn't impose my anguish; it was mine to deal with. I could only hope that time would eventually heal everything. But now, I had my doubts.

The pungent smell of decayed leaves blended with the scent from eucalyptus and redwood trees, as I walked up the small magical mountain, my favorite place to hike after writing. I had programmed the mountain to give me answers. On the way up, I would think of a problem I needed to solve and on the way down I would always discover the solution.

I was thinking a lot about little Adam and how John had foretold his coming, when it dawned on me that I might be able to tune into my coming grandchild. Why not try? So on the way down the mountain, I sought out the grove of redwood trees I considered sacred, where I would often sit and meditate. Within the grove was a huge stone, the perfect place to sit. As I settled myself, bells from a distant church rang out three o'clock. Sunlight filtered down through the trees, and it did seem that magic was close by.

As I closed my eyes, I doubted anything would happen. I'm not sure how long I was sitting there, but suddenly I opened my eyes and there was a fairy child with blonde hair and light shimmering all around her. A feeling of great joy and wonder came over me. She was too real to doubt. And then she vanished, leaving me astonished. It was one thing to want to believe in such possibilities and another to have an actual experience.

One afternoon in late March, while I was finishing the book, I felt an overwhelming need to go out on the deck and soak up some sunshine. I soon fell asleep, even though I hadn't been at all tired. When I awoke, it was time for Kip to come home from school, so writing was done for the day. Brett was already in his first year at the University of Arizona.

Late in the afternoon, the phone rang. It was Jack. "It's a girl! We named her Mia Alexandra."

Anna was doing fine and they were both so happy. After three sons and a grandson, I was thrilled to have a granddaughter. Like with Dylan's birth, I must have been there somehow, because she had been born at the same time I'd fallen asleep outside in the sunshine.

Before I left to go down to see her and their new home, I sent the completed manuscript off to SoHo.

Little Mia was sweetly sleeping in the bassinet, when I arrived. Jack stood next to me, as I bent over the bassinet to take a peek. Suddenly, unbidden, I flashed on an image of Jack and I standing together on Mia's wedding day. Was I being shown the future?

"Dylan, Grandma Carol's here!" Anna called out.

I was Grandma again, just like that!

When Anna's family dropped by and then later Rosemary, everything felt lighter. Our issues had vanished. I was relieved that I hadn't made a fuss over them. Anna's mother was fond of saying that every baby brings a blessing when they come into this world. I was sure the whole family was hoping Mia's blessing would be a positive change in Jack and Anna's financial situation, but I knew her blessing to me was being back in the fold as one of the Grandmothers.

Morgan phoned when I got home from Los Angeles. Over the weekend, a forty-year-old woman named Robin, who had arranged an open adoption with a well-known and highly respected couple in Marin, had called in distress. It had been a week since she'd given them the baby and she couldn't stop crying. Did she have a right to change her mind?

On the way over to meet with Robin, I told Morgan about being demoted from Grandma and then elevated again, and she felt like I did that Jack and Anna's original fears had more to do with their own feelings than the impact the story would have on the children - not to diminish their feelings, which were quite understandable.

As we pulled into the driveway of Robin's small and neatly manicured house, Morgan and I agreed that, despite our own opinion that Robin should get her baby back, we had to remain as neutral as possible, that it was Robin's decision to make.

Robin greeted us at the front door. She was attractive, despite her eyes being swollen from so much crying. I was amazed, as I listened to her, that even at her age her reasons for not keeping her baby were much the same as ours had been. She was too ashamed to tell her family and friends, and especially mortified at the thought of telling her grown son about the baby, so she'd hidden her pregnancy from everyone.

"How do you know they would think less of you?" Morgan asked. Robin admitted that she just assumed everyone would react negatively.

"It could be that your fears are based on society's programming and not on how you feel in your heart," I suggested. "Who wouldn't love your baby?" I just felt in my gut that this was true for her, despite her worries.

When she asked if the pain would ever go away, we had to answer honestly, that she would miss her child for the rest of her life.

"But the adoptive parents are really good people," Robin said. "I would hate to hurt them."

"Are their feelings more valuable than yours?" I asked. "If you lose your baby, your sorrow will last a lifetime. This isn't to be cruel or heartless, but their pain won't be the same or as devastating as yours. How can it be? They can find another child, but you can't replace your own flesh and blood."

Robin was silent for a long time. We watched as her eyes became clear and her confusion dissipated. "Will you stay here while I call them?" she asked, getting up and walking toward the kitchen. "They gave me their phone number, knowing it would be hard for me. That's how kind they are."

When she returned, Robin asked if we would go with her to pick up the baby. The couple told her they could not possibly keep her baby, if she had such regrets, that they would not be able to live with themselves.

Morgan went into their home with Robin, while I waited in the car, feeling badly for the couple but knowing it was the right thing. Soon, Robin, with her baby in her arms, and Morgan, loaded with diapers, bottles and formula, came out of the house. I could see the faint shadow of the couple through the screen door, as they watched the baby they had thought was theirs disappear into the car.

Robin held the baby tight, as she settled into the back seat. "I asked them if they wanted to stay a part of the baby's life, but they answered no, it would be too hard," she said quietly.

That's the difference, I thought to myself.

We got Robin settled and left her to make her phone calls. The next day she called to say everyone was thrilled and offering support. To her amazement, they told her they couldn't believe she would even think they'd react otherwise. And her son was overjoyed at having a little brother. Morgan and I breathed deep sighs of enormous relief.

"I thanked God this morning when I saw his beautiful little face," Robin said, "and realized how close I had been to losing him forever."

Two months after sending the completed manuscript, the edited version arrived. I placed the package on a table in the living room and circled it for three days before opening it, trying to figure out the source of my apprehension. I remembered how Rosemary had told me that Jack had taken a long time to screw up the courage to open the package of letters and pictures I had sent him. Perhaps Laura had been right, the editing process would be like a mirror of the adoption. The book was my baby, and now someone had added their input and suddenly it was no longer my own. I had given birth to the book and had handed it over to someone else to rear.

Finally, on the third day I read the first page. This was not my writing! I was horrified and waited two more days before sitting down to read the whole thing.

In the meantime, I called my friend, Lynne, who was a librarian and avid reader, and asked if I could stop by her house so she could take a look at it. Lynne and I had gone to Baja together with two other tennis friends, Mary Beth and Shelby two years before, and they had been the first to read any of the book. Mary Beth had been the very first, and I had watched her intently as she read the first thirty pages while sitting on the beach a distance from us. The tears streaming down her face left me shaken and relieved.

"Lynne, what am I going to do? This doesn't feel like my book anymore," I wailed. "They even started the book in a different place in the story."

Lynne quietly read the first page. "I love that symbol you wrote about the light from the Venetian blinds making a pattern of narrow streaks on the ceiling, as you faced that social worker. Made me think of prison bars," she said.

Prison bars! I hadn't thought of that when I wrote that line. How clever of her to make that observation. I'd just gotten the most important lesson of my writing career. I wasn't in control in any way of how readers would interpret my words. They would bring their own perceptions and life stories to the reading of it. For each reader my story would be different. That was the revelation I needed, and I went home to read the new manuscript.

Still, the writing style was too different from my own to accept, and as I read further I seriously considered withdrawing from our contract. For some strange reason, I decided that, if they edited the scene from Sacre Couer, I would definitely pull out from publication. Otherwise, I would work with them no matter what. I guess a part of me still wondered if the shooting flame in the butter warmer had indeed been a visitation. Not a comma from that scene was changed.

I spoke honestly with Laura about my reservations, and she confessed that they didn't like the first version either, that it had been done by someone else and she would take over the editing now. Then she gave me my second lesson. "It's important to trust your story and not tell the reader how they should feel. Let the telling of the story illicit the reader's own feelings and you will have them hooked," she advised.

I had to admit that I did overwrite in places, not trusting because of past experience that others would understand. The next version was perfect and felt like mine again.

The next big issue was the title. Laura said, "Silent Love," as much as that title made sense to me, didn't convey what the book was about. The title was going to be *The Other Mother*."

By now I knew there was no arguing with Laura, once her mind was set. But I feared the implications of "the other woman," and my first reaction was shame. Of course, as I tried to accept the new title, I realized how much shame I was still carrying. How was I going to go out with the book still feeling so much disgrace?

The sky was an incredibly bright blue, as the plane circled then landed in Las Vegas. Laura and Juris were flying me there for the day to meet me for the first time, since they were attending the American Booksellers Association convention there. Laura wanted us to edit the last few pages together, and so I met her in her hotel room and we sat down to make the final decisions about the ending, before meeting Juris for lunch.

Laura's voice was child-like on the phone, the opposite of who she was in person – sophisticated and quite intelligent. I was afraid my brain wouldn't kick in as we began, but then the meaningfulness of our ritual and her kindness replaced all my self-doubts, and we finished the book together.

As we sat down to lunch, Juris surprised me with a copy of the book jacket. I loved it. "The artwork of mother and child is the same size as a holy card," I remarked.

"You're the first person to notice that," Juris responded.

I was happy I could impress them.

"You know, Carol, during one of your book signings," Juris said, a mischievous twinkle in his eyes, "a nun is going to come out of the shadows, pushing her walker, and it will be Sister Dominic!"

I knew he was joking, but a shiver ran up my spine anyway.

After lunch, Laura and Juris walked through the lobby with me to the entrance of the hotel, as I had to catch the plane home. A beautiful white limo pulled up as we exited, and Juris signaled to the driver that the car was for me.

"Get used to it, Carol!" Juris said, as I turned to him startled.

Nestled in the back seat of the limo, I realized there was no turning back. What in the world had I set into motion?

Over lunch, Laura and Juris had prepared me for the launch of the book and the publicity tour. Because they felt it was an important book, they wanted to delay publication until after the Christmas season to give it a chance to be noticed. So, the publication date was set for January 23, 1991. Much had to be done before then.

The most pressing item on the list, when I returned home, was to get releases from everyone whose name was used in the book. The nun's names and the names of the girls at the home had already been changed. I couldn't imagine what it would be like for someone to pick up the book and suddenly be reading her own story, so I changed some of the details of each girl's story and their names – all except one. Mary, who had been date raped and found herself pregnant, hymen still intact, had given birth on Christmas Eve to a daughter – our own version of the Virgin Birth. I couldn't resist the irony and only hoped she would never know of the book.

Otherwise, during the writing I had used everyone's real names, feeling that the honesty of my story wouldn't ring true to the reader unless I did. But, as I prepared myself to make each call requesting a signed release, my anxiety grew. Now I see I was being hyper sensitive, but at the time I needed everyone's unconditional support for strength. Nearly everyone, including Jack and Rosemary, agreed to have their own names used. My family was completely behind me.

But it was hard when Jack's father asked that his name be changed, as much as I understood his reasons. He wanted to be in control of who knew our story, and he wanted to respect his wife's privacy. Also, his parents still didn't know that Jack was back in their son's life. Still, I felt that if Ray could really own his part of the story, it would have been a deep healing for him. It took many years, but finally he asked that his real name be used, instead of the name we came up for him – Chris.

One person from the past was especially important for me to try to find. Jerry had been my knight in shining armor, when he defended my reputation at the Sigma Chi Fraternity at Davidson College. I doubted he even realized what his actions had meant to me, and now I needed him to know. It had been over twenty years since we'd been in contact, so my call was a shock.

"I can't believe it's you," Jerry said. "You won't believe it, but only a month ago, after keeping it all these years, I finally threw out the Rock Hill newspaper clipping of you as Winthrop Student of the Month." Of course, I could use his real name.

I soaked in everyone's remarkable graciousness, and no longer felt alone with my story.

The second big project was to help gather endorsements for the book. My dream endorsement, besides those of the experts in the field like B.J. Lifton, adoptee and author of *Lost and Found*, and Reuben Panner, author of *The Adoption Triangle*, was from Gary Zukov. His best selling book, *Seat of the Soul*, was the first one I read after finishing my manuscript, and I had been struck by how his teachings about reclaiming personal power were so similar to the inspiration I wanted to convey in *The Other Mother*.

So, I sent a letter to Gary through his publisher. A few days later the publisher called. Please send the manuscript. Gary phoned a week later. As it happened, he would be driving through Marin County the next day on his way to the airport from his home in Mt. Shasta. Could we meet for coffee?

As soon as he introduced himself, I knew our meeting was going to be about more than the book. After six years of being immersed in adoption issues, I could spot someone who had been impacted by the experience. I used to joke that it was like we all had a neon sign over our heads, declaring our involvement. But Gary Zukov? Maybe I was wrong this time.

Gary was a lovely man, and our conversation was fascinating. He had an extraordinarily calm presence that forced me to slow down. As we talked, I patiently waited to hear what he really wanted to tell me.

"Carol, I have never told this to another soul, but I had a daughter and the mother and I gave her up for adoption. Her mother went to a home like yours. I have never forgotten our daughter. In fact, I was going to dedicate my next book to Elizabeth - the name we gave her."

"Oh, Gary. You are going to be able to help so many people!" I blurted out.

Gary looked at me as if I had two heads and was silent for a long time. "Carol, I just told you something I've never told anyone and you have me out there telling the world." He was clearly upset. "You are going to be a very public person when your book goes out, and you have to be extra careful to really listen responsibly to the stories people are going to tell you. Just let them tell you, without adding your own opinions about what they should or should not do."

106

I apologized for my mistake, grateful for Gary's honesty and to learn such an important lesson from someone who could handle my insensitivity, before I made such a blunder with someone else who might be more affected. I had to control my need to make everything all right for others in pain.

Gary went on to explain that he wanted to wait for his daughter's mother to search, as he didn't feel it was his place. But, if she were unable after some time, he would try to find their daughter.

While Gary went out to his car to gather his thoughts and write the endorsement, I waited inside, absorbing and feeling grateful for all that I learned during our remarkable conversation. I had an even greater awareness of my responsibility, as I went public with the book, and hoped I was up to the task.

Gary returned to our table and handed me a piece of paper with his endorsement: "I recommend it with all my heart. Its courage, integrity and love make it a treasure. ... not only for adoptive families and birth families, it is for everyone who longs to know how deep the levels are that connect us, and how precious."

How had he known my greatest hope for the book?

Chapter Seven

One bright sunny morning in October, I received a frightening phone call from one of the mothers in our support group. Gail, who had been attending the group for the past several months, had become pregnant as a result of a date rape and had given up a daughter twenty-five years before. The boyfriend had denied they'd even had sex, and she never got over his betrayal and the loss of her daughter.

Her reunion had been difficult, because her daughter's materialistic values were so different from her own and how Gail would have raised her. Finding a child who had been raised with different values or a different religious faith is always difficult to reconcile.

In Gail's case, her daughter's adoptive parents were buying her love with a new car and a new apartment, after finding out about the reunion, and Gail couldn't compete. Nor, did she want to. But she felt she was losing her daughter all over again.

If she hadn't been raped and then abandoned by her boyfriend and then lost her daughter, Gail would have become a strong woman, full of life. Those qualities were still a part of her, but now she was fragile. She had arrived at the last group with a huge shopping bag full of gifts for everyone – all meaningful to each person, like baby booties and pink bubblegum cigars for one of the mothers who had just had a reunion. For me, she had bought a beautiful white silk designer blazer to wear for the book's publicity tour. We'd accepted the gifts at Gail's insistence, but we were worried for her. She didn't seem like herself.

I had just dropped off my car for a tune-up when the phone rang. In the beginning of the conversation, Gail seemed normal. But then she talked about the movie, *Five Easy Pieces*, and quickly deteriorated, until all she did was spell the number "5" over and over for the next twenty minutes. Then she switched to spelling my name. Nothing I said got through to her.

I felt paralyzed without a car and was afraid to hang up to call someone for help, in case she might harm herself. Finally, after nearly an hour, I realized that Gail was just going to keep on repeating the same things, and so I put the phone down and ran over to the neighbor's to call a friend of hers. When I returned home and picked up the phone, Gail was still spelling the number five. I stayed on the phone, until her friend arrived at Gail's house.

"I need to call an ambulance," she said. "She refuses to go with me to the hospital."

Gail's friend phoned in the late afternoon to let me know that Gail had been admitted to the psych ward of San Francisco General Hospital, and I went to visit her there the next day.

I found her in the locked ward for women. That morning's *San Francisco Chronicle* had run a story with pictures about a woman who was found wondering deliriously around the financial district with her baby in her arms. She was the first woman I saw, as I was let through the locked doors. "Where is my baby?" she kept saying over and over, just the same way Gail had repeated the number five.

When I found Gail, she was holding a blanket in her arms as if holding a baby and talking about Tinkerbell and other things that made no sense, until I made the connection to a one woman show

Gail had recently attended with some of the women from our support group. In her brave one woman play, *A Name You Never Got*, that was both funny and tragic, Rhonda Slater acted out her experience of having to give up her daughter playing all the characters herself, including the mean social worker.

At one point in the play, Ronda told of seeing the play *Peter Pan* when she was a child and being asked to "clap if you believe in Tinkerbell." From her vantage point, she could see someone backstage manipulating the light that was meant to be Tinkerbell, and refused to play along and clap, feeling betrayed and manipulated.

I realized that everything Gail seemed so incoherent about actually made perfect sense. I could tell that she was so caught up in her own mind that it didn't matter whether I was there or not, and so I went to the nurses' station to report my observations and give them Gail's background information. Otherwise, they would never be able to help Gail unravel all that was happening in her mind, and would assume anyone talking about Tinkerbell was completely nuts.

As I approached the nurse's station, I could feel the tragedy all around me. How many women were there because of the loss of a child, from all the many ways that can happen? Perhaps in this place the psychiatrists knew to ask such a question, but I wondered. Over and over, women coming into our group told of being in therapy, sometimes for years, and the experience of losing a child to adoption was never discussed. Many never brought it up to their therapist, so deep was their denial. Having the belief firmly planted at the time of relinquishment, that we could go on with our lives as if IT never happened, derailed the chances of making the connection between our profound loss and any psychological problems we may be having. But for those who did bring their experience up their therapists only briefly discussed the subject.

What could cause such a blind spot in psychological literature? I had been so fortunate to find Toni.

Years before, I had been a volunteer counselor at Planned Parenthood, hoping to spare women the pain I had gone through. I did and still do believe in a woman's right to choose. But, at that time, I hadn't gained any understanding of all the layers of my own feelings of losing my son, and so regrettably sometimes might not have given the best support. At least I knew that now. After a year of volunteering, I'd found I couldn't do the counseling any longer, the depression I felt was growing too strong and I didn't understand why.

At an anniversary celebration of Planned Parenthood I'd attended after finding Jack, thirty of us had formed a large circle and went around the group telling how we'd come to work at Planned Parenthood. Three quarters of the women had told their story before it was my turn, and I was surprised that not one had yet mentioned giving up a child for adoption. Statistics proved I couldn't be the only one.

As I told my story, no one stirred. I added at the end, that every one of the women I had met, who had experienced both adoption and abortion, felt that though the grief of abortion was great it was nothing compared to losing a child to adoption. I thought for sure now someone would feel safe enough to bring up her own experience, but no one did.

Afterwards, a woman who had talked after me approached me to say she shared my story. I wondered why she hadn't felt like she could be honest with the group, when I had opened the door for her. But from her breezy attitude I could tell she was only living on the surface of her feelings, since I had been there myself.

Then another woman came up to me, speaking loud enough for everyone in the group to hear, and cheerfully told of having become a social worker helping unwed mothers give up their babies for adoption. The impact of my loss had not made a dent in her defenses. I saw that for the system to change in any profound way professionals needed to honestly examine their own misguided thinking, instead of repeating the same mistakes in order to protect their own egos and past mistakes. We all had a journey to take.

That evening I became even more determined not to go out still wounded with my book, so that I could help others without my own blind spots interfering.

A nurse turned to me from her position behind the nurses' station and patiently listened to my explanation about Gail's obsession with Tinkerbell. She seemed to appreciate my insight, but I got the impression she didn't really grasp all I was telling her about Gail's traumatic losses.

A week later, Gail called heavily drugged from the medications she'd been given and frustrated at her psychiatrist's lack of understanding. She'd been diagnosed manic/depressive. "That's why I went on that crazy shopping spree," she explained. "They think it's a chemical imbalance in my brain." She said she had no choice but to go back home to live while she recovered.

When I hung up the phone, I was nearly undone by her tragedy.

Laura phoned with exciting news. The publicist they'd hired had contacted *Good Morning America*, and they wanted us on the show. But we had to agree that they would be the first to interview us. Us? Apparently, the publicist was finding that without Rosemary and Jack on the publicity tour with me the book had no credibility. After all, which woman was the *other* mother, and how amazing that Rosemary had let me into their lives? After all the blood sweat and tears of the writing, the story was suddenly all about Rosemary and not about the experience of being an unwed mother and losing a child to adoption, a reality that was difficult for me to accept. But all along I knew that I had to let things play out the way they were meant to, whether or not I agreed. At the time, I had no idea just how many adoptive mothers would be inspired by Rosemary's openness, and how many reunions would be successful as a result.

When I called to ask Jack and Rosemary if they would be willing to be part of the publicity and appear on *Good Morning America*, they were excited. We were going to be flown to New York and put up at the Ritz. What wasn't exciting about that, except I was really worried for them both, especially Jack. He would have to sit between his two mothers and not say anything to offend either one. What a nightmare for any adopted person to contemplate! I was worried, too, because neither Jack nor Rosemary had any interest in the issues inherent in adoption and wouldn't be prepared for the likely difficult questions they'd have to handle. As it would turn out, my fears were warranted.

My job, Laura said, was to come up with five bullet points that I wanted to convey from the book. Marketing research had proved that five ideas were the most listeners could take in. The bullet points would be used in all the publicity and what I needed to stick to in any interviews. Even if the interviewer strayed, I could always take charge by returning to the original points I wanted to make.

Of course I wanted to speak about the homes, what the times were like back then, and help others understand why we needed to find our children. I wanted to explain how we were severely impacted by our experience and help our children to know that they had never been forgotten. And, I wanted to advocate for Open Records.

But, if I only had one point to make, I realized it would be my hope that people could come together in love and not fear.

After years of writing in solitude, suddenly so much was happening. Galleys were sent out for reviews, and the publicist was arranging television and radio interviews and book signings on both coasts. Press releases were sent out to all the adoption support groups and national organizations.

Despite the positive responses coming in, I was worried about the general public's reaction. Would I be stoned by going out with my story? The three books published before mine by a mother who had given her child up for adoption had not received the level of publicity that mine was going to have.

By chance, some time in the seventies, I'd turned on the television and received a shock. A woman was speaking anonymously from behind a curtain, telling of her experience of being in a home for unwed mothers and being coerced into giving her infant up for adoption. Hearing a story so similar to mine, when I had never spoken with another mother with my same experience, left me reeling for weeks after. That the woman was interviewed from behind a curtain and used a fake name left a clear message that it was still not safe to reveal our stories. Her shadowy image became burned in my brain. My plan had always been to search for my child when he turned eighteen, but seeing that the stigma still ran so deep I began to feel the chances of a positive outcome were bleak.

Now, years later, with the prospect of being so public with my book, one of the first questions people asked was whether or not I would use my real name, and most reacted with surprise when I said I was going to. But what would be the point of writing a book about all the secrecy and shame imposed by society on an unwed mother if I hid behind a fake name, I'd bravely respond. Deep down I felt shaken by their question.

Morgan and I sat in the circle of seats that surrounded the sunken fire pit of a cheesily decorated bar, so untypical of sophisticated Marin County, which made it even more fun. We were having our ritual glass of wine there after the support group meeting. Despite the over the top décor, the pit felt like a throwback to pagan times, the roaring fire seeming to elicit a deeper wisdom.

Brett was soon to arrive home for Christmas break. He'd spent the night before at Jack and Anna's, as he always did now on his trips to and from the University of Arizona. It was good that they were able to establish their own relationship, without all my emotional baggage getting in the way.

The night before, when I called there to see if he'd arrived, Anna answered the phone. "You know, Carol," she said, "speaking of the book tour, I should be on Oprah. I need her to put her arms around me and say, 'Hey girlfriend, what's it like having three mothers-in law!'"

Morgan laughed when I told her Anna's wish, but we both knew Anna really did need that hug. Search and reunion changed people, sometimes profoundly, as adoptees integrated new knowledge about themselves and their mothers became whole from confronting all they had been through. Husbands, wives, partners, family members were suddenly living with a new person. The healing process is intense and preoccupying, consuming beyond anything anyone is prepared for, and adoption literature was still in its infancy and had yet to extend its focus beyond the immediate triad of birth parents, adoptees and adoptive parents.

Jealousy was an understandably common reaction, as significant others had to stand by and wish they, too, could impact their loved one in the same powerful way. Feelings of betrayal and abandonment were a natural result of so much preoccupation with the new relationship and all the inner changes that were occurring. For many it was difficult to accept the necessary changes their loved one was going through, and there was nowhere for them to go to find help with all they had to cope with.

John Bradshaw's books, *Healing the Shame That Binds You* and *The Family*, had been a great resource for me. Though his work was about addictions, I found his wisdom easily applied to adoption issues. He often used a mobile to illustrate how, when one family member changes, everyone else is forced into the uncomfortable position of having to change, and hopefully grow, as well. The very least that is required is patience that comes from the knowledge that the dust will settle eventually.

On our minds this night, as Morgan and I stared into the flaming pit, was not only our group but also the frightening possibility of a war in the Gulf.

War had been brewing since August, but fear of it had increased dramatically over the Christmas holidays. Worry that there could be a draft was escalating, I was terrified of the prospect of my sons going to war, and I began reliving memories of the draft during the Vietnam War. I kept thinking we unwed mothers should have been a strange footnote to that war, as it seemed nearly all of us were asked to wear fake wedding rings and lie that the father of our children was away at war in Vietnam.

President Bush had given Saddam Hussein a warning that, if he didn't withdraw from Kuwait by midnight January fifteenth, the United States would use force to insure he did. The drama was being played out on television live and, as I watched, I felt guilty about worrying that my book launch could be derailed.

A week before publication, I went to my favorite bookstore, Book Passage in Corte Madera, to get a sense of reality about all that was about to happen. I was scheduled to give a book signing there the Tuesday before Mother's Day, the first real public acknowledgement that we were mothers, too. Since I never considered the book to be just mine, I hoped that every mother who had lost a child to adoption would somehow feel empowered by the inroads into the collective *The Other Mother* made.

"Oh, your book is already on the shelf over there," one of the employees said. "But the strangest thing keeps happening. It's been removed from the shelf three times and hidden in different places in the store! Each time, we've had to spend hours looking for it."

Who would have done such a thing? A mother who shared my story, who wanted to read it privately, too ashamed to buy it for fear of exposing her secret? An adoptive mother who didn't want anyone to read it? It had never occurred to me that the very people, whom I'd hoped would benefit by reading the book, would be afraid of buying it. But, of course they would. Should the book have been packaged in a brown wrapper?

I followed the directions and there it was on the shelf of new releases, ironically right next to a book about steamy sex, by an author whose name followed mine alphabetically. But there it was! I was thrilled.

Saddam Hussein did not back down by midnight on the fifteenth, and the country was held in terrified suspense the whole next day. The evening of January sixteenth, five minutes into the evening news, the first bombs were dropped on Kuwait. From that day on, all media coverage was dedicated to Operation Desert Storm. For the first time, war was primetime live.

Laura called the next day to say I needed to be braced for the likelihood that the publicity tour could be cancelled. Coverage of the war and constant war briefings obliterated anything else that might be happening on the planet. Who knew how long the war would last and what the outcome would be.

But two days before publication date of January twenty-third, Laura got word from the publicist that *Good Morning America* wanted to go ahead with our story and use it as the first bridge to regular news. Apparently the story was serious and tragic enough to ease viewers out of the constant barrage of war news, without causing emotional bends.

The *Good Morning America* studio was heavy with tension from the constant war coverage, when we arrived. Jack, Rosemary and I nervously waited in the Green Room, still uncertain if a war briefing would eclipse our segment. A stone-faced five star general sat with us. I was wearing the white silk jacket Gail had given me, even though I knew wearing white was going to add ten pounds for the camera. Needing to honor Gail's struggles and remind myself of all the people in adoption reform who were rooting for us to do well trumped my vanity. I was well aware of the countless video recorders poised and ready to capture our segment.

We were to go on live the second hour, the first hour being dedicated to news of the war. Joan Lunden was to do the interview. But, just minutes before we were to go on, the show was indeed preempted for a war briefing. The general arose from his seat, his huge frame towering over us and filling the doorway as he left. Not once had he made eye contact.

We stared at each other, deflated. Then an aide came in and asked us to follow her into the studio. Charlie Gibson was on camera, and we were quietly ushered to a set, where Joan Lunden was sitting. Jack was positioned between his two mothers. I could see his mouth was already dry as parchment.

As soon as the red light was turned off, Joan began to explain that they'd been on the phone with the publisher, trying to decide whether to tape and then air our segment at a later date, or go live for the West Coast only. What were my thoughts? There was no question in my mind that we should tape for a later date. I had no way of knowing then that, over the next two and a half months until the show finally aired in April, miles and miles of video tape would be wasted, as people set their recorders only to be disappointed by another delay.

As Joan Lunden spoke with us, while the crew prepared, she was giving all her attention to Rosemary and Jack. I felt she was uncomfortable with me, seeming to look at me as if I had two heads. I told myself not to be paranoid, but I felt uneasy. Only after the interview was over would I find out why she seemed so wary of me.

The taping began with Joan Lunden reading from the teleprompter. "When Carol Schaefer was nineteen ... "

Everything began to feel surreal, as I watched my story scroll down the screen. She then turned to me and asked for more details of my story. When it was his turn, Jack was nervous, as he explained that he had never planned to search himself but was happy when I found him. Later he said he felt his tongue was like the sole of a shoe.

"Rosemary, what was it like for you when Carol called. How did you decide to let her into your lives?" Joan leaned forward with much more interest, as she questioned Rosemary.

Rosemary was poised and confident. "Well, you never know if you'll be opening a can of worms?"

Can of worms! I hadn't expected her to say that, and I hoped my hurt didn't show on my face. I knew she had said it innocently and that most of the viewers would agree with her trepidation, but I was hypersensitive about how we mothers were going to be perceived. Rosemary went on to say that I had done everything right by allowing them to take the time they needed before we met.

"Carol, what would be the one thing you hope the readers take from your book?"

"My hope is that both mothers and their children will be able to come together in love and not fear." I felt strong saying my main "bullet point" and then the interview was over.

Charlie Gibson gave us the thumbs up from his desk, and I became aware that everyone standing by in the studio had been mesmerized and powerfully affected.

Joan sat back in her chair. Something was on her mind. She turned to me with much more warmth and began to tell us that her mother had had several miscarriages and was told by the doctor that she shouldn't try again. So, they adopted a baby boy. Four months later, her mother was pregnant with Joan. "My brother always felt like my twin," she explained. "We were so close in age. I have to say, though, I cannot imagine my mother ever wanting to meet my brother's other mother."

There it was. To her I did have two heads. I only wish she had told me before, so that I could have felt more comfortable during our interview.

A few members of the crew came up to us, deeply emotional, and revealed their own stories, giving me a glimpse into the intensity of all that was to come.

A limo was waiting outside to take us to lunch with Laura and Juris, before flying home. After knowing Jack and Rosemary so intimately while editing the book, they wanted to meet them. Over lunch, they read some of the reviews that were coming in, and they were great – all we could ever hope for. One from the reviewer at the St. Petersburg Times meant so much because it was accompanied by a personal note telling of how she'd stayed up all night reading it, something she never did.

This time, two limos were waiting outside, as we all said our goodbyes. Jack and Rosemary were flying back together from a different airport than me. We would see each other again in Los Angeles in a couple of days to launch the West Coast publicity tour, where our relationship would nearly come unglued.

I was packing for my trip down to southern California, when Laura called with surprising news. Two producers, Dr. Larry Horowitz and Michael O'Hara, were interested in making a television movie based on *The Other Mother*. In fact, there was an article in that day's *New York Times* that talked about their plans.

I wasn't sure.

"Apparently, Larry Horowitz knows your ex-husband," Laura informed me.

I called Ron right away.

"Yes, I'm Larry's investment advisor," Ron said.

Did you tell him about the book?" I asked.

"No. But Larry had recently called me and said, 'Ron, I have a book here on my desk, written by a woman named Carol Schaefer. Her ex husband's name is Ron. Do you know her?'"

I was floored.

"Larry's a great guy," Ron explained. "He's a physician at Stanford Medical Hospital, who got involved in the film industry when his friend Senator Ted Kennedy asked him to produce a movie about his son and the tragedy of losing his leg. An unauthorized movie was being made on the subject, and Kennedy wanted to make sure the story was told accurately. You can trust him."

Such an incredible coincidence could have only been heaven sent. Ron had been my major critic about writing the book, understandably concerned that I was wasting my time at the expense of the kids. What a sweet victory!

Still, I was reluctant. Made for television movies were popular at the time, and the dramatic formula usually involved pitting one person against the other, the last thing I wanted for our story.

Before leaving for Los Angeles, I called Laura back and asked her to thank Larry for his interest, but that I was declining his offer. I had given my first baby to strangers and I wasn't going to do such a thing again.

Our next appearance was on the *Michael Jackson Show*, a talk radio program that reached millions in Los Angeles. As with *Good Morning America*, we were to be the first non-war story in two weeks.

Jack was again deliberately seated between his two mothers, despite the fact this was radio and not television, and no one could see us. Jackson was sitting in a chair that was twice as high as ours. His sharp features and penetrating eyes were like a hawk's looking down at his prey from his perch.

Jackson, who was known for his intelligent but blunt interviews, lulled us in the beginning with nice easy questions. Then, suddenly, he asked Rosemary, "What would you think if Jack wanted to call Carol "Mom.""

Rosemary was taken aback by the question, but answered she wouldn't like it at all.

"Why not?" he asked her, pushing. And my mind went blank. I didn't hear her answer.

Then he blindsided Jack.

"You're sitting between these two women, which one is your real mother?"

Jack was furious and wouldn't answer.

Jackson pushed further. "I would have thought that at this time in your life, you would have made that decision."

Fortunately, they had opened up the phones for listeners to call in, and the next caller was a male adoptee, who expressed sympathy for Jack being put in the hot seat like that, and got him off the hook.

Jackson informed us that the phone lines were so jammed with callers they'd like to extend the show for another hour. But we were scheduled to do an interview for a Long beach newspaper and couldn't stay. We left the station shell-shocked.

I could see that Jack and Rosemary were boiling mad, but they said nothing, as they climbed into Rosemary's car for the drive to Long Beach. I was mad, too, but the difference was that I was prepared for anything that would be thrown at me, including the proverbial stones, where they knew little about adoption issues and were vulnerable. I wished I could go with them to Long

Beach, instead of in the limo, but I had five more interviews scheduled and this would be their last one.

I felt so alone sitting in the huge back seat, as the limo driver made his way through traffic to Long Beach. Where would I find the strength for the rest of the interviews, when it seemed our relationship had suddenly been damaged, maybe even beyond repair?

Rosemary and Jack were already in the parking lot of the newspaper office when I arrived. I could tell their anger had not dissipated. I'd never seen either one of them angry, so I didn't know what to expect. Clearly they did not want to be there.

But, like real troupers, they pulled themselves together and the interview went well. Still, when we said our goodbyes, I felt everything had changed between us. We had one last interview scheduled together the next day on *AM/LA*.

The picture that appeared on the front page the next morning showed Jack standing again between his two mothers. Jack and I were staring straight at the camera, and Rosemary was looking adoringly at Jack.

As I settled myself into a chair, waiting to go on the *George Putnam Radio Talk Show*, the third interview on my own, I was exhausted but elated at the same time. The interviews were going well, perhaps because the war had primed people's raw emotions and lent a sense of the futility and absurdity of keeping secrets against the backdrop of death and destruction. I loved doing the interviews, as it turned out. But then I tuned into the talk radio conversation going on ahead of mine.

Putnam had been the voice of the thirties newsreels, and if God were to speak to us from the heavens He would sound just like the legendary George Putnam. The debate that day, with his extremely conservative Orange County listeners, was whether or not the United States should use the neutron bomb and get the whole mess in Iraq over with right away. The majority of callers believed the bomb should be used and Putnam was agreeing with them. I was horrified. I began to fear a neutron bomb was about to be dropped on me. All I wanted was to escape from there, and as fast as possible.

After a long half hour, I was escorted into the studio. During a commercial break, while George and I were putting on our earphones, our eyes locked and he told me how he remembered those girls who had disappeared from his high school, and about one in particular whose sad eyes he would never forget. I was shocked, having prepared myself for the worst and not this enormous compassion. At the top of the interview, he repeated the same story for his audience. Our interview was electric and our eyes remained locked the whole time. I was sure that many of his conservative listeners were shocked as well by his views, and wondered how many of them were thinking of their own daughters, who had been hidden away and forced to give up their baby, in a different light.

As George thanked me and asked me to come back on his show any time, it seemed we were both left a little shaken by the intensity of our conversation.

The last radio interview of the day occurred during rush hour, and again phone lines were jammed with people hungry to finally be heard about their great losses. I found that listening through the headphones created an almost supernatural focus and intimacy, as if I were sitting right next to the callers as they told their stories, finally given a voice. The show was extended another hour.

By the time I returned to the hotel, I was flat out exhausted. Fearing the worst, I decided not to call Jack and Rosemary to see how they were doing and fell into bed. We were scheduled to appear on the *AM/LA* morning show the next morning.

But sleep brought a terrible nightmare. Through a strange filter of red, I saw Jack as an infant lying alone in the nursery of the hospital after I'd left him behind. I could feel in the very core of my being his terribly broken heart and confusion, and I was ripped apart by it. Finally I was seeing for myself in stark reality what I had done to my baby.

The phone rang, and it was Laura. *AM/LA* had been cancelled because of new developments in the war. But the taped television interview for a highly respected show about authors would go on.

I still hadn't shaken my nightmare, which had seemed to go on all night, when I dialed the phone to let Jack know of the cancellation.

Anna answered. "Jack isn't here," she informed me. "He spent the night in jail."

Apparently, Jack had been driving home after going to the cleaners to get the clothes he planned to wear for the *AM/LA* Show and running other errands, and was caught going over the speed limit near a local park. The cops, discovering unpaid traffic tickets while doing their background check, had roughed him up a bit, and Jack instinctively resisted. At the time, LA cops were notorious for their abusive tactics. Rosemary had bailed him out using her credit card.

When I asked Anna why they hadn't informed me, she bluntly responded, "What makes you think you have the right to know?"

What? Obviously, the pressures of our being public had brought to the surface all their unresolved feelings. Devastated, I hung up the phone and sank down on the bed. Why was I doing any of this? Why had I written the book in the first place?

How could I make them understand that I had never lost my motherly instincts for Jack? In fact, I couldn't sever them even if I wanted to, which I did not. Obviously, on some level I had known something was wrong with my son. Perhaps the deep groove of our separation had caused me to be more in tune, but my terrible nightmare had been a warning. Had Jack's lonely night in jail mirrored his feelings, as an infant, of being abandoned by me?

From my work with Toni, I remembered again to look for the deeper cause of intense feelings and see them as an opportunity to become more conscious of myself, instead of merely reacting. I had learned that I was much more than my painful story and not to get lost in it for too long, and that greater part of myself was where strength lies. But, in that moment, I needed all of that strength to go on with the book tour, when I was beginning to feel like a sham. I was scheduled to tape the next interview in a half hour and somehow had to pull myself together.

The host, an elegant and erudite man, welcomed me to the studio. By now, I had learned never to be nervous going into a show, as all the interviewers had a special gift of making a person feel comfortable. I could put myself in their hands and trust that all would go well.

Somehow, I was able to set aside the morning's drama, as the interview began. In fact, being on this show was a treat, since it was about books and writing and not about any issue. The host remarked that he rarely showcased memoirs, but he had found mine especially compelling. We talked about my writing the book, which I found an enormous relief.

Before going home the next day, I had one more event, a book signing at a popular bookstore, my first. As I sat at the table, surrounded by copies of *The Other Mother*, I waited and waited, and nobody came. That night was President Bush's State of the Union address, and we were at war. Everyone had naturally stayed home to see what he had to say.

Just as soon as the owner and I decided I didn't need to stay any longer, one woman came in, a copy of the book already in hand. She had picked up the book the day before, after hearing the

Michael Jackson Show, and had already read it. "Your story is my story," she said. "I've never told a soul."

When I returned home to San Francisco, there was another round of radio and television interviews and book signings. I was finding the public recognition of our suffering and need to find our children had become an unexpected healing, and I hoped so much that other "other" mothers and their children felt the acknowledgment as well. At the time, our plight had never been so public. We were no longer pariahs.

After the last round of publicity in the Bay Area, I phoned Laura to fill her in on all that happened. She told me that she'd relayed my decision to decline the movie deal to the producers, and they had asked that I wait to make my final decision, until after the airing of their upcoming movie *Switched at Birth,* the story of two families who had unknowingly reared each other's daughters when they were accidentally switched in the hospital.

"We think Carol will change her mind after seeing it," they said. "There's a scene where one of the mothers is praying that reminds us so much of her story."

I doubted I would change my mind, but I agreed to wait until their movie aired to make my final decision. The money offered didn't matter. My family mattered most.

No stones had been thrown during the entire tour. Somehow, I had been protected from any negative backlash. When I was speaking publicly, I had applied Laura's advice during the editing process, to trust my story and allow the reader to react emotionally without direction from me, and presented our story in a neutral manner. People were not put on the defensive and could really take in what I was saying. My apparent success had lulled me into believing this would always be the case, but I found out I was very wrong.

By then, my friends John and Kathy had moved back to Marin, and I ran into Kathy one day. John and Kathy had been great supporters of the book, which I had valued, especially since they had no connection to adoption. So, when Kathy said she had talked to her book club about the possibility of their choosing *The Other Mother* to read, I was excited, still needing to be acknowledged as an author as well as a birth mother.

"You won't believe it," Kathy said, "but the club nearly disbanded over the idea of reading your book."

I was shocked and hurt, as I would have known all the women. Apparently, one of the members threatened to leave the group if I came to speak, and those who had wanted me to come were thrown into turmoil over how vehement she was. In the end, they decided the group was more important than making a stand.

I was left to wonder who was that person and how many others in my community felt the same way?

Chapter Eight

The moment I walked into the hotel lobby, I was disoriented from the plethora of glass, mirrors and pink plastic flamingos decorating the place.

I was in Garden City to speak at the American Adoption Congress's annual national conference, for me a great honor. The pioneers of the Adoption Reform Movement had begun speaking out in the seventies about the need for recognition of our issues and the necessity of opening sealed adoption records. Many great writers, thinkers and activists had come before me, and I'd had their wisdom to draw on in my search for my son and in my own healing. All the research and writing that's followed has been based on the solid foundation that they originally established.

I had not yet reached the check-in when several people rushed up to me, cradling their copy of *The Other Mother*, eager to have me sign the book and to tell their story. One woman began hers midstream, as if we'd already been having a conversation. I was finding the book had created a special intimacy between the readers and me, and they felt safe telling their personal stories. One woman showed me her book, which was highlighted throughout in places where she began remembering her own story. Another showed me how she'd written her own experiences in the margins and planned to send that copy to her family to read. I was overwhelmed. I had hoped so much the book would be of help, but never dreamt it would create such raw emotions and strong reactions.

As I made my way to the elevator, I was stopped all along the way with one account after another, some almost too heartbreaking to take in, and I was struck over and over by the courage it had taken these women to even survive. Compared to most of the stories I was hearing, mine was benign.

Completely spun around by glass and mirrors and all the emotions, I got off on the wrong floor. The disorienting effect of the mirrors and glass was becoming a metaphor for emerging from the cocoon of our secrets, finally alive with our truth but not knowing what could happen next as a result.

After finally finding my room, I had only a few moments to pull myself together before I was expected down in the book room to sign copies of the book. Jack and Rosemary had been asked to speak with me, and I'd hoped they would get to experience the impact their openness to me had made, but they had declined. I wouldn't see them this trip, and I could only hope that time would heal our rift. But I wasn't sure.

A long line awaited me, as I arrived at the book room and settled myself at the table piled with my books. I had a great need not to have my story be a one-way conversation and so wanted to hear a little bit of each person's story before signing a more personal note with my purple felt pen. When a mother knew her child's name or an adoptee his or her own mother's, I included it, so they could see in print an acknowledgment of their relationship, perhaps for the first time. I began to feel like a priest hearing confession.

Back then, searches were far more difficult and most of the stories were about the pain of not knowing where their child was and the lack of acceptance by family and friends of the need to find their children in the first place. For me, as a writer, one woman's story meant a great deal. She told of reading the book while on a long train ride one night. "I'd been in denial," she said, "about all that had happened to me and had never cried, but the gentle rocking of the train and the cries of an infant seated with its mother behind me as I kept reading finally wore me down. I began sobbing, finally acknowledging all I had been through."

The line was still long, because I was taking so much time with each person, when the scheduled workshops were ready to begin. Just as the book room was about to close, I noticed an older woman in a plain gray suit approaching. She introduced herself as a nun with Sisters of Charity in Fayetteville, North Carolina. Oh, no.

"Carol, I just checked your book out of the library. I haven't had a chance to read it, but I wanted to meet you anyway."

Whew! She hadn't read it.

The sister explained that she had worked at a maternity home in North Carolina in the sixties, and had visited Seton House several times back then. To meet someone who had actually been to Seton House, when I'd never returned nor had met anyone else incarcerated there, turned me white as a sheet. What if all my memories were in fact a product of my imagination after all?

I took a deep breath and asked her what she remembered about the layout of the home. Her description matched mine exactly, which was a great relief. Then, fearing that I had maligned the nuns, that my memory had twisted my perceptions and I was wrong about how harsh they'd been when actually they had taken good care of me, I asked. "How would you describe the nuns at Seton House?"

Her kind eyes looked directly into mine. "In one word – cold."

Wow. Whew.

But she had her own story to tell. "Unlike the other nuns in the home for unwed mothers where I was assigned, I risked caring about the girls. I'd sit with them during labor, until they left for the hospital."

When I told her how I'd been pretty much ignored during labor and put in an ambulance to travel alone to the hospital, she became visibly shaken.

"We were never allowed to accompany the girls to the hospital," she recalled. "I don't know whether it was to punish the girls or because it would be considered sinful for us to witness birth. In truth, it was probably both."

We became aware that the room was empty and someone was standing by the door to lock it closed, while the workshops were taking place. The sister and I parted ways. I was left to ponder how any woman, even a nun, could possibly believe witnessing birth could be considered a sin. What were the origins of such a twisted idea?

That afternoon, one of the workshops was packed to the rafters. An adoptive mother, Nancy Verrier, was to present from her masters thesis in Clinical Psychology, which she had entitled *The Primal Wound: Legacy of the Adopted Child*. The title alone filled the room.

Nancy had two daughters, one she and her husband had adopted and the other she had given birth to. She explained that, until her adopted daughter was a teenager and in therapy and her daughter's therapist made her aware of the special issues her adopted daughter was dealing with, Nancy believed there was no real difference between bringing up an adopted child and a child one gave birth to. Once she became aware, her thirst to understand took over and her thesis was the result.

What she had to say was radical. She believed the mother/child bond was established during the first nine months in utero through communication between the two that was unconscious, instinctual and intuitive and that the bond was, therefore, extremely profound on all levels - physically, emotionally and spiritually. Thus, the severing of that relationship causes trauma in the infant, a wound that is primal and very real, though unconscious.

"Naturally, the child's growing sense of self is severely impacted by the original perceived abandonment by the mother," Nancy went on to say, "causing unexplainable feelings of loss and a lack of a sense of trust that results in anxiety and depression, emotional and/or behavioral problems, and difficulties in establishing intimate relationships with significant others. In addition, and on top of that," she said, "a child growing up in a family other than his or her original one had no genetic mirrors and thus was put in the position of having to adapt to what they perceived were the needs of those around them."

The explosion after her talk was telling. She had hit a nerve, and the truth of what she was saying rang throughout the room. Everyone was asking her for copies of her paper, which she didn't have, but she handed someone the one she'd used for her talk and they ran out to make copies. Even before she thought of writing a book based on her thesis, now a classic in adoption literature, *The Primal Wound* was already being published.

My extensive reading about pre and peri-natal psychology had tilled the soil and helped me accept her conclusions, as much as I wanted to bury my head in the sand of denial. As horrific as it was to hear about the great impact separation from the mother created for our children, especially when we had been assured the opposite – that our children would be better off without us – I was grateful to Nancy for clarifying the truth of what we were dealing with. How else could we begin to heal, except through the truth?

As I was waiting for a copy of Nancy's talk, I flashed on two adoptees, who had recently come to our group. One was able, since she was a little girl, to see energy around her, and told us

133

that, when she first spoke to her original mother, she could actually see her DNA being activated like sparklers on the Fourth of July, which was how many would describe the feelings during the first phone call or meeting.

I had to wonder if some of the overwhelming feelings during reunion were actually caused by dormant DNA being activated for the first time and all at once, when the process was meant to naturally occur over time through the mirror of the mother and other family members, as a baby grows older. "I finally feel part of the planet and not an alien anymore" was a universal statement by adoptees after connecting with their original mother, whether or not they liked whom they found. I had to think that perhaps that wasn't an abstract idea, but based on nature's design. That the late discovery adoptees, who only found out in their teens, twenties and even much later, that they had been adopted, also had the same feelings of emptiness as those who'd known all along was for me a validation of the Primal Wound theory.

Another adoptee had come to the same meeting of our group. All her life she'd had an image in her mind of a small town surrounded by rolling green hills, a place she longed for. She could only conclude that maybe some day she would live in such a place. But, when she found her original mother, she learned that she had lived all her life in a small town of the same description. "To think," she said, still in awe, "I always knew where my family came from."

Sometimes I wondered if all our pain and suffering was serving to unlock the secrets of the universe.

That evening a few of us sat in the lobby, having a glass of wine to unwind from the intensely emotional day of workshops and talks. During conferences it often felt like we were the walking wounded and downtime was essential. At the same time, our mutual understanding of each other created fast and often lifelong friends.

A woman came over and tapped me on the shoulder. 'I'm going upstairs to read your book," she said.

As she walked away, I looked up at the layers of glass and mirrored floors that surrounded the open space above me and realized she might not be the only one up there reading my story.

Sure enough, more than I had imagined had stayed up almost the whole night reading the book and seemed to be waiting for me, bleary eyed, with lots of questions the next morning. So many said that I'd told their story. Details may have been different, but our similarity derived from having the same feelings. My book was all I had hoped it would be.

Yet it was still so hard to acknowledge what I had created, first because of the enormity of it and second because, no matter what I accomplished, I still felt shame. If only I could have written a book about anything else but giving up my baby.

There was much to reflect upon on the drive home. The workshop presenters and keynote speakers had offered much stimulating food for thought. It was exciting to be at the forefront of a new movement.

Early in April, *Switched at Birth* aired two nights in a row to high ratings. What struck me the most about the production was that no one was portrayed as a "bad guy." Each family's reaction to finding out about the switch was portrayed as completely understandable, despite their conflicting emotional needs, which left the viewer to decide whose side, if any, they were on. This was exactly the approach I wanted O'Hara/Horowitz to take, if they produced *The Other Mother*, not only because I was afraid of losing my whole family if we were portrayed badly, but also because I believed everyone had done their best at the time – everyone except the nuns at Seton House that is, and maybe even some of them.

So, I called Laura and asked her to find out if the producers were still interested and if they could guarantee our story would be handled with the same fairness. They promised we were in good hands. During their discussion with Laura, they asked if I had mentioned the scene where one of the mothers was praying. They seemed to have unusual compassion for our story, and so, with a deep, still anxious breath, I gave them my okay.

After many cancellations, our *Good Morning America* segment finally aired in April. I was pleased with how well we did, though my heart went out to Jack. He looked so miserable sitting on the hot seat between his two mothers, obviously nervous about offending either one of us. Immediately after the segment was over, the phone rang. It was my mother congratulating us. She hadn't told anyone about the show. But each time she thought it was to air, she ended up late for work waiting for it. She was glad it finally was shown, since she'd run out of excuses.

I was going to be late for work, too, and flew out the door, as the phone began ringing off the hook. My scalp felt stretched taut to the point where I could hardly think, as I parked the car and walked the few blocks to the Marin Education Fund, where I was working again. The whole day I felt wired. When I got back home, my answering machine was full with congratulatory messages. By chance, my friend, John, who'd used up so much video tape trying to record each cancelled show, just happened to turn *Good Morning America* on from his Atlanta hotel room that morning, instead of watching the *Today Show* as usual, and our segment had just begun. Had word spread through the ethers?

Just as I finished listening to all the messages, the phone rang. MH, the nickname I had given her, which was short for Mary Hobson, one of my two best friends from high school, was calling to congratulate me. Our friends nicknamed us - MH, Linda and me - The Three Musketeers, because we were always together.

136

MH and I had been in her father's powder blue Buick at the legendary Boar and Castle drive-thru in Greensboro, North Carolina, when her boyfriend brought a friend of his along during the evening break from their summer job – Ray. Two summers later, the summer after our freshman year in college, I would discover I was pregnant. Linda was also pregnant, a few months further along than me and in the Florence Crittendon Home in Charlotte. All those years later, MH was able to finally tell me the devastating impact our pregnancies had on her life.

"Keeping Linda's secret was difficult emotionally, with no one to talk to," MH said. "But then learning my other best friend was in the same situation was devastating. I felt abandoned and afraid of an unknown future."

When a couple of friends of MH's mother told her of Linda's pregnancy, her mother forbade her to see Linda again. Otherwise, the neighbors would think her daughter was "like that" as well. Her mother's demand, however, contradicted all MH had been taught about being a loyal friend, throwing her into confusion, unable to reconcile the need for secrecy with religious teachings about compassion.

"Did the nuns at the unwed mothers home ever pray for the girls?" MH asked. "Or were they just there to enforce the secrecy with lies?"

"If the nuns did pray," I said, "they said the wrong prayers."

Keeping our secret and remaining our friend strained MH's relationship with her mother. "My mother never found out about your pregnancy, but what if she had?" MH asked. "What would she think about me having two friends in the same boat? What if I had gotten pregnant?"

Meanwhile, another friend had become pregnant around the same time but married the father of her child. That friend's mother had refused to attend her daughter's wedding or have anything to do with her again.

"The message I got," MH said, "was that if you want to be loved you'd best be perfect. My world was rocked."

Ten years passed before MH told anyone about us, and that was Brian, her future husband. "He didn't think any less of me," she said, "nor less of you or Linda. And now, there's a book review in the Greensboro paper for all the neighbors to see, and you were on *Good Morning America* for the world to see," she exclaimed. "That's very exciting and very scary at the same time. Now, no one is going to tell me you can't be my friend! But I think I have some work to do to chip away the Sixties beliefs that had been burned into my brain."

I was seared by all MH had been through and the fact that, as much as she had been there for me, I'd been unable to be there for her, never even realizing the shame she was forced to carry for the sake of our secret.

AM/LA called, wanting us on their show after their initial cancellation because of the war, and Jack and Rosemary were willing. Hoping to avoid another disaster, I sent a copy of Nancy's talk to both Jack and Rosemary, so that they could think through some of the issues that might be brought up this time, instead of being blindsided. But, on the drive down to Los Angeles, I couldn't shake an uneasy feeling that instead of preventing a disaster I had actually created another one by sending Nancy's paper.

We all met at the studio the next morning. Rosemary had brought a friend, and Anna came with Jack. I was happy Anna could finally feel a part of it all, even if it wasn't Oprah giving her the understanding bear hug she longed for. Jack greeted me warmly, but I realized right away that Rosemary was pretty angry still, though she said nothing. This time, as my story scrolled down the teleprompter, I felt alone with it. No one watching would have detected the tension between us, however, and the woman who interviewed us was enthralled with our story, as was the studio audience. Jack was much more comfortable and, in the end, the segment turned out to be a pleasure to do.

Afterwards, the five of us went to lunch before I had to head back to San Francisco. I was feeling hyper sensitive and wished I had an ally with me, too. Jack and Anna had news. They were expecting again. The baby was due the end of November. Then, halfway through lunch, Rosemary finally brought up what was on her mind.

"Do you really believe that business about the primal wound?" she challenged me.

I explained that I had sent it, not as something personal but to prepare her for how others might be feeling.

"Well, I don't believe in the primal wound, and I don't know why you do either," she said. "I believe love can make up for anything, and you know Jack was well loved."

I told her that it wasn't that I wanted or needed to believe in a primal wound, but the idea had struck a chord in many adoptees I knew. Listening to her side, I didn't get the feeling that she was defending her abilities as a mother as much as she needed to say that Jack was fine and that being adopted was not a factor in his life, as she had even forgotten that she had not given birth to him.

After lunch, we were all standing at a street corner about to say our goodbyes, when Anna and Rosemary began talking about Rosemary finding a list of Jack's firsts – first words, first steps, etc. - and a journal she had kept when Jack first came to them. Anna was encouraging Rosemary to write her own book, because she was a good writer and had her own story to tell. Since it had never been my intention when writing, I hadn't realized until then that my book might have been threatening. In fact, I'd always perceived Rosemary as having everything. If I were asked to choose between having only given birth to Jack or only raising him, without a doubt I would have chosen to raise him. My voice sounded weak in my own ears, as I encouraged her to write a book, too.

When I asked if she would mind sending me a copy of the list of Jack's firsts, that it would mean so much, and got no response, I thought I must not have spoken loud enough. I made my request again.

After a long pause, when I still thought I might not have been heard, Anna turned to me and asked, "Shouldn't some things stay sacred to Rosemary?"

I tried hard to cover up my hurt and quickly explained that I needed to get back on the road. I had to get away before tears betrayed me. We left in opposite directions. When I'd crossed the road, I turned back and watched the four of them walking away together. Was I not important to my son after all?

My grief was suddenly overwhelming, and I found myself still standing in the same spot on the sidewalk, wanting to end my life, not certain how I could go on. Only once before had I had such thoughts of wanting to die, and that was the night after Jack had been born, when I could not imagine how I would go on living without my baby with me.

Just as back then, when I ironically couldn't imagine leaving my baby all alone in the world, thoughts of Brett and Kip snapped me right out of my black hole and gave me strength to go on.

I still felt too shaken to drive and decided to stop by a neon shop run by a close friend of my friend, Lee. Before I'd left, he'd suggested meeting Linda and seeing the shop, if I happened to be in the area.

When I walked into her store, Linda looked at me startled. "Didn't I just see you on television this morning? I never watch those things, but you all had such a positive story!"

Just at that moment, Lee called. Lee had given me advice and support about handling the publicity, from his many years working in the theater as a director. His best advice, not to pretend I wasn't nervous but simply set the jitters aside, had carried me through everything. Funny how similar his advice was to Rob's. In most cases it seemed best to ignore the mind and all its dramas and just come from the heart.

"I hear you've become as notorious as Daryl Gates," Lee teased. LA Police Chief, Daryl Gates, was under fierce criticism after the recent violent beating and arrest of Rodney King by Los Angeles police, revealing suspected LAPD racism and brutality – something Jack had experienced himself.

Linda's compliment and Lee's joke thankfully brought me back to myself.

When I returned home, I had hundreds of letters to answer, heart-wrenching letters that all needed a response. And there was news from Larry. After their great success with *Switched at Birth*, they easily sold the rights to CBS to produce the movie version of *The Other Mother*. At the time, I was naïve about Hollywood and expected I would soon have to make myself available for the movie, as I had for the book. The five thousand dollar advance would float me for a while, so that I could take the time to answer all the letters, while waiting for production to begin.

As I settled myself back into a more normal life again, I found myself wanting to write another book, as I learned I loved becoming immersed in the writing process. But what would I write about, and how could any book I wrote ever mean as much to me as *The Other Mother*?

From my seat near the podium at Book Passage, I watched the audience taking their seats and felt like I was coming home. I'd been out in the world with my story, somehow given the strength for it all, and here I saw familiar faces finally. The room was packed.

We'd been invisible for so long, our stories little understood and meant to be hidden away, even to ourselves. But from the promotional tour, I had learned how important to our healing it was to own one's story and to feel the public acknowledgment of it. So, after Elaine Petrocelli introduced me, I stood up at the podium and asked how many there had lost a child to adoption? The question suddenly felt taboo the moment I said it. As I scanned the crowd, I could see some of the women there were startled and frightened, some close to tears by my question, and I wished I could take it back. But then a few raised their hands and then more, until the majority of the women in the room had their hands up.

After briefly telling my story, I read a passage from the book, one that I knew I could get through without breaking down in sobs, and then opened the reading up for questions. The room was silent and thick with emotion.

Finally, one woman got up and revealed she'd never told a soul, not even her best friend, she said, turning to the woman who was sitting next to her, whose eyes were wide open in surprise. As the speaker sat back down, her friend, eyes now full of tears, too, gave her a huge hug.

One by one, women found the courage to tell their story, as they gained strength from each other. Some there were adoptees, who spoke of never realizing that their original mothers had ever thought of them, much less suffered for not being with them.

We could have stayed there half the night. Just as Elaine Petrocelli got up to announce it was time to sign books, a man in his sixties emerged from the atlas section, amazed at all he had overheard. "I'm adopted," he said. "Do you think it's actually still possible for me to find my family, or is it too late at my age?"

Everyone turned toward him. "Yes you can," I answered, as others offered encouragement. "It's no accident that you happened to wander by." I could see a whole world had just opened up to him, as he stood there among the atlases.

Elaine apologized for having to stop the discussion, and said they had never before had such a powerfully moving event in the store. From the back of the room, her husband, Bill, nodded in agreement.

Again I felt like a priest hearing confession, as I signed books. Reaching for one book offered with trembling hands, I saw it was the woman seated in the front row who'd spoken of having given up her son in 1968 and had never thought she had the right to find him, much less know him. I looked straight into the pain in her eyes. Years later, Debra Baker said that when I didn't look away from her pain, she knew she herself couldn't look away from it any longer either. In fact, soon after, Debra began filming what became an award-winning documentary, *Broken Ties*, in which she bravely stepped out further than anyone so far and interviewed her mother and her sister about their feelings about Debra's unwed pregnancy and the relinquishment of her baby son.

It had been a great acknowledgment of us as mothers, too, to hold the book signing Mothers' Day week. But that Mothers' Day I wouldn't hear from Jack.

Sadly, the powerful urge to search for each other and reunite does not always guarantee a fairytale happy-ever-after ending. Because of the losses that have to be grieved, the secrets and lies that must be confronted, the forgiveness that needs to happen, relationships can end up shattering. The ripple effect of such a profound meeting inevitably stirs the lives of those we love, sending us all into unanticipated directions with crucial issues to confront and few guidelines.

We are intimate strangers, able to affect each other's lives in the most unexpected and far-reaching ways. But, when even mutually joyous reunions invariably create some measure of pain, it is natural to question whether or not these relationships are worth the risks. Is it selfish on our part to put innocent bystanders in such potential jeopardy? Does the need to reconnect stem from mere curiosity or from a need deep within the soul? What was this journey all about? Where would it lead? As our relationship floundered, these questions were again on my mind.

Through magical thinking I'd let myself believe that by writing the book I could pull heavenly strings and we would be spared the pain and troubles inherent in creating a relationship after reunion. But I was learning that certain parts of the journey cannot be avoided, nor should they be. Through these intense relationships, with strangers with whom we are profoundly connected, there is an opportunity to heal and experience love and forgiveness at a deep level - .a level far deeper than if we were never so wounded in the first place. But it was only an opportunity.

No way could I imagine abandoning Jack again, so I simplified my expectations and decided to call him when I felt the need. Otherwise, I would have begun to feel like a powerless, unwed teenage mother again - a place where I never wanted to return. The work of the relationship seemed to always fall on the one who searched, as the one found needed the time to process what the relationship meant to them. Instead of taking things personally, patience was required. And hope.

In hindsight, I was able to see that I needed to go through all the sorrows and pitfalls, not just for myself but also in order to help others with true compassion for whatever they were going through.

Our movie wasn't going to be made after all. After waiting six months with no word about when production would start, I called Larry. Apparently, CBS decided to produce another story, one about an adoptee, a minister who presided over the marriage ceremony of his original parents, who had met and fallen in love again after reuniting with their son. Larry hadn't called to let me know because he didn't want me to be disappointed. The huge wave I'd been riding had suddenly dumped me unceremoniously on the shore.

This was Kip's senior year in high school. His college application process was complicated because he was also hoping to play college football, preferably on a scholarship. The whole process became consuming and helped me get back to real life.

But my old reality was no longer completely satisfying. The need to begin another book gnawed away at me. Was I only meant to be a one-book author? One day, while sitting out on the deck, watching Buffy lying in the shallow water, a tennis ball floating inches from her nose while ducks swam all around her, I remembered how I felt while writing a particular passage in *The Other Mother*, when for the first time I began to wonder what I would write if I just let myself go.

I had been writing about a trip our psychology class had made to the South Carolina State Mental Hospital and being shown the belly of the place. Remembering the ancient soft pink brick buildings, crumbling from age, and the insanity housed there had struck a deep chord. One patient in particular had affected me, and I remembered even then how I knew she was a part of me.

> *"She was wrapped in a straight jacket, lying on her side as if she had been flung there. Her sandy blonde hair was matted and fell over her face. Her long, slender legs were tucked up under her chest. She looked to be my age. Her face, the chiseled line of her cheeks and jaw, bespoke a lost beauty, though her wide-open blue eyes were sheer emptiness. Mine filled with tears. I wanted to go into the cell and talk with her, help her. I asked a million questions about her, as we were whisked off the ward."*

I understood, as I wrote about her, that she had been a part of my unconscious, asleep from the trauma of losing my baby. Thinking of her now was opening me up somehow to something deeper in myself that needed to be expressed. But what that was about was a mystery. A good enough place to begin, I decided.

I found Jack standing on the sidewalk outside of the arrival area at the Los Angeles airport with Dylan and Mia. Mia was wearing the little green and white handmade smocked dress, stitched by a black woman from Charleston, that I had sent her. Her blonde hair was like spun gold in the sunshine, and she looked like the little fairy child I had envisioned before she was born. Jack seemed really happy to see me, and Dylan and Mia ran up to greet me. All was well again, miraculously.

With Anna's huge family, there was always a party going on. This time I was there for Dylan's third birthday, and Jack and Anna were throwing a barbeque. By now, I was an accepted part of the family, which meant so much. I was glad I had hung in there through the naturally uncomfortable times in the beginning when they didn't know me. I was growing so fond of everyone.

We were all sitting around the living room, when Rosemary arrived late. I found myself feeling like all the blood was draining from me, as she came through the door, even though she greeted me as warmly as she did everyone else. I knew it was my problem, not hers, but I couldn't get over the feeling and couldn't figure out its source. I only knew that I didn't feel I had a right to be there, that I couldn't be myself with Jack when Rosemary was around.

At one point, Rosemary and I wound up talking with Jack while he was tending the barbeque. It was Rosemary who had the courage to comment to me on our situation. "Isn't it funny how we can get along so well, unless Jack is around," she remarked.

I wished then that we could have gone over to a corner in the back yard and talked everything out, but I didn't know how and I

146

was afraid of saying the wrong thing. After all, to my mind she did have all the power. She could very easily have made it uncomfortable for me to be there. Being the other mother was very much like being the other woman. Maybe we just had to accept our feelings, until we understood them.

As usual, I was staying the night at Jack and Anna's. Early in the morning, before the sun was even up, Dylan climbed into bed with me and woke me up. He laid his head down on the pillow next to mine and we talked until everyone else was awake. For that little while, time was suspended and unfettered by feelings of adoption loss.

"From the sin of a broken condom ..." The simple line from Patricia Holt's review of *The Other Mother* for the San Francisco Chronicle haunted me still. Even after finding Jack and being accepted into his life, after the long four years of trying to understand my story and writing the book, I was still searching for the lost pieces of my shattered soul.

Reading books and research about our trauma had helped validate my feelings, at least intellectually. Books on spirituality gave me a greater perspective from which to view our journey. Working with John, Toni and Rob helped me to validate how the bond with my son had never been severed, which was consoling. Walking in nature always brought me peace, at least temporarily. My family's complete love for Jack and support of my book was invaluable. The new friendships I made, forged by our common experience, were indispensable. I knew now, from talking with so many birth parents and adoptees that one trauma does not fit all, that some were able to either shake off or let go of the effects of their experience. So, why wouldn't the pain just finally go away for me and for others?

One sunny morning, I went for a massage. I had met Darla, a clairvoyant healer, through John. As I knocked on the door of her apartment, I wasn't even sure why I was there, since I was feeling so good and it was such a beautiful day.

Layers of stress I wasn't aware I was carrying began to lift, as Darla began the massage. I had learned a lot about energy from John and all my reading on the subject, so I knew that working with someone who understood energy and could increase his/her own vibration facilitated healing.

We were laughing and catching up on each other's lives, when Darla began to work on my right leg. I found myself talking about how my legs had felt like two beached whales, after being given an epidural while in labor with Brett. Memories became as fresh as if I were still right there in the delivery room.

Then she moved around to work on my left leg, the one where I had had a melanoma the year before searching for Jack. As soon as she began to massage the part of my leg where the melanoma had been, I began sobbing and my whole body shook uncontrollably, something I had never before experienced. I was shocked and alarmed that I couldn't get control of myself.

This time, I was in the delivery room giving birth to Jack. I was asking the anesthesiologist to stop whatever anesthesia he was giving that was making me dopey and sleepy. I had only wanted a spinal to relieve the unbearable pain from the back labor, nothing else, as I wanted to be fully awake for my baby's birth. I'd always remembered that part. The part I hadn't remembered, and was now seeing as if my legs were still high up in the stirrups and I was peering through them, was the doctor's silent gesture to the anesthesiologist to up the dosage instead. I was horrified at seeing how I had been so deceived.

Despite the comfort that Darla was offering, I felt terribly embarrassed to be so out of control and fought hard to gain my composure, instead of allowing the horror that was trying to escape run its course. After letting me talk the whole scene out, Darla explained that the energy of the trauma had become stuck near my knee, eventually becoming physical with the melanoma. After my extreme reaction, when she released the energy still stuck there, I had to believe her.

Darla explained that, while talk therapy can be helpful, to sit week after week talking about the same issues only adds more energy to the problem and perpetuates suffering by causing us to constantly relive our painful experiences. "Once suffering or trauma has become a part of us, the memory can be literally stuck in our body as dense energy that begins to cause physical problems," she explained. "For example, a person who continually stuffs their feelings can become overweight as a result. Combining therapy with physical release, even by taking a hot bath with sea salts, speeds healing tremendously," she said.

On the way home, I found myself feeling ambivalent about letting go and becoming free of my perpetual sorrow, which made no sense at all. Didn't I want to be happy? Didn't I want to be free of the past?

When I got home, I called John. "I'm afraid to let go of my memories," I told him. "If I forget, how will I ever prevent the same terrible thing from happening again?" I was actually panicky just thinking about the prospect of letting go of the pain.

"Think of your memories as a color snapshot," he advised. "On an energy level, emotions have color. We humans know that when we say someone is green with envy, or when rage is always depicted as red, or blue as calming, for example. Now, in your mind's eye, drain the color from the snapshot, until all you have is a black and white image. Now you have a memory that will protect you, but you don't have to have all the emotions attached to it that are harmful and keep you stuck in the past, instead of being fully in the present moment."

I was eager to try anything. My pain was like a grain of sand in the proverbial oyster, opening me up to worlds of thinking I would never have imagined existed otherwise.

That night was our monthly support group meeting, and I was eager to share my discovery of how the mind and emotions have a direct impact on our bodies. In those days, Marin County was where much of the original what was called "New Age" thinking was rapidly evolving, so I wasn't afraid to offer my new insights to the group for fear of being thought a "flake."

But that night we heard an incredible story of healing. Adam, an adoptee, had been coming to the group off and on for several years, as he searched for his mother and sought understanding for himself. Just the last month he had found her, and in that meeting debated about whether to call or write her a letter.

I always advocated for a phone call over a letter because I believed in the power of our voices to convey so much more. Besides, what if the person never received the letter and the lack of response was perceived as a rejection? Early on, when one of Kip's teachers told me his sad story, I also advocated against having an intermediary call, and instead to wait until enough healing was anchored in to make the call oneself.

Fifteen years before, Bill had tried to contact his mother, using a social worker as an intermediary. The social worker informed him that his mother didn't want contact. After we talked, he called himself, only to learn that his mother had always talked about him with her five other children and had wished so much to meet him. Unfortunately, she had passed away three years before, heartbroken that she never knew her first child.

In the early days, it had been advised, when calling, to ask the person if they had a pen and paper handy and to please write down this name and number. That approach would have frightened me, so my recommendation had always been to start the conversation off by saying: my name is so and so, and I'm looking for someone who's very special to me. I'm wondering if you can help, or words to that effect. That opening would set the tone and allay fears, and it worked.

But Adam felt quite reluctant to call, and after much debate decided to write her a letter instead. He had felt in his gut that was the right way to go. We all encouraged him to follow his intuition.

By the grin on his face it was clear Adam had good news. "I'm so glad I trusted my instincts," he said. "When my mother received the letter, she was on life support and would never have been able to talk on the phone."

Adam had found his mother in a tiny town in Oklahoma and learned that she had never left the town limits, since giving him up. She was married but lived like a recluse, and before receiving his letter was thought to have only a few more days to live.

But, since receiving his letter, she was having a miraculous recovery, was now off life support, and they'd talked several times on the phone. Her husband hadn't known of Adam, but facing death she had nothing else to lose and shared the letter with him. Her husband was only upset that his wife had kept such a secret from him. Over the months ahead, they would meet and before long Adam's mother blossomed. Her health was restored, and she began to travel extensively. It was like she was reborn, Adam would say. The irony that he gave life in a way to the woman who had given him life was not lost on him.

Jack and Anna's third child, Asia Madison, was born on Thanksgiving Day, and I went down soon after for a visit. Jack had filled the house with yellow roses he'd picked from behind a gas station. 'No one was paying attention to them," he explained.

They were beautiful, but Anna was naturally upset that he risked getting caught. I was touched.

As he had the previous visit, Dylan climbed into bed with me early in the morning. This time, Mia climbed in, too, and they both nestled their heads on the pillow. "Grandma, tell us the story about you and Daddy and why you didn't keep him," Dylan whispered.

His question caught me by surprise. Somehow, he must have overheard conversations and was fascinated. The story, after all, had all the elements that children love in fairytales.

Anna had already made it clear to me that she wanted she and Jack to be the ones to tell the kids, and she wanted to wait until they were old enough to understand. As much as I wanted to explain things to Dylan, I respected her wishes, so I tried to change the subject. But Dylan insisted. I didn't want to lie, nor did I want to upset Anna, so I told them simply that their Daddy had two mothers, that Grandma Rosemary was wonderful to raise him when I couldn't. They seemed satisfied. After that, each time I came for a visit, the same ritual was repeated, each time the questions becoming more complex. My simple answers seemed to satisfy them, but in a few years the kids would really put me on the hot seat.

Now it was Kip's turn to get all the publicity. He'd just been named to the 1992 Mizuno Baseball All American Dream Team, the same team as future New York Yankee greats Derek Jeter, Alex Rodriguez and Jonny Damon. Scouts for various major league baseball teams and colleges, who would come and stand along the first base line to watch him play, were recruiting him, and articles were being written about Kip in the *Marin Independent Journal*.

But he was torn between going professional or taking a college scholarship and delaying his career. A dream settled his decision. In the dream, he was walking up a hill. Others were walking up the same hill, but they all drifted away. When he reached the top of the hill, he saw a small blue church – Chapel Hill and Carolina blue.

Ironically, I had wanted to attend Carolina and study journalism, but in those days women were not allowed to attend until their junior year, unless they were nursing students, since they would be too much of a distraction to the guys. In the South, in fact, girls who attended a coed school were not considered good marriage material. Guys dated girls in coed schools, but married those from women's colleges, the medieval assumption being that they were still virgins.

Before he left for Carolina, Kip gave me instructions. "Mom, I don't want you to make my room a shrine that I feel like I have to come back to. Just focus on your life now."

Easier said than done!

Chapter Nine

As much as I loved my home, it suddenly felt too big, now that the nest was empty with Kip away at Carolina. Where I had loved its openness to the sky and its spaciousness, I now felt strangely exposed, raw, unprotected. At least I was aware my feelings were a bit too extreme to be explained by the "empty nest syndrome."

I was willing to try anything, tired of the roller coaster: for a while feeling I'd dealt with all my issues only to be blindsided by some triggering event. So, when John called to tell me about a shamanic healer, I thought why not, I had nothing to lose. I'd been primed for the idea after reading Sandra Ingerman's book, *Soul Retrieval,* the most important book I'd read so far, in which she described how parts of the soul split off during a traumatic event, such as rape, in order to preserve itself. All the symptoms she listed of signs of diminished spiritual energy matched the effects of our trauma exactly. As a licensed Marriage and Family therapist and Professional Mental Health Counselor, as well as an expert on traumatic stress, Sandra's work as a true shaman in that ancient tradition bridged the culture gap between the modern and the ancient worlds, making the idea of lost parts of the soul believable.

Still, I was quite nervous as I left my name and number on the woman's answering machine, half hoping she wouldn't call back. Instinctively I knew to trust the process, but the other part of me thought traveling to unseen worlds in search of lost parts of the soul might be a little too far out. Unseen worlds? Lost parts of the soul?

I did know, though, that in order for any wound to heal properly, the core cause had to be reached and dealt with. Leaving the origins of the wound unattended would only create a scar, at best. I had come to understand, too, that when a trauma has occurred and hasn't been healed its effects broaden over time and anything that feels similar becomes like the original trauma. Even a slight rejection, for instance, can then have enormous weight. So, I was willing to try anything.

Two days after leaving my message, I was in the kitchen doing dinner dishes, when I looked up and saw what was distinctly a golden eagle high up in the cathedral ceiling, the same place where I'd seen an angel when I'd walked into the house the first time. The sound of the phone ringing startled me. It was the shaman.

"You won't believe it," I told her, naively, "just before your call I saw a golden eagle in my living room."

There was silence on the other end. Why did I say that?

"A shaman is never to reveal their power animal," Christine explained reluctantly. "But I have to validate your vision. Shamans work with power animals when they travel to the other worlds, and the golden eagle is my power animal."

We set a time to meet in the evening a few days later.

By the time I arrived at her apartment in Berkeley for our appointment, I was quite nervous and very skeptical. Christine didn't look like anything I would have expected from someone who practiced this ancient art. She seemed more like the quiet librarian type. I sat on the edge of the couch, my eyes huge as I

155

took in the array of crystals, rattles, incense and feathers on the long table along the opposite wall.

Christine was explaining that, whenever someone has experienced a trauma, whether from a serious accident, a sudden loss, rape or abuse, for example, a part of their life force or energy might split off and go to other worlds in order to survive. Soul loss is the result and can be experienced as anger, depression or apathy, physical or mental illness, even suicidal thoughts. The job of the shaman is to travel to one of the worlds, either the upper, middle or lower worlds, to find and retrieve the part of the person's soul that feels it needs to retreat from the physical world in order to survive.

I had decided not to tell her my story, as I wanted to see what might come up naturally, if anything.

"First, I need you to lie down here on the floor, while I use the rattles to call in the helping spirits and both our power animals to assist me while I journey," Christine explained. "As soon as they are here, I will lie down next to you and journey. When the journey is complete, I will tell you what I saw and then we will journey together. I do have to warn you, however, sometimes, but rarely, the spirits decide not to come."

I felt extremely uncomfortable as I lay down on the floor and Christine began to shake the rattles and burn incense around the room. The only feeling that would have been worse would have been the embarrassment of running out the door. The longer she shook the rattles, the more concerned I became, certain that I would be the rare one the spirits would decide not to show up for.

Finally, Christine lay down next to me, and I kept still, eyes wide open for what felt like an hour. At last, she came out of her trance and began to blow her breath through the top of my head and over my heart. "I have to apologize," she finally said. "It took longer than normal, because my golden eagle had a lesson for me.

He said I was taking too much pride in the fact that he was my animal spirit, that he could just as easily be a rooster."

"Different animals spirits are with us during different times in our lives," she explained, "depending on your needs at the time. Yours is a tiger, and he took me to an ancient temple, where there was a white marble statue of a Madonna and Child. Does that make any sense to you? There was a great deal of decay around the statue, and it took a long time to clean it all up."

"Yes, your vision makes complete sense," I said, astonished, and then told her my story.

"Now, you will journey with me, so that you can "see" for yourself and welcome back this part of your soul." Christine turned on a tape of drumming music, and we lay back down side by side. Soon, I was able to have my own vision of the temple with the statue, which was remarkable.

"You must make this part of yourself feel safe and very welcome," she said. "Celebrate! And, expect others to sense a difference in you."

I left her apartment feeling quite disoriented, but at the same time feeling a profound inner peace. The next day, Jack called. I hadn't heard from him in a while. We were both finally at complete ease with each other during the whole conversation. After hanging up, I knew that on some level he had sensed a shift, and that finally I wasn't still unconsciously trying to find what was missing in me through him.

The next time I sat down to work on my novel, I couldn't believe how much my creative mind had opened up after the shamanic healing. Writing was now a whole new experience.

Everyone had settled down around the aluminum table, ready to begin our support group meeting, when Angela arrived late, an angry scowl on her face. A few members of the group started to get up to leave, just as they told me they would should Angela ever come back to a meeting. Angela's anger was consuming and disturbed everyone. As much as I didn't like having her there, either, I believed that everyone was there for a collective reason and couldn't ask her not to come, as others had requested. Please stay, I asked those ready to leave. Two left anyway.

As we tried to settle back down, Angela kept silent, but everyone could feel her anger. I was as uncomfortable as the rest, as I began the meeting by telling my story about the shamanic healing, in case anyone might want to try it. When it was Angela's time to speak, she retold her story with rage and indignation, as she did every time she came, about how her son hadn't talked to her in three years and how the adoptive parents must have turned him against her. It was as if she pushed the replay button - she told the same story again, with the same wording as always, like the tape was stuck. Now, I knew I was going to have to ask her not to come back, as I could no longer ignore the effect she was having on everyone.

But, after the meeting was over, Angela surprised me by asking for the name of the shamanic healer. She was the last person I thought would be interested. I had to give her the name of a different shamanic healer, because Christine was out of town.

Three days later, Angela called to let me know she'd had an incredible experience with the shaman, who had discovered her soul hiding in a dark cave being protected by the Weaver of Time. The shaman explained that a common reaction to having a part of one's soul missing was uncontrollable anger – we want to be whole, not split off, and we're angry about the situation. Angela said that, after her healing session, her anger simply disappeared. To top it off, after not hearing from him in three years, despite living a mile away from each other, her son called the very next day. Now, she wanted everyone's address, so that she could write a note of apology for all the stress she had caused the group. I was shocked.

When she came to the next meeting, she apologized again and said she and her son had reconnected and all was going better than imagined. She was like a different person.

I began to wonder if it might be possible that our children could be angry with us for holding onto a piece of their souls. Many mothers had found adult children who had a great deal of anger towards them, anger that could be naturally explained from having been abandoned, but anger that ran so deep that they couldn't get past it. What if we literally had held onto a piece of their infant soul, as an instinctive way of staying connected or as a result of our own trauma? Physics was proving what ancient cultures had always taught, that we are all connected within a field of universal energy, and thus even our thoughts can impact others.

I offered the idea as a possibility, since I wasn't a shaman and so didn't know for certain, and suggested those mothers with angry children sit in meditation and "give back" to their children whatever part of their child's essence they still held onto. What did we have to lose by trying? Some realized to their surprise that they were afraid to let go at first, when they hadn't even realized they were hanging on in the first place. All, who tried, found the exercise had reopened their relationship with their child, as if by magic.

It seemed as if the deeper we healed the more life's mysteries were revealed. Unfortunately the process seemed endless. Would it be possible to ever heal completely? I doubted it. One woman, who'd been coming to our group for years, had access to all the great healers in the world. Liana was married to the highly respected Buddhist author and teacher, Jack Kornfield, and through him had met them all, but she still suffered. She and I would often wonder what it would take.

The house sold. One night, as I was packing to move, I found myself staring blankly at the television screen, even though the TV was turned off. I was exhausted. Suddenly, a gold light seemed to emanate from the empty screen, and I somehow knew then that the movie was going to happen. The whole week before, I'd seen commercials that could have been straight from the portfolio I'd put together when looking for a job in advertising before deciding to write the book, which made me frustrated. Even as I argued with myself that the film finally being made was impossible now, with so much time passing, a certainty remained. Maybe I *was* meant to take a different path, but only time would tell.

As seemed to be my habit, I became good friends with the couple who bought my house. Mark and Nancy loved it, and it suited their needs perfectly. Knowing they could take better care of it than I could at the time gave me peace of mind, and I could let it go. The irony of how the house sale mirrored letting go of Jack was completely lost on me at the time.

I had always loved visiting Morgan and Patrick at their home on Christmas Tree Hill. The pungent smell of eucalyptus and redwood trees, the protection provided by the dense woods there was like a nurturing balm, and so I bought a small fixer upper near the top of the hill. My new home was again opposite from my former home in every way, and, instead of feeling like a victim of my own poor choices, I began to see that perhaps I needed each new house to mark a new phase in my life.

Deer and raccoons replaced the sea gulls, ducks, geese and egrets of my former home. In dreams, houses and their various rooms represent different parts of our unconscious minds. But this house, dark and gloomy as it was, was real, not a dream. The power of a festering unconscious mind to create outer circumstances that scream out its need for healing cannot be underestimated. Brightening the house with paint became a Zen practice.

Since my shamanic healing, I felt the novel I was writing was even more personal than *The Other Mother*. I loved getting lost in the writing of it, but the book made me afraid at the same time, as it was a thinly veiled version of my own spiritual journey and the discoveries I made while seeking answers to how my life had gone. As much as I loved being caught up in my imagination, I felt vulnerable, since I was sure it would be considered too far out. I had yet to become aware that vulnerability was a good sign that I was bringing something new into the world. Instead, I felt fragile and wanted to keep the book to myself.

In *The Other Mother*, I wanted to connect with the reader through shared feelings. With the novel, I explored archetypes, having had a fascination with symbolism since studying *The Old Man and the Sea* senior year in high school. So when I discovered Joseph Campbell's books, I was in nirvana. I found tremendous inspiration from all of his teachings, especially his writings about the Hero's Journey.

However, if I had read only one particular statement of his that would have been enough. In it, he was discussing rites of passage and initiation. While pregnant, he explained, we are "expectant mothers," and still very much who we've always been. But giving birth is a rite of passage, an initiation, he explained, and after bringing life into this world you are never not a mother again - never again the same person you were before. Everything suddenly made sense about how we could never just simply return to our former lives after giving birth, as was promised.

Soon after, a friend called to let me know that Bruce Rappaport, founder of the Independent Adoption Center, was going to be on a popular radio talk show in the Bay Area. The full hour was going to be devoted to his trailblazing efforts to create open adoptions, where pregnant women were able to choose the parents for their children, as opposed to the closed system of adoptions in the past.

As I listened to the show, I became increasingly upset, as Rappaport explained how the "birth mothers" were counseled to make an adoption plan, and how they were to refer to that plan and the reasons for it whenever they began to waver in their decision, and especially when their feelings might change after giving birth. Counseling was even offered to the grandparents to help shore up their daughter's resolve.

I phoned in with an innocuous question, in order to get on, as the whole show was devoted to singing the praises of open adoption. Three callers were ahead of me. Just before my call was taken, Rappaport was discussing how they were trying to pass a law that would shorten the time for signing the surrender papers to seventy-two hours for the "benefit" of everyone, especially the "birth mother."

"Carol from Corte Madera, you're on."

When I introduced myself as a "birth mother" and author of *The Other Mother*, I could tell they knew who I was and were dismayed that I got past the gate.

"First, I need to point out that a woman does not become a mother until after she brings life into this world," I said. "While still pregnant, she is an expectant mother, so to refer to her as a "birth mom" before she gives birth is not only incorrect, but also takes advantage of her vulnerability. Words are powerful. In light of that fact, expectant mothers should make two plans: one for adoption and another for keeping her baby, as giving birth is an initiation (I probably shouldn't have said that!) and, therefore, the new mother, with entirely new feelings, may very well change her mind, as she is just getting used to her new role."

"Well, she'd never give up her baby then," Rappaport responded.

"Well, there you go!" I managed to say, just before being cut off.

I actually didn't have such an empty nest after all. Brett asked me to take care of his dog, Tory, because the apartment he was moving into in Tucson didn't allow pets, as the previous one had. So, I now had three cats and Kip's bird Magic, plus Tory. Buffy had died just before my move.

I had no idea that Buffy had meant so much to others, until a neighbor had yelled over to me from across the creek, wondering where Buffy was. He missed watching her daily morning walk down the pier. Now, in the new house, the mailman and Magic had formed a special relationship. Every day, as he walked up the hill to deliver the mail, he would whistle to Magic and Magic would whistle back.

When Jack called to tell me they were expecting again, he confessed that he'd scheduled a vasectomy, ironically he said on my birthday, but chickened out while sitting in the doctor's office. The baby was due the end of October. With four little ones under the age of five, they were under all kinds of stress financially and had to move in with Rosemary.

Tess Miranda was born October 29. As with each of the others, she brought a gift.

Just before Thanksgiving, I received a call out of the blue from Maureen McCormick, who played Marsha on the *Brady Bunch*, wanting to know if the rights for *The Other Mother* had been sold. She had loved the book and wanted very much to produce the movie version.

Brett and Kip and their friends were quite impressed with me, when I told them I'd been talking with Marsha of the *Brady Bunch*. Once Kip answered the phone and got to speak with her. What young boy of that generation didn't have a crush on Marsha Brady? What young girl didn't want to be like her? During one of our conversations, I told Maureen she should run for president, she had such a devoted following.

Maureen wasn't able to put any money down for the project, and I was advised to wait until she could, so as not to tie up the rights in case another offer was made. But I liked her very much and she had such a passion to make the film, I had a difficult time holding a hard line over the next year, while she tried to figure out a way.

In February, my Aunt Marge, Joanie's mother, passed away suddenly, and many in the family gathered for her funeral. I was not related by blood to either my Aunt Marge or my Uncle Jack, who was also my Godfather, and thus not to their children, my cousins, either. My mother's father had married Aunt Marge and Uncle Jack's mother, after my mother's own mother had died. But they were family to me as much as if we had been blood relatives, and so I have always had an understanding of how deep the love in adoptive families can run.

As much as I wanted to attend the funeral, I was unable to go financially. My new job working in the designer department at Macy's brought in only enough to cover basic expenses, if that. I made the sacrifice working there to be able to continue to write. Ever since I had faced death, with the discovery the year before searching for Jack that I had a melanoma, I no longer took my life for granted and took to heart Joseph Campbell's advice to "follow my bliss." Some could easily have called me reckless, but I felt I had no choice.

Mom called when she got back from her sister's funeral. "Well, now everybody knows," she said.

"Knows what, Mom?"

"About Jack, about your book."

I couldn't even say, you mean they didn't know before? How could she not have told them? How anxious she must have been then that they all would find out.

Apparently, during the wake, Joanie's oldest son, Bruce, had begun talking with Mom about the book. Mom was surprised that he knew about it. He said he had known through Joanie, and that he was frankly tired of all the family secrets. He himself had just come out that he was gay.

While he was talking to Mom, Joanie rushed up. "Please, don't let Janet overhear you talking about Carol's son and the book. It was Mom's dying wish that Janet never know."

That's when Mom first found out that her own sister's daughter had also given up a child. Even though Marge had known about Jack and the book through Joanie, they had never discussed anything. Mom was floored, but as usual didn't say much. Maybe she didn't even know how she felt about Marge never telling her, or maybe she understood completely. They were, after all, from the same generation. But Bruce was clearly not. I sensed Mom was relieved that the secret was out, and that no one was judging her.

My Aunt Peggy, Uncle Jack's wife, had been to the funeral, too. Uncle Jack had passed away a couple of years before. They had adopted their first child, whom they'd named Jack Jr. So many Jack's in the family.

The Chosen Baby story rankled most adoptees I'd met over the years. For so many, being told when they were little they'd been chosen made them feel special - until their rude awakening when conveying such proud information to little classmates when first entering school. Their special bubble burst when their little classmates informed them that that meant their first parents had given them away. The unexpected teasing that followed was devastating.

When I first heard the little book discussed, I was reeled back in the past to when we'd visit my Uncle Jack's family and he invariably gathered everyone together in a circle in their living room, with himself and Jack Jr. in the center, and told the story of how of all the babies they could choose from they had picked Jack. My uncle had told the story almost like a fairy tale, but I found myself, even then at such a young age, feeling uneasy about the story and embarrassed for my cousin, despite all the love with which the story was told.

Everyone knew never to bring up my Jack or the book with Aunt Peggy. But little did any of us know then just how public our story was to become.

Jack and Anna continued to struggle financially, and I worried about them. Jack never seemed able to get on his feet long enough to find a career, after having one baby after another. Instead he had a series of low paying jobs. There wasn't any way anyone could have known that all those seemingly random jobs were preparing him for a successful career, where he could finally use all his creative abilities and all he'd learned from what appeared to be meaningless work.

They were lucky that Rosemary had a house, so they had a place to live, but the arrangement created a great strain on their relationships. Though Ray and I didn't talk on the phone very often anymore, sometimes I needed to talk with him about my concerns. Despite the fact we weren't Jack's "legitimate" parents, I couldn't banish my instincts as a mother or the fact that Ray was Jack's real father. Even though neither the law nor those who loved us acknowledged our little family, our bond as family was still real and sacred to me, and Ray's wise and insightful advice was valuable and necessary at times. We knew Jack in a way no one else could, because he was from us. How could any law ask us to negate that?

I found it sadly ironic that Ray had provided Jean's son, whom he had adopted, the best education possible. He'd graduated from Duke University and was now attending law school. Ray would have done the same for our son, despite the warnings of those who'd told us we would deprive him of all that was good in life if we kept him. I was always fighting the instinct to reclaim what was ours, knowing that was impossible and unfair to Jack. To wish for a magic wand that would erase the past would be to negate his life. We all had to deal with the hand we were dealt.

During our conversation, I mentioned to Ray that Kip was attending Carolina. At the time, Ray was traveling back and forth between Virginia Beach and Greensboro because his father was ill, a trip that passed by Chapel Hill.

"What do you think if I stop by and meet Kip?" he asked.

I could understand why he would want to meet his son's half brother and told him it would be fine with me, and that I was sure Kip would be receptive. But, with everything going on, I forgot to tell Kip about the possibility.

A few days later, Kip called. "Mom, you won't believe who I met today – Ray!"

Kip had just finished baseball practice and was walking off the field, when Ray and a friend of his approached Kip and introduced themselves. Kip was pleased that Ray got to see him play a little baseball. DeAnna, Kip's girlfriend, joined them, and after walking along Franklin Street, they had dinner at Hamm's, a popular North Carolina restaurant chain, where Ray and I would often eat when we were dating.

'What did you think? Was it okay that Ray stopped by?" I asked.

"It was cool that he had the courage to do it," Kip said. "He was really nice."

I had to wonder what DeAnna thought of our family. Hers was so normal.

Ray called the next day, excited and full of praise for Kip and DeAnna. I so hoped that Jean didn't worry that I had romantic designs for her husband, because we talked occasionally. Our relationship hadn't ended naturally, it had been tragically cut off and there were loose ends to heal.

Two days before Thanksgiving, I was shocked to get a call from Larry Horowitz. Was *The Other Mother* still available to be produced? Actually, yes it was! NBC had contracted O'Hara/Horowitz to produce a series of what they called Moment of Truth movies, and the network was interested in our story. In fact, they had already sold the idea to them.

Remarkably, less than twenty-four hours later, Maureen McCormick called to say she had found the money. I hated having to tell her she was a day late, but I had to believe things were working out the way they were meant to.

Soon after, Steve Loring, the writer the producers had hired to do the screenplay, called from New York to arrange a visit. When I told him my worries, that someone would have to be the bad guy and then I'd lose my whole family as a result, Steve gave his word that he would keep the book's integrity. However, he said he had to confess that besides being a guy, he was Jewish, had never married, never had children and knew little about adoption. But he was funny, sensitive and smart, and I trusted him right away. As it turned out, he became like our family rabbi.

As excited as I was about the actual creative process, I wasn't looking forward to Steve's arrival, imagining I would be thrown back into the past and sobbing the whole time he was there. As it turned out, I ended up in tears of laughter most of the time, as being with Steve was like hanging out with Woody Allen. They both have the same sense of humor.

Steve spent four days interviewing and researching, carrying his tape recorder everywhere. After an impromptu mothers support group meeting at my house, Steve was shaken. "This was truly like the Holocaust," he said. He'd really gotten it, and I felt reassured that the script was in the right hands.

Before he left, Steve asked if we could arrange ⌐
my therapist. Toni was willing. I hadn't seen Toni in a few ye⌐
and it was nice to be back in her nurturing presence. Somewhere
along the line, while Steve was interviewing Toni, I found myself
in the midst of a therapy session talking about anger, a subject that
made me extremely uncomfortable. Before I knew it, angry
feelings were coming up that I fought hard to push back down.
When I was a child, we were punished if we got angry. So I
learned to know when I was angry, but I wouldn't let myself
express it. But for a brief moment with Toni and Steve, my anger
was laid bare and it frightened me. As it turned out, our session
became a powerful scene in the movie.

Only once before had I inadvertently tuned into the full force
of my rage over all that had happened. I was reading Rickie
Solinger's book, *Wake Up Little Susie: Single Pregnancy and Race Before
Roe V. Wade,* in preparation for a keynote address we were giving
together at Joe Soll's CERA conference in New York City. Rickie
was to offer the academic side of our story, and I was to provide
the more personal, emotional side.

I was handling reading the book, until I came across a passage
that left no doubt as to the extent of the coercion applied to us to
give up our babies. Always before then, I had protected myself
from the truth about the forces arrayed against me by blaming
myself - if I had only been stronger. I could never face the fact
that I had actually been powerless, and that there had never been
any hope that I could keep my baby. I had put the book down
slowly and deliberately, got up from the sofa and, fueled by pure
adrenaline, walked for hours on the mountain trail behind my
house, until I could calm down again.

After Steve returned to New York to write the script, he
interviewed members of my family and Ray and Rosemary by
phone. Where in *The Other Mother* I was careful to speak solely
from my point of view, now everyone in my family would have

their own voice, which I was happy and unnerved about at the same time.

The interviews went well, Steve said, until he spoke with my mother. "All she could say was that she didn't remember much, that the priest and nuns told her it was for the best, and that you were a lovely daughter. What can I do with that?" he asked, at a total loss given my mother had to be a central figure in the story.

We talked on the phone nearly every day. The conversations were usually intense. Late one night, I came home from work, exhausted. The phone was ringing, as I opened the door. Steve had some questions about the hospital scenes, particularly what happened during delivery. I accidentally sat down on a chair with a broken leg and landed hard on the kitchen floor, where I stayed, as if frozen to the spot, for the next two hours as we talked. It was impossible to prepare for the whole process of seeing my life through someone else's eyes.

The script was nearly finished, when Steve called to read the final scene.

"Wow, Steve, you must be feeling adopted yourself now to have written such dialog," I remarked.

"No, Carol," he said. "Jack wrote those lines."

Such a gift! Jack and I never discussed his feelings, and so I didn't have a clue what he was thinking.

After the script was completed, it was sent to NBC for approval, and Steve began to get notes about changes. One afternoon he called upset. "They want to make the nuns nicer! I can't do that."

"What are we going to do?" I wailed. "I'm going to lose all credibility!" I was feeling enormous pressure about representing the adoption community well.

A compromise was finally struck. One nun would be cold and heartless, the other beautiful and sweet like Audrey Hepburn in *A Nun's Story*.

Soon after final approval of the script by the network, Larry called, excited. Frances Fisher, who was in Clint Eastwood's film, *Unforgiven*, had agreed to play me in the movie. I had no idea who Frances Fisher was and hadn't seen the film, but I didn't tell Larry that.

As soon as I got off the phone with Larry, I called Jack. "Do you know who Frances Fisher is?"

Jack said she was the prostitute that had her face cut up in the film.

I ran out the door to rent the movie and watched it as soon as I got back home. When I saw the actress he was talking about, I thought she was great, a good choice. But when the actress, who played Strawberry Alice, the madam of the "house of ill repute," came on the screen, I was shocked and then relieved and grateful it wasn't her - she was so much like me somehow, and that would have been too much.

For two weeks, I imagined the other actress playing me, until one evening Steve set me straight.

"No, Frances was Strawberry Alice."

I practically had an identity crisis.

I had asked Larry before if I could go to Vancouver for the filming, but he had declined, saying the budget was so low there was no extra money to cover such an expense. But, hearing his joy over getting Frances Fisher to star, I decided to take advantage of his happy mood and asked one more time if I could go.

"Well, okay," he said, "but only for one day."

Chapter Ten

The fog shrouded day revealed little of Vancouver. As we headed toward Stanley Park, where the day's filming would take place, the driver described the close by mountain ranges, and I could only imagine them.

"We all feel this movie has a special blessing," he informed me, his voice raspy from years of smoking. He looked at me kindly through eyes that had seen it all and would not be surprised by anything, yet still held a twinkle.

The two days scheduled for outdoor shooting were the only two days it had not rained, one of the little miracles that kept occurring. This day was one.

His eyes had sized me up quickly, as he took my suitcase from me at the airport the night before. "They are going to like you. You'll fit right in."

It was the first time I thought about how odd it would be for everyone having me on the set, even though the movie was about my life. After already filming for a week and a half, most must have formed their own opinion about me. It was strange to think that people who did not know me were recreating my life. I was experiencing in many ways the ultimate creative process and, at the same time, the ultimate identity crisis.

A bouquet of flowers with a welcoming note was waiting in the Meridian Hotel's richly furnished room when I arrived. The set was closed that day, as Frances Fisher was filming the scenes with my therapist, or rather her therapist, and it would have been too difficult for her to let go with me there. Actually, she probably let go better than I ever did in therapy. Perhaps I should have brought Toni along.

That night, as I read the final working version of the script, an envelope was slipped under my door. Inside was the "call sheet," listing the scenes to be filmed the next day. At the bottom of the page were a large asterisk and an added note, "Carol Schaefer, the REAL Other Mother! will be on the set!" Sleep was nearly impossible.

"We call the area over there, where you see all the trailers for the actors, wardrobe and makeup, 'The Circus'," the driver informed me.

My sons' names were written on the sides of two: one for Jack, and one for Brett and Kip. They would have gotten such a kick out of seeing all this. Signs reading "The Other Mother" were everywhere. To think for four years I had written my book in solitary, and now all this. I found it difficult to keep tears back as I took it all in.

We hurried along, past The Circus and along the edge of the bay, toward the tip of the park, to where the crew was setting up the lights and camera equipment for the first scene of the day. Thick black wires snaked along the ground. A bridge in the distance framed the view. It was freezing cold. Vaporous breath mixed with steam from cups of coffee held close to the chest, as people huddled in various small groups. From my years in advertising, I knew to expect long waits between takes. I wasn't sure what I was feeling, as I let myself out of the van, so I searched for the source of the coffee.

Marion Dodd, on the set to film a press kit for NBC's Entertainment Tonight, introduced herself. "You know, Carol," she said. "There isn't a person on this set who cannot relate to your story in some way. We all feel it touches something in our lives."

Suddenly, I felt connected to the production, instead of strangely apart.

As I began to breathe again, I noticed that the cameras and crew were surrounding a car parked at the edge of the water. We walked over to a vintage Ford Galaxy with huge tail fins, the same make of car that Ray used to drive. I told the people surrounding me that, if they had found an *aqua* Ford Galaxy, I would have passed out cold and that would have been it for me for the day. I was losing the battle to stay cool.

Corrie Clarke, the actress playing "young Carol," was standing by the passenger side of the car preparing the scene. Our eyes met for a long moment as we were introduced. She wore her hair in a perfect blonde flip, just like mine used to be. And she had a dimple in her chin like mine.

While I watched the scene unfold through a small black and white monitor, reality began to blur. I was there in the car again, and it was 1965. My mind flipped back and forth between admiring the lighting and framing created by the cinematographer, Lazlo George, to seeing my own face from twenty-nine years before. Ray was telling me that we were not going to get married, that someday we would when we finished college and were on our feet and could take care of a baby. This was not the right time. Our baby should be with parents who could offer him so much more.

"Oh God, Ray. How will I ever tell my mother?" Corrie pleaded, turning away from the camera.

I caught myself wanting to tell her to fight harder, keep your baby no matter what. Nothing would ever make up for such a loss. You will find a way. People will still love you. You just don't know that yet. I was surprised I didn't scream my thoughts out loud.

Then I became aware of a huge NBC camera six inches from my face. I found myself hoping the earphones had not messed up my hair and, at the same time, wondering if the camera had captured my powerful feelings. What in the world would be required of me emotionally to get through this day? As I was being filmed watching my life being recreated, I was literally standing in the past, the present, and the future in the same moment.

That was Corrie's only scene for the morning. As the cameras were moved to a different area of the park, Corrie and I got to know each other. It was a conversation between a young woman of the nineties and a young woman of the sixties. I couldn't get over the difference.

"I hope you don't mind, but I played you a little on the wimpy side," Corrie said.

Was I wimpy? I never thought of myself as anything but strong. But then how could anyone, who had not lived in the sixties, imagine how controlling society was, how difficult to imagine rebelling back then, when the most complex family on television had been the Cramdens?

I wanted to ask Corrie what it felt like to play an unwed mother, hidden away in a Catholic maternity home. Could she possibly relate? Yet I was afraid to know Corrie's answer, since I could barely understand anymore myself. Times had changed so much. Would the audience get it?

Corrie volunteered that her family had similar issues, and she understood them from a deeper place now. And, she knew herself as a woman in a way she hadn't before the filming. Corrie's sensitivity played all over her face. Each thought that passed through her mind registered in her expressions.

I laughed as she described an entire afternoon spent with a rubber doll between her legs for the delivery scene, fighting my painful memories of the scene she was portraying.

"But the moment they placed the real baby in my arms in the birth scene, my life changed forever," Corrie said. "It was the most powerful experience."

My life had changed, too, when my son was born. Would I ever be able to watch that scene?

Corrie said that she had not decided how she should play the love scene, the one that led up to my son's conception, which was to be filmed that night.

"Just remember I liked it!" I said. "I was not a wimp, and I was not a victim!" She laughed, a little surprised.

The veil of fog had lifted enough to reveal a line of ships waiting for a turn to enter the harbor. Still, the snow capped mountains remained hidden. I already felt comfortable on the set, as if I had been there for the entire shoot. In fact, it felt like I had come home in a way. We walked along a path to the area of the park where they were to shoot the opening scene of the film, when I would meet Frances and the actors playing Brett and Kip.

As I was walking back from the espresso truck, Frances arrived. I separated out from the others and walked over to meet her, knowing she had only a moment before beginning work. Enormous sky blue eyes were all I saw at first. Then I noticed how much she and Corrie looked alike, except Frances didn't have the dimple in her chin. For a split second, it seemed our spirits merged.

As if we were picking up on a previous conversation, she looked deeply into my eyes, assessing what she saw there, and said she wished the script had included a scene with the psychic and more about Jack's father, a neglected part of the story, she felt. I told her I agreed completely, and then she had to rush off to film the opening scene.

In the scene, Frances was photographing Brett and Kip while they played football. Art began to imitate life at the same time life imitated art. I photographed Frances photographing my sons, her sons, while she was being filmed. The boys were being photographed by the photographer, who was taking the still pictures that Frances was supposed to be taking and would, in another scene, be developed in my/her darkroom. I photographed him taking the pictures.

Before lunch, Marion interviewed me for the press kit. Seeing the cameras, a group of young boys rushed over for an autograph. But then rushed over to where Frances was standing, when they realized I was not she.

Throughout the morning, whenever there was an opportunity, someone from the crew would come over to me and share their story. Filming *The Other Mother* was stirring memories. Long dormant issues, kept powerful by being too shameful to discuss, bubbled to the surface for many. This I had experienced when the book was published, when I learned the truth connects us all at a deeper place. Busting the stranglehold of the taboo by telling of my love for my secret child, others felt safe about revealing themselves. They felt no need to judge me, so why go on judging themselves about whatever secret kept them captive?

I was beginning to wonder if there wasn't a little Divine Intervention in the selection of scenes I was going to get to see filmed. The final scene, between Jack and me after we first met, had already been shot by the ocean, just like what happened in real life, but the sound of the surf had ruined too much of the dialogue, so they had to reshoot at a quieter location. They chose a beautiful duck pond, surrounded by ancient trees and their brilliantly colored changing leaves.

I felt the cold from the tree run through my back, as I leaned against the trunk for strength. The scene began with Jack and I walking along a path that rimmed the pond. Ducks quacked and leaves rustled, yet everything felt still, poised. Cameron Bancroft, who played Jack, was amazingly like him. They both have a touch of the magical prince from some fairy tale about them. When filming began, Frances and Cameron walked toward where I was standing. When they reached the camera next to me, they turned and walked over to a bench to continue their conversation. To my increasing discomfort, the only line I was able to hear as they passed by for each take was Jack's: "Was it your choice to give me up? Was it your choice to give me up?" Several of the crew sobbed.

Now, I was chilled to the bone. When they talked on the bench, I could only see Cameron's face on the little black and white monitor, but that was enough. Finally, I was able to see objectively why those who loved us must have been so concerned about our meeting each other. The reunion had felt only right to me, but our meeting again was powerful and momentous. I had not wanted to hurt my son for anything, but I could see where others had thought I might unwittingly. Nineteen was an awfully young age to deal with so much.

As Cameron and Frances began another take, there was a sudden disruption in the pond. Out of nowhere, an enormous swan landed close to where Frances and Cameron were walking. Bethany Rooney, the director, cut immediately to the swan floating serenely by, bestowing a mystical blessing that everyone seemed to absorb. For the swan to appear then was astonishingly perfect. *The Ugly Duckling* in many ways tells the story of how it feels to be adopted.

Just as Frances and Cameron got up from the bench and began walking arm in arm back down the path, the sun came out from behind the clouds for the first time since filming began, and shone on their backs as they walked away. Everyone was stunned at what seemed like magic and cheered as soon as they heard the word "Cut!"

Light faded quickly and the air was getting colder. Hot soup was put out, and a crewmember handed out hand warmers to everyone. He found an extra pair of gloves for me. Everyone was working hard. All the equipment was moved back down to the tip of the park, along the shore looking out to the bridge. Two scenes remained to be filmed.

Frances sat alone on a park bench. Carol had returned to the scene of the "crime," where she got pregnant in the first place. The next scene filmed would be the flashback to the night Jack was conceived, which Carol was now remembering on the park bench. After several takes, Frances walked over to two of her friends and me. She was feeling the need to connect to find the strength to portray my churning emotions. I felt split off, as I watched her feeling my feelings. Seeing her so poignantly alone on the bench amidst the camera, lights and crew mirrored a place inside me. That take was a wrap.

The crew swooped in to set up for the next scene. The Ford Galaxy was brought back and parked on the secluded beach. Two other vintage cars were parked alongside. Inside, actors were "making out," steaming up the windows. One actress had teased her hair into a beehive. Much more equipment was needed to shoot this scene, so it was taking a while to set up.

A young man, only a month older than Jack, came up to me. As the sixties were being recreated before our eyes, he told me how difficult it had been for him, when he read the script, to relate in anyway to the sixties. The story almost seemed implausible. Why had I not simply walked out of the Home, told everyone to take a hike? This was my fear. It had been my fear when I tried to explain it all to Jack, when I met him again. As I attempted to answer his questions, my eyes kept being drawn to the beehive hairdo bobbing in the back window of one of the cars. No one of his generation could imagine trying to make out passionately and needing to keep every hair in place at the same time.

A bonfire had been lit, the lighting created and the cameras positioned. Corrie sat on the beach with Kavan Smith, playing Ray, in a few moments to become Jack's father, too. Steve, the writer, had created a little schtick that they were to do with French fries, something reminiscent of the sixties innocence, while we debated whether or not to go "all the way." A microwave was close by to keep the actors supplied with warm fries. But, as soon as the actors progressed to more passionate kissing, the airport changed the flight pattern and the sound of planes flying overhead ruined every take. Just as soon as they had figured out the timing and began filming the scene during the lull, a flock of geese honked overhead.

Between takes, Corrie came over shaking her head, joking. "I have never had so much foreplay in my entire life!"

"But the sixties were nothing but foreplay," I laughed, as the younger members of the crew looked on a little incredulous. "You could date someone for two years and never get past first base."

Did I really say "first base"? How in the world had we found any passion in that terminology?

"No wonder the condom broke," Corrie remarked. "It must have been dried up from being in Ray's wallet for so long!"

Corrie was called back for another take. By now it was icy cold. I found myself pulling away, needing to be alone to etch in my mind all that was happening. For a moment, I stopped feeling the cold. In awe, I scanned the scene before me: the lights, the crew, the cameras, all these people, even the extra with the beehive hairdo, were all assembled to tell our story. I watched the scene being filmed through the filter of my own memory, as we succumbed to a force too great to control or even to comprehend - the power of creation.

Then it struck me. What would have happened if the condom hadn't broken? This scene would vanish into thin air. The little beach would be inhabited solely by the geese complaining overhead. One little twist of fate - a faulty condom - changed not just our lives and the lives of our families, it might now possibly change a great many more.

My return flight was scheduled for early the next morning, but Frances sought out the producers to see if I could stay for the next day's shooting, and they granted her wish. During the filming of the emotional scene on the bench, Frances had asked if we could have dinner together that night, and so we met in the hotel's restaurant, when filming was done for the day. She brought along her friend.

As I sat across the table from her, the feelings were difficult to describe. I felt such a kinship with her, not simply because she was becoming me in order to portray my life, though that would be enough right there. She was just a very real, smart and deeply caring person.

She and Clint Eastwood were living together at the time and had a daughter, Francesca, named after the character in the film he was directing and starring in while our film was being made - *The Bridges of Madison County*. Frances told me of her life as a struggling actress in New York City, where, if she found a five dollar bill on the street, that would make her day. She'd met Clint at a studio party and said, when she first saw him, it was as if a piece of a puzzle she didn't even realize had been hanging over her head suddenly fell into place.

After Clint had read the script for *The Other Mother*, he'd called the producers and said, "This should be a feature film." But, that was six days before shooting was to begin, and so it was too late to change things.

When I told Steve later, he said, "Wow, to think my script was lying on Clint Eastwood's bed!"

Frances invited me to her suite the next morning before shooting began, so that I could meet Francesca.

Francesca was sitting regally in her baby stroller, when I arrived. She was adorable, a real combination of both her parents. After Frances gave the nanny instructions, we got into the limo that would take us to the house that was supposed to be my house.

The air was damp and the fall leaves just beyond their peak, as we drove through old residential streets on the way to the set. When we pulled up to the house, I thought it was uncanny how similar the house was to the one I'd sold to Cindy and Jim, as if the crew had really gotten into my head.

We found everyone gathered in the living room, where the stylist was arranging my mother's hair. I was horrified. "My mother never let her hair go grey," I exclaimed. "In fact, she was never anything but perfectly dressed." I looked in dismay at Debra May, the actress who was playing my mother, dressed in a scruffy sweater, wearing dark-rimmed glasses and appearing anything but glamorous.

"Tell me," he said. "We are all upset. We wanted your mother to look lovely, but Michael O'Hara came on set yesterday and changed everything. 'I know this kind of woman,' he told us, 'and she hasn't had sex in thirty years!'"

Oh, my God. How was I ever going to tell my mother, I joked, imitating Corrie's line from the day before. This might even be worse than when I had to tell her I was pregnant.

Everyone came up to welcome me on the set, and again I felt as at home as I had the day before. After getting the finishing touches on her horrible grey wig, Debra May introduced herself. I could see she was actually a striking woman underneath all the makeup used to age her.

"I have to tell you that I am the only one who didn't accept doing this movie right away," she said. "The pay was so low that I almost didn't consider it. But, I'm glad I did. It's pretty remarkable that no one turned it down."

There did seem to be a "meant to be feeling" about the film.

We were called into the kitchen, where the first scene of the day was to be shot. Steve had had a huge dilemma, as he considered how to write the script. "In the book, most of the drama happened on the phone," he said, "How do I make that interesting?" In the script, the truth was never bent, merely portrayed differently, he'd promised.

But, as the first scene of the day unfolded with Kip spilling the beans about Brett not being the oldest and my mother storming out of the house, I realized that my mother was going to be sacrificed as the dramatic foil. Creatively, I thought the portrayal was perfect and would ring true for many who had the same kind of mother. But, personally, I felt protective of my mother, who had been completely supportive of my search, and now worried more about her reaction to how she was being portrayed than about the wig.

After the morning's filming, Frances invited me to her trailer for lunch. Just as I was settling myself down in the chair, the phone rang. "You'll never guess who's sitting with me right now," Frances exclaimed. "Carol Schaefer!" She was talking to Clint.

When we returned to the house for the afternoon's filming, Lazlo George, the cinematographer, found me, excited to show me the dailies. I followed him up the stairs to where the monitor was set up in one of the bedrooms. He wanted me to watch a scene he'd lit in the therapist's office, where the rain on a windowpane behind a close up of Frances shadowed the tears she couldn't yet shed. It was beautiful.

As he began to show me the rest of the dailies, someone came rushing into the room to tell me that Frances needed me on the set. Filming was to start right away. Frances had requested a reshoot of a scene filmed a few days before. After seeing the dailies, she felt she could do better.

The room was hushed when I reached the bottom of the stairs. A makeshift kitchen had been set up at the far end of the room, meant to be my mother's kitchen. Frances looked relieved to see me. She had told me the night before at dinner that she felt Corrie had carried the emotional weight of the film. But, seeing the depth of her feelings in preparation for this scene, I felt Frances had short-changed her self.

Carol was confronting her mother, something I never did. She was showing her mother a picture her mother had taken of her the day she'd returned from Seton House. "Why did you take that picture, Mom, on the worst day of my life?" Carol asked. I flashed back to standing in the backyard for the real picture, picking up our toy poodle, Gigi, and holding her in my arms, so I wouldn't feel so empty.

Debra May reaches for a tin cookie can, handing it to Frances to open. Frances is startled to find the little red stocking ornament inside. My mother is telling me how she never forgot, that she'd hung the ornament on the tree every Christmas, in honor of her first grandchild.

"I was scared, Carol. Whatever I did, right or wrong, I did it out of love for you. Go find your son, Carol. You can do it because you're strong, much stronger than I could ever be."

I began to sob uncontrollably. Though the same words had been unspoken between my mother and me, I realized how desperately I had needed to hear them said out loud. We all needed that acknowledgment from our mothers.

After the final take, Frances came over to me, still deeply into the emotions of the scene. I was still crying.

"If I can make you cry, I can make anyone cry!" she said, gratified that she could deliver such a powerful scene. "Can you possibly stay until the movie's done filming?" she asked.

As much as I would have given anything to be able to stay, I knew it was impossible. Even if I were able to convince the producers that with the same money they'd spent flying me first class, having me stay in a beautiful hotel, driving me around in a limo everywhere, they could instead put me up in a Motel 6, I couldn't make up for three weeks of lost wages. But my heart was broken having to decline.

That night, a group of us went to dinner, including Frances, and then the limo arrived early the next morning to take me to the airport - to my real life, which now felt far less real than the last two days had been.

On the way to the airport, I asked the driver to stop at a Starbucks. As the limo pulled up to the curb, I felt I could get used to this. But, sitting alone in the huge back seat sipping coffee, I suddenly felt quite lonely. Whom could I talk to that could relate to the incredible and unique experience I had just been through?

As the plane took off, I sunk deeper into the plush leather seats of first class and stared out the window down at the beautiful city of Vancouver. I spotted Stanley Park, where filming was done the day before, and the ships lined up at the harbor. Now I could see the mountains that ringed the city, and I felt I was being wrenched away.

Such an enormous experience, how could I fit back into my normal life and go to work at Macy's, folding piles of clothes left carelessly on the floors of the dressing rooms? Something unexplainable inside me had changed. By the time the limo drove up the hill of my street, I decided to call in sick, something I never before had the nerve to do. But I had to savor all that had happened for just one more day.

My house had been on the market for a couple of months before filming began. My dream of renovating it to sell at a profit had been unrealistic. I should never have bought it in the first place. But I had no idea then that what was once a booming real estate market in Marin would tank.

I tried to figure out how in the world I could shoulder so much responsibility, with the movie coming out, and make the most of such a great opportunity while worrying about finances. I doubted my ability to even figure it out, since I had gotten into the situation in the first place.

One day, when I was being especially hard on myself, an adoptee friend called. After years of searching, Jim had found his mother had died years before. Now he was trying to meet her sisters, but they were resistant. He was a brilliant guy and had been successful in real estate, until his search and all the issues it brought up had derailed him. Yet, he knew he had to deal with everything before he could go on. Now he found himself homeless. But instead of succumbing to his situation, he found a way to live a full life by going to free lectures all around the city, mostly about art and philosophy, until he could find a way to get back on his feet. Even without a roof over his head, he worked tirelessly for adoption reform, and he had no regrets, despite his unsuccessful search. He didn't want to continue his life as a successful but false person. He wanted to know who he really was.

I felt I had no right at all to complain to him of all people, but I was learning that it was the people who'd struggled the most in life who were the ones that gave of themselves without question.

"Carol," he said, in a tone that insisted I take in what he was about to say. "All my life, I've studied military strategy, especially the Civil War and before. In military terms, Carol, you would be called the target, the one who draws the fire so that the rest can advance. With that much pressure, of course you made mistakes."

I wasn't sure Jim's analogy was correct in my situation, but his words were comforting, nevertheless.

After our conversation, I knew I had to take the house back off the market, with all that was happening with the movie. This was a once in a lifetime opportunity, and I didn't need any distractions. Besides, more than having to be available for any upcoming publicity, I didn't have the strength to be so public and, at the same time, have strangers walking through my house. It was a risky move, financially, but I felt a strong need to protect myself emotionally. In addition, I had a vague feeling, but didn't know how to deal with it, that old feelings of shame were behind my need to keep my home private. It wasn't like I was proud to be telling the world my story of giving my son up for adoption.

But then Laura called with wonderful news. *The Other Mother* had been listed in a new book, *500 Great Books by Women, a Penguin Books Readers' Guide*. The list went back to the eleventh century. Nothing, not even the upcoming movie, was greater than that acknowledgment in my mind. Our story was being understood.

The first interview arranged was a feature article for *McCall's Magazine*, due out in their March 1995 issue before the April seventeenth airing of the film. My mother had subscribed to *McCall's* and *Ladies Home Journal* for as long as I could remember growing up. The women's world they portrayed month after month: "Can this marriage be saved," the cleaning tips and articles on how to be the perfect wife, the endless recipes left me depressed about having to become an adult, if this was all I had to look forward to. Never would I have dreamt my story would be a featured article in one of them. There was no way of even imagining at the time that one particular reader would touch Jack's life directly.

After the holidays, Jack had gone alone to Virginia Beach to see again if they could make a life there. Jack and Anna needed to find a situation that would enable them to finally be independent. Besides, Los Angeles was a difficult place to live with four children. Whenever I went down to visit, we were always on the freeway visiting one family member or another, hoping the van would make it. Finally, it was all too much for Anna.

Jack stayed with Ray and Jean, and again rode a bike everywhere, as he worked waiting tables in a restaurant while looking for a job in advertising. The separation was hard on everyone.

In late February, Ray's father died. Though Ray was reluctant, Jean insisted that Jack attend the funeral. Jack had never met his grandparents, and Ray had always been reticent about explaining why. I hated to think why. I had never met them either, despite the fact Ray and I had dated for two years. Two people, whom I had never met, had changed the entire course of my life with their advice that Ray took, that it would be best not to get married.

Jack called afterwards to tell me how the day went. "There I was, sitting in the front row with the immediate family, and nobody knew who I was," he said. "When I looked into the casket and saw my grandfather for the first time, I thought, well now I know what I'm going to look like when I'm lying in a casket. It was eerie. I couldn't figure out how I could look like him, when I look so much like you."

Jack had been brought up in Rosemary's huge family, so the contrast to Ray's small one, one he well could have been a part of, gave him much to reflect upon. They owned a considerable bit of land outside of the Greensboro city limits that served as the family compound for generations, with several family members having houses on the property. Jack said it was strange to walk on the land of his ancestors, people he'd never known.

After Jack and Anna had visited Ray the first time, they both joked that Ray and I would have never made it. All the pots and pans in Ray's kitchen had to have the handles pointed in the same direction. The garage was as spotless and organized as the rest of the house – a striking contrast to my garage, where I usually just opened the door and flung something in.

Ray wouldn't let Jack see his father's basement, because he'd been such a packrat. "I probably could have spent days in that basement and been in heaven," Jack said. Jack loved anything old and unusual.

Somehow, the word finally got out about who Jack was, and the family was thrilled to meet him, accepting him unconditionally. A week after the funeral, Jack got an excited call from one of his cousins. She'd picked up the mail that day, and her *McCall's Magazine* had arrived. When she flipped through it, she was shocked to see Jack's picture in the article about the movie.

"To think," she said, "if I hadn't met you, I could have easily read the article, never knowing we were related."

Jack returned from Virginia a few weeks later. They wouldn't be moving. He hadn't found a good enough job.

Mark, a father who was in the fight of his life with his ex girlfriend and a Christian adoption agency for custody of his infant son, phoned one day for mental and emotional support. I'd learned from Mark, a Christian himself, the "adoption option" was preached about every Sunday in church as the "greatest gift" one could give.

I remembered being consoled by the nuns at the unwed mother's home with the exact same words, which I didn't buy even then. I wasn't voluntarily giving a gift. My son was going to strangers because no one was helping me to keep him. Now the seed was being planted in young women of a new generation, who probably hadn't even had sex yet, to choose adoption for an unplanned pregnancy, with an implicit message that they would be doing "God's Work." Such propaganda was alarming. Why couldn't they see that, until unwed mothers are no longer considered social pariahs and the undeniable bond between a mother and her child is honored and supported, there will always be a need for abortion, if abortion was what they were fighting against?

"By the way, Carol, I just saw you mentioned on the Information Super Highway!" Mark said.

"What in the world is that?" I asked.

When Mark tried to explain, I still didn't quite get it, but apparently a lot of people involved with adoption searches were using it to get around laws that prohibited them from finding each other. Soon I would realize the power of the precursor to the Internet myself.

Larry called with a suggestion. The "Moment of Truth" movies he produced rarely got much publicity, since they were low budget films. If I could get people to write a letter to the president of NBC before the movie aired, the network might consider adding more promotion. "Even ten letters would make a difference," he said.

I contacted everyone and every group I knew, and then remembered about the Information Super Highway. Why not try reaching people that way? I felt like it might be empowering for so many, who never had a voice, to feel a part of the whole process.

Little could I have imagined then the impact of our collective voice.

Three weeks before the film was to air, the network sent me a copy. I let the cassette sit on my coffee table for a day, before I had the nerve to watch it. Should I invite someone over to watch with me, or see it alone? Finally, I decided to watch alone. What if the film wasn't very good after all?

It took me a little while to push the play button, but finally I overcame my fears. From the moment the credits began scrolling down the screen, I found myself watching through a filter of layered memories and feelings. My own experience blended with the film's portrayal and all the conversations Steve and I had had while he wrote the script. The scenes filmed while I was on set held even more layers from the conversations I'd had with the actors.

Watching Corrie give birth and remembering her saying how the scene changed her life merged with my own memories of fighting the anesthesia and then seeing my infant son for the first time. As I watched Corrie's wrenching plea to my mother to let me bring my baby home, I became an outsider looking in, caught up in wonderment at how I ever went through everything alone.

At the same time, my creative side was appreciating how real and honest the performances were and how cleverly the flashbacks were handled. I almost stood up and cheered as the actor playing Sister Dominic was able to make her the nun of all nuns, down to the tiniest gesture.

I was able to keep myself together up until the scene with my mother and me by the kitchen sink, when I finally broke down in tears like I had when watching it being filmed.

After the movie ended, I sat still for a long time, letting all my impressions sink in. I was so proud of how it turned out. It was more like an art film than a made for TV movie.

Soon, I was out the door to get copies made for everyone. I wanted Jack and Rosemary, Brett and Kip, my parents and Ray to have the chance to see the movie before it aired, so that they could be prepared for the public response.

My mother called first after receiving it. "Of course, I cried," she responded, when I asked her what she thought. "Watching the movie was hard."

"Were you upset with how you were portrayed?" I asked, barely breathing, as I waited for her answer.

"Those who know me, know that's not me, and those who don't know me – who cares?"

What a transformation from the woman she used to be, so afraid of what the neighbors might think. I couldn't get over it.

As I hadn't been when I told him I was searching for Jack, I wasn't really worried about my Dad's reaction. He was probably responsible for more sales of *The Other Mother* than anyone else and loved bragging about it, especially the line in the book where I had told him, when he picked me up from Seton House after the baby was born: "Dad, I just want you to know that I will never, ever do anything to disappoint you again."

Each time he mentioned that line in the book, I cringed but said nothing. To me, such a promise revealed how damaged I had become. But he didn't understand what he was always implying, until years later when once again he brought up my promise, but then at long last said, "Actually, Carol, you've never disappointed me." I was glad that I hadn't demanded that he "get it," and instead allowed him the time to come to his own understanding,

"Sort of funny the actor who played you wore a hat," I joked. "You always hated hats!" I felt the need to deflect the raw feelings of the scene in the film where he'd dropped me off at the maternity home. Frances had told me that everyone cried as that scene was being filmed, it was so touching.

I'd always accepted the fact that my parents felt they were doing what was best for me, given the times. Still, holding two different realities as true was difficult. Deep down, I didn't feel loved, I felt abandoned, but I wouldn't let myself go there anymore.

One day, while writing the book, I had had a "Shirley MacLaine" moment. Shirley found that a book she was meant to read would literally fall off the shelf to get her attention. The same thing happened to me one day, when Rollo May's book, *The Meaning of Anxiety*, caught my attention. When I opened the book to get a sense of it, I was surprised to find myself staring at a page describing his research at an unwed mother's home.

Not wanting to use animals or put other humans in an anxiety-producing situation, he decided to study girls in a home for unwed mothers. Going in, he believed he would prove that the girls who were rejected by their parents would have the highest levels of anxiety. Instead, he discovered the opposite - the girls who were told they were loved and supported had extreme levels of anxiety, from their inner reality of abandonment and sorrow contradicting the reassurance being offered. Those girls went back out into the world unable to trust themselves, let alone anyone else, where the girls who knew they were rejected had no need for rose-colored glasses and could better deal with their lives realistically.

So much of myself was finally explained. And, it did seem from all the women I had met that those who had been kicked out of the house had a much more practical attitude. Before reading Rollo May's conclusions, I would wonder how they survived. One of the worst stories I'd heard was from a woman in our group whose parents had put her in an insane asylum in Louisiana, a horrible place, and refused to sign for her release until she surrendered her infant. A nurse there had even tried to help her keep her baby, but her parents made it impossible. She had such courage and strength to survive it all, heart intact and eager to meet her child.

Brett and Kip both liked the movie, though Brett was disturbed that I was portrayed as having such a messy house when that wasn't really the case, at least most of the time. Watching the film, it was obvious that Brett had been honest with Steve, during their interview, much more so than with me. In the beginning, I had been afraid I couldn't handle what everyone might say, but I finally could put down my own rose-colored glasses and appreciate the truth.

In the movie, their comment that their brother might be John Elway was changed to: "Maybe he's Joe Montana!" Of course I had to tease them about that, since I was the only Forty-niner fan in the family.

I was feeling relieved about everyone's acceptance, when Ray called after watching the film. "I look like such a bad guy," he said.

"I didn't see it that way," I reassured him. But I could tell he was upset, even as he wished me well.

I was feeling enormously relieved and supported, and proud to have such a great family. Both Laura and Larry had been shocked that no one had come forward asking for money for their participation. I did feel that everyone should be rewarded, but there wasn't so much money to go around. So, I gave Jack, Brett and Kip some of the earnings, feeling that everyone was connected to one of them and so somehow compensated, too.

Steve, on the other hand, being a pure artist by nature, was upset with the ending especially, which the producers had changed. Enveloped by the sunset, Jack says, "Thank you for finding me Mom." Carol responds, "You're welcome!"

"I would never write anything so corny," Steve complained.

After all his research, he knew reunions were much more complicated.

"But, at least I was still alive in the last scene," I joked. "I'm the first birth mother ever portrayed in a movie that didn't conveniently die at the end!"

I had little private viewings with Rob, Lee and Morgan and Patrick, just to get their opinions. Encouraged by everyone's reactions, I felt ready to take on the world.

Larry called, surprised and elated. NBC was going to advertise the movie three times a night in primetime for a full week before it aired. 'The network must have received hundreds of letters," he said.

I was struck by the power we had.

Could I arrange to come down to Los Angeles to do a network feed to stations around the country with Frances? Of course I could!

A week before the movie was to air, I flew to Las Vegas to speak at the American Adoption Conference's annual conference, not the best place to hold an adoption event. As always, the workshops and talks brought up heavy emotions, but then we'd have to walk through the casino with all the slot machines clanging, still raw. The incongruity was too much. Still, being there was essential. Anticipation of the movie airing was high, and I felt tremendously supported.

While I was unpacking after returning home from the conference on Sunday night, the television was on in the other room. Suddenly, I heard the commercial for the movie and ran to see it. There I stood in the middle of the living room, staring at a part of my life portrayed on my own television screen. How was I ever going to process all that was happening? I could barely feel my feet on the ground.

Chapter Eleven

The movie was to air the following Monday night. On Thursday, I flew down to Los Angeles for the network feed on Friday. The NBC affiliate in Los Angeles wanted to do a segment with Jack as well, and so we were put up in a hotel in Studio City. Anna came with Jack, a treat for them to be alone without the kids. I was happy they were getting something out of all they were being put through.

The next morning, an aid led me into a small dark room next to the recording studio. Frances was already there, and we greeted each other like old friends. Then the aide instructed us about what we could expect. The network feed would take about three and a half hours. Some of the affiliates would be interviewing just Frances, some just me, and some wanted the two of us together. Some of it would be live and some taped.

Inside the studio, we were settled into chairs next to each other, as another aide wired our mikes. Then the taping began. Where the radio shows I'd done created an intimacy with the audience, now it was like I was speaking into a void. Disembodied voices asked questions, as we spoke with one affiliate after another for the next three hours.

196

When the taping was finally over, we met Jack and Anna for lunch, before being interviewed by the Los Angeles NBC affiliate for the evening news. Frances was thrilled to finally meet Jack.

The news crew met us after lunch and took us outside for the interview. The sun was glaring and I became self conscious, thinking about how harsh the light was going to be.

"Could you do something to soften the light," I asked the cameraman. I rarely was so bold.

"I think we've created a monster!" Frances joked.

Everyone was laughing.

"I'll do the same lighting I'd use for Elizabeth Taylor," the cameraman promised.

"Good!"

Monday at long last arrived. I'd just finished my morning coffee, when the doorbell rang. There stood a young man with a dozen yellow roses. They were from my mother. I was touched that she would send them, and fought back regret for all the years wasted from when she was unable to be there for me when Jack was born in the same way she was now. We'd both come a long way.

Laura called to wish me luck and to tell me there had been several positive reviews, one from *Variety*, another from the *Hollywood Reporter* and a recommendation in the *New York Times*. That was unexpected and a thrill. The fact that Frances Fisher was the star had caught their attention.

I pondered options about how to watch the movie when it aired: have some friends over or watch with the support group? But, in the end, I decided to see it with Lee and his daughter, Sarah, at their house. As a director in the theater and Artistic Director for the Marin Theater Company, Lee had lived through the agony of reviews and public reaction more than anyone I knew, and I needed his strength and sense of humor to keep me balanced and somewhat sane from all the pressure I was feeling.

The day was long, as I counted the hours until six o'clock when the movie would begin on the East Coast. Over the next couple of hours, before going to Lee's, a surreal image of the film rolling over the country like a wave kept filling my mind, and I worried most about the women, who shared my story but had never told a soul, tuning in unexpectedly and the shock they must be feeling.

I got to Lee and Sarah's just before the movie started. By then I was a bag of nerves. The wine Lee offered helped, and then the movie started. It was strange to see it with commercials; strange to imagine it was actually my story. But I drew strength from the fact that the movie wasn't just about my life, that countless others shared the same story. I could only hope the movie helped with their healing and brought awareness to our issues. But it was a lonely business putting myself out there like that. What if no one liked it?

Even though Lee had already seen the movie, he was still moved watching the second time, as was Sarah, so by the time I left to go home and face the results I felt somewhat reassured that all would be okay.

As I walked through the little forest behind my house, down the stone steps from the parking space above, I wished now there were friends there to celebrate. The cats met me at the door. I was happy to see the answering machine was flashing its red light, indicating a message. Hoping for the best, I pushed the play button and listened to one wonderful congratulatory message after another, from friends, my parents and people from the adoption community. Thank God!

The next morning, I'd barely awoken when the phone began to ring with one call after the other, that didn't stop the whole day.

Late morning, Larry called. "Carol, you won't believe it, but your movie beat out Murphy Brown and came in first in the ratings last night – with twenty-five million viewers! You would never have reached so many people if it had been a feature film." Larry, still a practicing physician, was in the business of producing movies that had an impact on people's lives and he was thrilled.

After hanging up the phone, I sat for a long time trying to grasp the irony of having been banished to a home for unwed mothers, so the neighbors would never find out about my illegitimate pregnancy, to now having twenty-five million viewers know everything. The opening line of the movie was "My name is Carol Schaefer, and this is my story."

The most important phone call I received, however, was from Jack. He had watched the movie with Anna and a few of their friends. All morning he had been getting calls from his adoptive family, expressing their compassion and surprise at all he had gone through. From the sound of his voice, I sensed that Jack had changed somehow from all the acceptance and love he was receiving, that he could now value his own feelings about being adopted.

Rosemary was pleased with the movie, too, and joked that she wished she had a beautiful house by the water like how she was portrayed living in in the movie. I let out a sigh of relief. Everyone in the family had put so much trust in me, without having a clue how the movie would turn out.

The next night, Kip called. He'd just gotten off from work, bussing tables at Chili's in Chapel Hill. "You'll never guess what happened tonight," he said. "I was clearing a table, and at the next table three women were discussing the movie. When I told them the movie was about my Mom, they didn't believe me. It took a lot to convince them."

"Once someone is on the little screen they can't be ordinary people anymore I guess," I replied, laughing at the odds of that happening to Kip, and imagining the confusion the women must have felt.

For the next three weeks, the phone never stopped ringing with calls from people all around the country. Then one morning I woke up to discover the phone was dead. No dial tone, just silence. It took two weeks for the phone company to discover the problem – a squirrel had chewed the wire.

As awful as it was to be so suddenly cut off from all the gratifying calls, the squirrel had actually done me a favor. Coming down from such a huge wave was difficult, but I had a lot of reality to face, after being consumed with the movie for so long.

The man who had sold me the house lived next door. He held the mortgage. From the time I moved in, I could feel he resented me, and I always believed it was because I was a projection of his ex wife, who had forced him to sell the house during their divorce. His resentment grew as I put the house back on the market, and he made it unbearably difficult as I tried to sell it, harassing possible buyers as well as me. The longer it took to sell, the more I fell back on mortgage payments and the angrier he got. I would tell him about the book and the movie, hoping to reassure him he could count on me and that everything would work out. But my efforts at putting his mind at ease only served to inexplicably enflame him even more.

It felt like I had used up every ounce of my energy with the movie and had little strength left to make anything else happen in my life, much less battle the man next door. Writing was the only source of renewal. I had found a part time job working at Nancy Ann's Flower Shop in Sausalito, until I could find something else. Arranging flowers was the last thing I would have imagined I would ever be doing or enjoying, but I needed to take any job and fast. At least the hours would allow me to write in the morning.

Once a week at Seton House, the volunteer ladies would come and teach us different skills that were ironically meant to make us a good little housewife one day. Flower arranging was one of those skills we were to master, one which I associated with being trapped, playing out a woman's role according to society's standards instead of finding my own way of being in the world. Since the sixties were such a transition time for women, my need to break out from the mold of what would be expected of me was confusing, though undeniable.

As so many discover, once they get connected to their adoption issues and launch a search or have a reunion, people related to adoption seem to come out of the woodwork. They sit next to you on the plane, confess in a super market line, tell their story at the beauty parlor. Adoption had followed me everywhere for years now, ever since searching for Jack, and so it turned out that Nancy Ann was adopted. When I first started working there, she had no interest in searching. Nancy didn't realize whom she had just hired.

Late one night there was a huge storm. As I lay in bed, I heard the trap door leading underneath the house banging. I'd always made sure the door was closed and knew it should be, but the idea of going outside in such weather, when I was so cozy in bed, was too much, and I rolled over and fell back asleep.

The house had two floors. The lower floor was a small room that I used for writing and as a guest bedroom. The next morning, as I worked downstairs on my novel before going to work, I heard scratching in the ceiling above me. Uh, oh. Over the next days, all my attempts to scare the raccoon away proved to no avail. My biggest concern now was to keep the critter quiet whenever the house was being shown.

A week later, I went downstairs, cup of coffee in hand and ready to write, when I noticed a strange odor in the room. As I settled down at my desk, I heard little cries from the raccoon in the ceiling above me and realized she was giving birth. Oh, great! If I didn't have the house on the market, it would have been sweet. Now, I couldn't force her out and decided to give her a couple of weeks, before trying anything else. However, the combination of the noise she and her babies were making and the harassment by the former owner, as potential buyers came to look at the house, was driving away any possible sale.

Finally, a friend told me that, if I soaked a towel with ammonia and placed it under the house, the raccoon would leave. She was gone in less than an hour. If only the same method could work on the guy next door.

Soon, another but this time horrible odor developed in the house. I called a professional to find the source, but he couldn't. The smell grew worse, until I could barely stand it, and I was having an open house Sunday. That's when I learned who my truest friend was.

I met Jeanne when Brett was little and Ron insisted I find someone to help clean the house. Ron had grown up with help, but I hadn't and so was reluctant. Finally, I searched the help wanted ads and found one that said: "Have broom will travel." I could relate to someone with an ad like that, and so I called. Jeanne was an artist and cleaned houses to support her work.

We became great friends, and spent much of the time she was supposed to be cleaning talking and smoking, until the ashtray between us was piled to overflowing with butts. We talked about everything but the subjects we both mentioned in passing one day, that I had given up a child and she was adopted. At the time, we each were both clueless about our issues, as hard as that is to believe, given their enormity lurking just below the surface of our conscious awareness.

Not until twelve years later, when I began my search, did we begin to discover the impact of adoption on our lives. By then, Jeanne had become sober for many years. We'd both quit smoking, too.

The percentage of birth parents and adoptees suffering from addiction is far higher than for the normal population. In the early days of adoption reform, blame was placed solely on genetic predisposition, until research revealed that discovering relief from the feelings of emptiness and loss and the resulting pain of separation was a significant catalyst for developing an addiction.

When I had finally forced myself to go out on a date, upon returning to college after losing my baby, I had my first drink. With the first sips of Jim Beam, the pain of all I had been through was gone, and the relief was beyond words to describe. Fortunately, I learned early on that too much alcohol or any use of drugs would bring up all the terrible memories, and so I never became addicted to alcohol or drugs, as studies found fifty percent of birth mothers had to some degree, as a means of coping.

However, the first semester of my senior year in college, I became hooked on amphetamines. With the help of speed, I was able to accomplish a great deal that led to my being listed in "Who's Who in American Colleges and Universities."

But the amphetamines were causing angry outbursts that I couldn't control. Now I would say that my suppressed anger was revealed through drug use, from the drug destroying my defense mechanism against my natural rage. Friends intervened, and I stopped using. But the anger went underground, instead of being dealt with, only to show up in the future at odd times that never had any direct relevance to the circumstances. I increasingly relied on cigarettes to push my anger back down and only was able to quit when I began my search and thus was able to take some power back over my life, and the anger began to dissipate.

At least the mothers could trace the origin of their pain, but studies were proving that a great number of adoptees had lived with the painful fears of abandonment and rejection and constant sense of emptiness in their hearts all their lives. Not understanding the origin of their feelings or that the feelings weren't normal made them more vulnerable to finding a buffer from them with drugs and alcohol.

Jeanne found that alcoholism had run in her family, when she discovered her roots. By then, she had been sober long enough to see and acknowledge the pain of growing up with a seriously mentally ill adoptive mother. From knowing her over the years, I observed that the more Jeanne became aware of and dealt with the troubles in her life, as difficult as that journey was, the more in control of her life she became.

When Jeanne met her original mother for the first time, she was severely tested. Her mother was from the generation of birth mothers who were more likely to reject their surrendered children, from needing to go to their grave with their "terrible" secret, rather than trust that the world had changed and they would be supported. Jeanne approached her mother's rejection with determination to hang in there, for her mother's sake as well as her own. "You brought me into this world, and I'm going to make you deal with me!" she told her.

However, that Sunday morning before the open house, neither one of us knew what we were going to have to deal with, and the fact that we could handle what we found without a drink or a cigarette was a testimony to the strength we both had acquired over the years.

Jeanne was all business when she came in, wanting to go downstairs right away to investigate. After five minutes of looking around, she asked what the lump was in the wall behind the bookcase.

"I don't know."

"Well, it looks like one of the raccoons fell through a space between the wall beams. The body has swelled from being there for two weeks already. We have to cut it out."

"Cut it out?"

"Yes! Cancel your open house."

Jeanne went out to her car, and I ran around the house gathering the necessary tools for the job. The stench when she began to cut into the wall was unbelievable. I began to scream in anticipation of the horror we would find. "Lawsy, Miss Scarlett, I don't know nothin' 'bout getting dead raccoons out of a wall," I tried to joke, my screams getting louder.

"Shut up!" Jeanne yelled back, as we both fought back our need to gag.

It took a couple of hours to clean the whole mess up. I could think of no other friend who would have gone to such great lengths for me and was in awe of her courage. As I tried to imagine a way to repay her, I was humbled to realize she didn't want any reward. As soon as she left, I poured myself a big glass of wine.

The house finally sold, but with the contingency that I create a parking space out front, which meant that the hill by the side of the road had to be dug into - a huge job. It was a race against time before the house was foreclosed on. Every day my neighbor stood by in his sleeveless white tee shirt, licking his chops like the big bad wolf, hoping to get his house back.

John, the contractor who had seen me through so many projects and the emotional toll they took, was able to finish the job just in time to save me. However, the cost ate up any profits.

"Carol, I don't know if I should tell you this or not," the loan officer said, as he handed me the closing papers, "but your mortgage holder was adopted. I've never witnessed such an abusive situation as you have been through."

Oh, my God. Not only had I been the projection of the wife who'd left him, but I was also the mother who had abandoned him at birth. I was shaken, as I realized all the times I'd tried to reassure him with tales of my book that could only have served to add salt to his wounds. I was lucky to get out of the deal alive.

Soon after I moved to an apartment down the creek from my former home on Lucky Drive, PACER was to hold an adoption conference in San Francisco, and Jack was asked to speak with me on a panel. I could tell he felt conflicted about doing it, and only decided at the last minute to participate. He would be staying with me, the first time we would have time together alone, since we'd first met ten years before.

Jack was greeted like a rock star, when we walked into the hotel lobby, the site of the conference. He seemed surprised, but handled all the attention well.

The room was packed, as we took our seats behind the long table for the first panel discussion of the day. Just before the presentation was to begin, Brett arrived to watch with his fiancé Jessica. When it was my turn to introduce myself, I pointed Brett out to the audience. Suddenly there was a clamor for Brett to be on the panel, too. Rarely were the issues for siblings addressed. I was grinning with pride, as Brett took a seat with the other presenters without hesitation.

After we each made a short presentation, the panel was opened to audience questions. The first question was to Jack, by a woman sitting directly in front of us. "Jack, did you experience genetic sexual attraction when you met Carol?"

I would have strangled her, if I could have. Jack and I had never discussed any issues in depth, and now this one. I wasn't even sure if Jack knew what the term meant.

During one of the first adoption conferences I'd attended, Barbara Gonyo spoke before a large crowd on the topic no one wanted to mention, the sexual attraction sometimes felt when family members: mothers or fathers and their lost children or siblings with their lost brother or sister, reunited as adults, after not growing up together. In the unchartered waters of adoption reunion, few were prepared for such a traumatic reaction, and so were swept up in feelings they didn't understand and were unable to control, causing devastation for all involved.

Nature provides the hormone Oxytocin when we fall in love and during the birth of a child, as a bonding agent to hold families together. Oxytocin is released at birth and causes the feelings of falling in love with one's baby. But, over time, close proximity desensitizes family members to the powerful chemistry that naturally bonds them to each other. None of us in the early days of adoption reunions were aware that Oxytocin was released at the time of reunion, as it should have been if we had not been separated from our child or mother and father and our siblings, as if it had simply been stored and waiting.

Such a taboo subject has had little research, so it is not known whether the adopted person, for the first time experiencing powerful mirroring by blood relations, is more vulnerable than the parent or whether the feelings are as common for the mother or father. It has been proven that hormones can "freeze" at the time of trauma, and, at the time of reunion, the mother or father regresses back to the age of the trauma, when the hormones are "thawed." If the child reminds either the father or mother of their lover, much projection can occur, at least initially. Education is the key to managing the feelings and preventing the devastation that results from giving into the overwhelming sexual impulse.

Nancy Verrier instead coined the term "genetic *sensual* attraction," which to me made much more sense and gave a healthier context in which to channel the primal feelings evoked in reunion. Part of the bonding between mother and child is naturally created from skin to skin contact, and perhaps serves to transmit and establish the infant's DNA. When deprived of such vital yet subliminal information because of separation from each other, it only makes sense that a grown child and mother in reunion feel a strong attraction to the very essential DNA information he or she needs and has been deprived of. Even if the sudden transmission feels sexual, it's not. Instead, it is serving to heal the necessary process that was interrupted.

The audience had become tense with the woman's insensitive question, which I deflected with a joke. I was too flustered to offer anything but a brief explanation of Nancy's rephrasing from sexual attraction to sensual attraction, but part of me wondered if this woman was buying the switch in thinking. Too often, and understandably, those of us wounded by our adoption issues prefer to hang onto the drama of being a victim, instead of taking the difficult steps toward genuine healing.

When I asked for more questions from the audience, worried about another bombshell, lots of hands were raised. As it turned out, many of the questions were directed toward Brett, concerning his reaction to finding out about Jack. So much necessary focus on the issues of the immediate triad in those early years had unwittingly left out the needs and issues of significant others, and the audience was hungry for Brett's impressions. At first I felt myself becoming like a protective mother bear but, as Brett handled the questions with poise and honesty, I relaxed and my anxiety was replaced by pride. He spoke of his initial shock and then his happiness knowing his brother, that finding Jack had only been a positive experience.

After our panel, I decided to skip the rest of the conference and have lunch with Brett, Jessica and Jack, instead. It was such was a rare opportunity for being together like that.

That night, when we finally got home, Jack and I sat facing each other on opposite ends of the couch, and finally had a real talk.

"What did you think of that first question?" I asked him nervously, yet finally brave enough to listen to his truth and possible confusion. My lack of courage before had derived from not wanting to face the harm I had done to him and all he'd had to deal with because of it.

"Well, Anna did understandably get jealous sometimes," Jack offered in his quiet way.

I'd learned to listen to Jack's comments carefully. He could say something quite meaningful yet spare few words. I wanted so much to help him and speak as freely as I had with hundreds of adoptees by then. But I was his mother, not his therapist, and the words didn't flow like I wanted them to. He admitted that the situation had been difficult for Rosemary at times, and that he often felt caught in the middle. It felt like, if we were to light a match, the whole place would explode, as we finally got to a new level of honesty and understanding with each other.

Soon after, there was another conference in San Francisco held by APPAH, the Association for Pre and Perinatal Research. By then, I had read everything I could find on the subject. During my research, I had stumbled across a book, *The Tibetan Art of Parenting*, in which authors Anne Maiden Brown, Edie Farwell and Dr. Dickey Nyerongsha wrote about the ancient Tibetan belief that the spirit of a child can be known even before conception, and that the dreams of the mother can meld with those of her child after the twenty-sixth week of the pregnancy. I was excited to see that the authors would be speaking at the conference, as I had a big question for them.

My interest in metaphysics had never waned, as I tried to find a deeper explanation for and perhaps find the key to healing our deep wounds. Highly respected psychics of the time unanimously claimed that we choose our parents before conception to learn the lessons we came to Earth to realize and to fulfill our karmic debts. Thus, adopted people had chosen their adoptive parents. Their opinion rankled me no end. Not only did it appear to erase our importance to our children, it also seemed to give carte blanche to those seeking to acquire a child through another woman's grief.

The resultant devastation emotionally and spiritually did not seem at all productive, if a lesson was to be learned.

I had been interested in past lives since I could remember, since I was a little girl sitting in church and wondering how heaven could be such a wonderful place when it must be so crowded. I'd even debated the idea in ninth grade, and was thrilled to finally learn how ancient and extensive the belief was in my class, Religions of Man, in college. My work with Rob solidified my belief and little Adam had certainly been a teacher, so I was vulnerable to the psychics' notion of choosing our parents. How could there be reincarnation without rebirth, without profound connections with other souls we'd known before?

The authors sat in folding chairs before a handful of us. From their lecture, it was obvious they had extensively researched the Tibetan science of conscious conception, pregnancy and birth.

Finally, in the face of their scholarly intellect, I tentatively raised my hand with a question. "Is it possible that the spirit of the coming child, as it approaches birth, could actually intend to help straighten out family problems?"

"Absolutely," they answered.

Ah hah. Reunion could be considered a chance for rebirth. On a spiritual level then, if, for my family what others thought were not as important as welcoming a new member of the family wholeheartedly, Jack would never have been lost to us. We had an opportunity and blew it. But we had rectified our mistake when Jack came back into our lives. Now everything made sense.

At our next triad support group meeting, I offered the idea that perhaps adoptees could be considered what I jokingly called "Buddhas," as their reappearance in their family of origin stirred up the very emotional issues that surrounded the time of their surrender, offering again a chance to finally heal. I was astonished at their reaction to the idea. None of the adoptees present had thought of such a notion, but for all of them in the group the

210

theory rang true. I sensed the idea was empowering, too, as it allowed them to let go of the feeling that their presence was more than anything disruptive to their family of origin.

Chapter Twelve

An opportunity unexpectedly presented itself to visit my own personal "Ghost Kingdom," and discover what was real there.

The profoundly wise author and adoption reform advocate, Betty Jean Lifton, had coined the term "Ghost Kingdom" in her groundbreaking book, *Journey of the Adopted Self*, to describe the multifarious phantoms of the very real "what-might-have-beens" that live in the psyche of adoptees, their original parents and their adoptive parents, disrupting our ability to be whole.

Kip and DeAnna were getting married, and the wedding was going to be held in the Outer Banks of North Carolina in the summer. We all would be flying into Norfolk, Virginia, not far from where Ray lived. I needed to find closure, despite the fact the word had always grated on my last nerve.

After finding Jack, people would comment that I must be so happy to "find closure." For me, that was the wrong word to use. Closure implied ending, termination, conclusion - the last thing I wanted. But it was a popular term, so I heard it all the time.

Closure probably wasn't the right word even now, as I contemplated asking Ray if we could meet again, for the first time in thirty years since five months after Jack was born. Full circle felt more like it. What I wanted more than anything was to be with my original family just once in my life. In a way, Ray and I had created so much together, not just a son and now four grandchildren but also the resulting book and movie and all the good for so many that resulted.

My original family had lived in my "Ghost Kingdom" ever since Jack was born. What would our lives have been like, if we'd stayed together as a family? Who would I have become? How would Ray's life have been different? What would Jack's life have been like if he were reared by us? Would he have struggled just as much? Who would he have become? A million questions with no hope for answers. All I knew was that I still felt our bond as a family, even though we could never be one.

Ray refused. Jean would be too upset. But, two weeks before the wedding, Ray's mother died and something shifted. Ray agreed to meet at the airport, when I would be picking up Jack and Anna and the kids to take them to the beach house for the wedding. He hadn't seen them for seven years. We were to get together a half an hour before their plane arrived. It was my fiftieth birthday.

By now I was quite used to traveling the road between the Outer Banks and the Norfolk airport, having made the trip three times already to pick up Kip's friends who were coming to the wedding. I had grown fond of this stretch of road, with its little stands and especially the homes with family gravestones randomly dotting overgrown front yards. The now familiar scenes were comforting as I sped down the road on a pilgrimage to retrieve that part of myself self still stuck in "Never Never Land," where our little fantasy family still happily lived.

I arrived ahead of schedule. Before rushing to the ladies room for a last minute primp, I scanned the airport for Ray, not certain if I would even recognize him, and remembering how one mother in our group had discovered the father of her child, whom she had been in love with, now had a pot belly and wore a hideous "rug" to disguise his bald head. She was horrified. We'd all been frozen in time and still young in our minds.

By now, I was quite excited and so only took a quick glance in the bathroom mirror before rushing back out to find him. We nearly collided into each other. Ray looked exactly the same - same weight, same twinkle in his blue eyes that had attracted me to him in the first place, except his hair was now completely grey. We were so happy to see each other, as the years melted away in an instant.

We found the gate and sat down in the metal chairs to await the plane's arrival. Ray could hardly sit still his anticipation was so great. He'd never seen his granddaughters, Mia, Asia and Tess, and had only known Dylan as a baby. Dylan would soon be eight years old. Mia was six, Asia four and a half and Tess two and a half.

How to broach the subject of the past, clear things up, state my truth?

"Didn't everything turn out well in the end?" Ray commented. It was not a question.

I just stared at him at a loss. How could he dismiss everything, at least all I'd been through, so easily? Was it that he simply couldn't bear to deal with the loss, or was he right - why keep dragging the past along with me, why not enjoy the present moment? His approach was the same as Jack's, so why couldn't I be more Zen about the whole thing like them?

"You were blessed with two more sons. I have had a happy marriage with Jean and have been a father to her son, Jimmy. We've both made the best of a bad situation."

"Yes, that's true," I responded, feeling stonewalled, though I knew that wasn't Ray's intention. All I knew, as I stared back at him helpless to explain, was that I'd grown richer and all my relationships had become more profound, from delving deep into all that had happened. And yes, I had been blessed in many ways after. The only way I knew to deal with it all was to hold both realities true, just as I was doing now – feeling unsatisfied with our conversation and, at the same time, so happy to see him.

Ray was explaining that he didn't have much time, because he'd taken off from work and he didn't want Jean to know we'd met. I felt guilty about deceiving Jean with my desire to close the circle, and wished she could understand I would have no need to see Ray again. Jack and Anna were planning to stay with Ray and Jean for a few days after the wedding. Hopefully, the little ones wouldn't spill the beans.

We watched as the plane arrived, and then there they all were approaching us through the gate. The kids ran up to me, giving me a big hug, and then Jack introduced Papa Ray, who was now grinning from ear to ear. After collecting their bags, we walked out to Ray's car in the parking lot. The kids were starved, and Ray suggested we go to the nearby Wendy's. But first we should take pictures. So, I took one of Ray with Jack and Anna and the kids, and then he took one of me with everyone. Finally, we were off to Wendy's.

As we sat around the table, I wondered how Jack was feeling about being with both of his original parents at the same time. It was something I had wanted for him as much as I had wanted it for myself, but I wasn't sure if he had such a need or could even handle it.

Ray joked that he and I had met at a hamburger joint, and now here we all were together having hamburgers. We were all having a good time, as if being together were the most natural thing, though I wondered if Jack's "deer in the headlights" expression derived from the situation or from a cross country plane ride with four small children.

Finally we had to go. As I said goodbye to Ray, I thanked him for granting my request. All of us being together this one time had meant so much to me. I watched him drive away believing I would never see him again.

Our whole side of the family was staying at a beach house on the ocean at Kill Devil Hills. We'd been gradually arriving since Sunday. Brett and Jessica were already there, and my brother Bob and his wife had brought my mother with them. My Dad and Lucy would arrive Friday and would be staying in a hotel. Fortunately, Mom had met Lucy briefly on a golf course a few years before, so there wouldn't be any awkward moments. Joanie and her Dad would be coming, too.

I was crushed that my sister, Janice, and her husband couldn't make it to the wedding. We'd all offered to help financially, but they refused. Perhaps she couldn't handle the emotions, but I was upset.

Bob would be meeting Jack for the first time, but he wasn't at the beach house when we arrived from the airport. A problem had developed over the first few days we were all together. His wife was acting irrationally, criticizing everyone for no reason. Though none of us let ourselves get caught up in her drama, it was still unpleasant, and he'd decided to spare us any more difficult scenes by moving to a hotel up the beach.

It was Wednesday, three days before the wedding. The kids couldn't wait to go out on the beach. While the others helped Jack unload the car, little Tess followed me into the kitchen where Mom was making my birthday cake. Tess took one look at Mom, then looked back at me and said, "Your Mom," though I hadn't told her yet. It was as if she'd seen a ghost. Then she ran out the door. I couldn't imagine what caused her reaction, but Mom took it in stride and patiently waited a few days for Tess to finally warm up to her.

Soon we were all out on the beach. Kip and DeAnna stopped by to fill us in on all that was happening and made plans to go out with Jack and Anna after the kids went to bed. Most of Kip's friends had flown in from California and were staying in a beach house down the road, and they were to meet up there.

"Dolphins!" the kids yelled out, jumping up and down with excitement.

A huge number of dolphins were circling in front of the kids, playing close to the shore.

"Dolphins are drawn to the sounds of children," Kip said.

The dolphins lingered a long time, circling and circling, as if inviting the children to come play.

"Wow, I feel that's a great blessing for our wedding!" DeAnna exclaimed.

It did feel like a special blessing.

Little did I know, as I watched the children calling out to the dolphins, that they were soon to give me one of my life's greatest lessons.

After the plane ride and long afternoon at the beach, the kids were tired and ready to go to bed without a protest. They were propped in a row on two double beds that had been pushed together, waiting for me to tell them a bedtime story. I racked my brain trying to come up with a memorable one and made several suggestions, but they only had one story in mind.

"Tell us again why you gave our Daddy away, Gramma," Dylan asked, wiggling his front tooth that was hanging by one stubborn root. He was hoping so much the tooth would come out before he was ring bearer in the wedding.

"What did you do, Gramma?" Asia's voice was softer than the others', like one of the little animals in Bambi's forest. She was intensely quiet and thoughtful. It was her first time hearing the story.

A soft salty breeze, skimming off the ocean, feathered the Venetian blinds. Once in a while, the edge of the blind twisted and banged loudly against the pane.

There was just enough light from the crescent moon and the porch light to illuminate their beautiful faces. The sultry Southern night and the darkness enveloped us, intensifying our closeness. It was horrifying to think I might never have known they existed.

"Tell us the story, Gramma. Please!" Dylan's eyes looked calmly and steadily into mine.

"Why did you give our Daddy away?" Wisps of curls escaped the 'hair pretty' that swept up Mia's long wavy blonde hair, which was just like mine when I was her age. At that moment, her large brown eyes held a knowing far beyond her years. "You didn't have to give him away. You could have kept him, Gramma." Since first telling her the story when she was little, her awareness had evolved.

The dreaded question I thought I'd get when they were much older. How could I make sense to them about something that still made no sense to me? The children knew about financial struggles and surviving them, so I couldn't use lack of money as a reason for not keeping their father. That might frighten them. Maybe they could be given away? Mentioning the strict nuns and the punishing attitude of the Catholic Church would confuse them, since Jack and Anna were raising them Catholic, and trying to explain society's rules back then was impossible. I felt stuck in a fairy tale.

Despite having written a book about my story and having a movie made about it, and even though I'd helped many thousands of mothers and their children who shared the same story grapple with the same questions, I was helpless to explain myself in the face of their innocence.

As I groped for an explanation my young grandchildren could understand, I knew there was none. Not really.

"People told your Papa Ray and I we were doing the very best thing for your Daddy, to give him to a family that could take care of him better than we could. We were really lucky that Gramma Rosemary loved him so much and took such good care of him."

Having none of my pretty story, they pronounced, "Gramma, you could have kept him."

"Gamma, yes, um hmm. I know." Tess shook her head in agreement, not knowing what any of the talk was about, but sensing the emotions.

I felt I was sitting before the Fates in a Greek tragedy. They were not going to let me off the hot seat until they heard the truth from me. My heart sank, as I sought the right explanation. Then, from somewhere deep inside the true answer came clearly for the first time.

"You're right, I could have kept your daddy. I just didn't know how to back then."

Instantly I sensed I was off the hook. They were satisfied, and so was I.

As I tucked them into bed, Asia whispered, "But Gramma, what did you do? Did you just keep walking when you left my Daddy behind?"

I didn't want them to see my tears, so I gave each one a quick kiss and barely managed to say, "Sweet dreams, I love you!" as I felt myself falling back into the same dark pit that had engulfed me when I returned to Seton House, leaving my baby to an unknown fate.

The early morning sunshine enveloped us, as we sat around the wooden table out on the deck, and the dark place I'd fallen into the night before melted away. The kids had discovered a hose and were busy filling their buckets in the sand below. Bob arrived with a bag of bagels and a huge bowl of shrimp he'd gotten right off the boat that morning.

As we settled down to devour the shrimp, I was surprised to notice that Jack and Bob had similar gestures, despite their meeting for the first time. Jack had inherited Bob's flat feet, which had served him well in water polo, but gestures? And, they both had the same easy, calm presence. Since Bob never had children of his own, it was nice to know that some of his special characteristics had been passed along the gene pool nevertheless.

As we made plans for the day and arrangements for how all of us were going to get to the cruise DeAnna's parents had arranged for the immediate family and the wedding party, we had no idea we were about to face a harrowing experience.

The beautiful clear sky all day didn't offer a clue about the violent storm that struck, just as we were leaving for the cruise. Our little caravan was already on its way, when the torrential rains began. All of a sudden, we couldn't even see the hood of the car, much less the car in front of us, as we approached the bridge to Manteo. Not able to see where we were, there was no way to pull off to the side of the road, as we inched our way across the bridge, certain one wrong move would send us over the side and into the water. Then, just as swiftly as it started, the storm was abruptly over. We'd made it over the bridge and already the sky was clearing.

As the boat took off for our evening cruise, a spectacular rainbow appeared, and I grabbed my camera and took a picture of Kip and DeAnna with the rainbow arching over them. The intense little journey now felt mythical.

At one point in the evening, as the sun was setting, I spotted Jack leaning on the boat rail by himself and went over to him. He was watching Ron's Aunt Perry, who obviously still had it all even though she was in her late seventies, enchanting all of Kip's groomsmen.

'How are you handling all this?"

Jack had kept his deer in the headlights expression since his arrival, and I'd grown concerned. But now he seemed totally at ease.

"It was overwhelming the first few days," he admitted. "Being with the whole family and Kip's friends were so accepting of me. I couldn't let it all in. But I was finally worn down and had to give up resisting it all. Feels great!"

Even after all the years of being immersed in adoption issues, I still couldn't get over how seemingly orchestrated "from above" healing moments could be.

One of the struggles I'd always had was in understanding why many adoptees never wanted to be with more than one member of their original family at a time after a reunion. Wouldn't it be the most natural thing to want to know all your blood kin? But it was the rare adoptee that couldn't wait to attend a family reunion. More common were stories of adoptees desiring to keep relationships separate, sometimes to the point of creating a wedge between two or more relatives. Some mothers had a difficult time accepting their child's stance, and the relationship suffered and sometimes ended as a result. Off and on, I'd bring up the subject in support groups and conferences and was met with blank stares.

Finally, during our support group just a few weeks before the wedding, the adoptees there were able to articulate the reason for their reluctance. Being surrounded by people who felt so familiar felt like annihilation to them, they explained, when their whole identity had been structured from being in another family. On top of that, they had developed a certain pride in the fact that they were unique, not like anyone they knew – self-made in a way. They'd spent their lives figuring out whom they were without any mirrors to go by, and feared losing themselves by being among familiar people. The root of the words family and familiar was the same after all.

Only one of the adoptees in the group had risked his sense of self by attending a family reunion. His fears were the same as the others' before attending, but he soon found, when he let himself go through the feelings of annihilation, he was more of who he was and not less as feared. I was so grateful to the group for helping me become sensitive to all that Jack was going through, instead of feeling he was rejecting the family.

The day of the wedding finally arrived. The night before, Ron and his wife had thrown an elegant and lavish rehearsal dinner. Afterwards, Kip, DeAnna and I had walked through the little town of Manteo to the quaint hotel where they would be spending their wedding night, before taking off for the honeymoon. We sat on high-backed wooden rockers on the wraparound porch and talked about everything.

The next afternoon, our beach house was a flurry of activity, as we all tried to get ready at once. Brett was to be best man and Jack a groomsman. Mia and Asia were flower girls, and Tess was to hand out silk and ribbon wrapped birdseed for everyone to toss at the bride and groom. The wedding was being held in the Elizabethan Gardens in the park of the Lost Colony, so it was necessary to replace traditional rice with birdseed.

The girls looked like fairy princesses in matching long white satin dresses and wearing a band of white flowers in their hair. They could hardly contain their excitement. Dylan, wearing a tux that matched the groomsmen, was still working on getting his tooth out.

The gardens were beautiful, and I was excited to be at the site of the Lost Colony, such an historic place in history. A mini disaster happened just before the wedding was to start. DeAnna had accidentally moved to a spot in the garden where there was a mosquito nest, and hundreds of mosquitos were now stuck in the netting under her wedding gown. Somehow, we were able to shake them all out in time for the procession.

As the ceremony began, I felt such gratitude for the miracle that had brought us all together, and for Kip and DeAnna's desire to have Jack and his family a part of the celebration.

After partying late into the night at the reception, held at the Beach Club, we all woke up late the next morning. The beach house was to be vacated by one o'clock. Jack and Anna were the first to leave, as they were expected at Ray and Jean's for a five-day stay before returning to California. We were all scattered to the winds again.

I came home to one of the most heartbreaking stories I'd heard in our group so far. Morgan's friend, Amy, had been coming to the group for a few months, preparing to meet her son. In the beginning she was almost afraid to meet him, since he'd seemed so needy during their phone conversations. Her own ambivalence confused her. How could she push away her own son, especially when he needed so much to know her? I quietly wondered myself, but had learned over time to just listen and not judge. Her son's raw emotions frightened her.

By coming to the group, Amy was able to see that she was terrified of facing the consequences to her son of her inability to keep him. He'd grown up the opposite from how Amy would have raised him, in a sterile home with white carpets and furniture that he would get punished for if he made a mess. His mother was a socialite, who cared little for him. He'd grown up a lonely little boy.

With our encouragement, Amy had written her son a beautiful letter, telling him of her desire to meet with him. They had set a date, but then she heard nothing from him for over a month, after hearing from him almost daily. One night, she received an anonymous phone call from a woman, claiming to be an adoptive aunt, telling Amy her son had been killed in a car accident the month before. She didn't want anyone in the family to know she had called Amy, but she herself believed Amy had a right to know. No, she would not reveal where her son was buried.

Amy was devastated and could only hope that her son had received her letter before the accident, but she would never know. Wouldn't it have helped the adoptive mother to meet his original mother, share pictures and stories of their son? In her own way, she must have loved him. Her meeting Amy might have healed both mothers.

My parallel metaphysical search, as I tried to find my son, had led me to one question. If it were spiritually true that ultimately we are all connected, wouldn't it then also be true that we are meant to strive to overcome all the issues that keep us from that realization? Wouldn't our souls then be liberated from our worst fears and our innate compassion and a new sense of confidence result? Yet society conspires to keep us in our fears, sealing us from each other in the name of protecting us from each other, enabling us to justify our fears by keeping adoption records closed. Why? Now Amy faced a future more ripped apart than ever.

All the stories people shared with me over the years were now a part of me, the tragic ones weighing especially heavily. My story seemed benign compared to many, and I was so lucky to have Jack in my life. Amy's situation put me over the edge, and I wanted and needed to give a voice to those less fortunate than me, but how?

My novel, *An Ancient Tear*, was finished, and I was looking for a publisher. As much as I had loved being immersed in the story, I still felt ambivalent about having it become public. Somehow, the book felt even more personal than *The Other Mother*, even though it was fiction, and I couldn't reconcile my feelings of being too exposed. I wasn't sure if it was actually badly written, naïve or too far out. But why would I deny my own experience while writing it? Sometimes I wondered if my reticence stemmed from old issues of shame from my first pregnancy, they felt so deep. After all, any creative act is much like giving birth. The root of my fear felt too deep to possibly understand, and pulling it out of the soil of my unconscious too soon might break off any chance of finally fathoming its source.

The advice of a good friend and healer, Kay Kamala, shook the root loose a bit. "Once you've given birth to a creative project, Carol, just like a child it has its own life, which you can't nor should control. Your book will have its own life apart from you."

Maybe that's what I was afraid of.

As the lights of the Marin Theater Company dimmed, I was tense with anticipation. I was there to see the play, *Kindertransport* by Diane Samuels, which Lee directed. He'd warned me that it might be a difficult play for me to watch.

As the threat of Nazi Germany grew before the outbreak of World War II, many Jewish parents felt they had no choice but to put their children on trains bound for the safety of Britain, a movement called the Kindertransports. At the time the families believed they would be reunited soon with their children and that the British families would be providing a haven until then. But as the war grew, the children were absorbed by their new British families and most never saw their original families again, in effect being forced to give up their original families and their identities in order to exist.

In the play, the story of the Kindertransport is told through one British woman in her fifties, Evelyn, now a Christian, and Eva, the nine-year-old German Jewish child she once was. Evelyn's daughter, Faith, has discovered her mother's hidden past, while rummaging through old letters in their attic, and confronts her.

Sometimes it is easier to see one's own story through another's work of art. I was gripped, as the complex play unfolded, watching Evelyn's denial of the self she was born to be, at one point tearing up into little pieces letters, some from her mother who wanted desperately to see her daughter again, and photographs of her original family, while sitting in the attic with her adoptive mother. It was impossible for me not to take her denial personally, despite knowing to the core all her issues. But Faith was relentless as she pushed her mother to get past her icy demeanor to her true feelings.

Evelyn became Eva again and confronted her first mother. "Why did you put me on that train? Don't you know I would have preferred to die with you in the gas chamber?"

The guttural gasp that escaped my defenses, as Eva's words seared me, rang through the silent theater. Some in the audience turned in my direction. I was mortified, yet at the same time strangely fascinated and grateful that my deepest feelings had been so starkly revealed to me. Only the movie *Sophie's Choice* had affected me more, but I'd seen it two years before searching for Jack and had not yet allowed myself to explore the depths of my feelings, fearing insanity without a resolution. I'd made a terrible mistake seeing the movie alone and was barely able to make it to my car before I let out a frightening scream. That night it had taken a huge effort and a good bit of wine to bury my feelings again, until the time when I could take action.

On the way home from the theater, I thought about the Jews in Nazi Germany, the slaves in America, the Native Americans and all the people throughout history who'd been forcibly separated from their original families – so much pain, too much to contemplate. I decided to write a play as a way of unburdening myself of all the tragedy I had been carrying with me, one that would hopefully enlighten people about our issues and rip off the romantic veneer adoption held for most of the public.

Writing the play would also afford me the chance to pick up another loose thread from the past, an attempt I'd made once before in the seventies, when I tried again to fulfill the thwarted desire from my college days to act. Then I had failed miserably.

We were to read a monologue before the class and I'd found it impossible to get up on stage.

When I was bemoaning my lack of courage to Morgan one day, she saw my failure differently. "You knew you couldn't reveal all of yourself up on the stage then, that you'd be lying in a way."

She was right.

One morning over coffee with Lee, I told him that story. "Use it," he said.

I went back home and began writing *The Sacred Virgin*.

Chapter Thirteen

Late August, Jack and Anna finally moved to Virginia Beach permanently, making the cross-country trip with the four kids, a dog and all their belongings in a van and a car. They'd decided during their visit with Ray and Jean after the wedding. More than getting away from Los Angeles, they wanted time to be their own family, without being constantly immersed in Anna's huge one. They'd found a house to rent and both found jobs right away, and suddenly life became a little easier for them.

I didn't want to feel jealous of Ray and Jean, but I was. Several times over the years, Jack and Anna had considered moving up to the Bay Area, most recently when Anna's sister, Angela, and her boyfriend had moved there, and Jack and Anna were coming up more often to visit them, too. Now the hope of developing a more normal relationship someday, by their living close by, was dashed.

Before they left, I flew down to see them one last time. Sensing that this time the move was permanent, I knew I had to risk doing something I'd debated about for a long time. It took until the very last minute to screw up my courage, and I almost didn't do it then.

Rosemary was driving me to the airport with Anna and the kids in the car. Could I say "I love you" to them in front of

Rosemary? What was I so afraid of? Of course Rosemary knew I loved them. She wouldn't expect me to feel otherwise. But the idea of saying so in front of her terrified me nevertheless.

I'd gotten out of the car. The windows were down and they were waving goodbye. I took a deep breath. "Bye guys, I love you!"

Nothing horrible happened. "Love you, too!" they all said. Rosemary was smiling. She hadn't fallen apart.

As I sat in the plane waiting for takeoff, I felt the most enormous relief, as if I had moved a mountain. My crazy fear was too complex to comprehend, so I simply let the mountain go, feeling whole for the first time ever, owning my place in their lives and finally feeling equal.

With Kip back east and Brett in Las Vegas I felt adrift, aimlessly floating down a meandering river leading nowhere. I didn't want to work in a flower shop forever, as much fun as it was. Besides, it barely sustained me. But my writing was not sustaining me either, at least not financially. One path that was logical meant going back to school to become a therapist. By now I knew a great deal about adoption issues and had laid a good foundation to go in that direction. But the idea of studying other people's ideas, when I had already developed my own over the years, felt too frustrating. Perhaps I needed to look at my issues regarding authority, but I didn't.

In the heat of my personal debate about what to do with the rest of my life, I came across a quote from the Gnostic Bible, attributed to Christ, that offered a rudder to guide me: "If you bring forth what is within you, what you bring forth will save you. If you do not bring forth what is within you, what you do not bring forth will destroy you." Okay, I'll continue to write I told myself, despite having no guarantees.

In spite of my resolve, I still felt stuck - like my life, after so much good that had happened with the success on so many levels of *The Other Mother*, was never going to mean as much anymore, and I couldn't shake off the resulting depression.

Then one day I received a call asking me to speak to a fourth grade class on being an author. People from all kinds of professions were asked to speak at schools around Marin County. I happily accepted. But as the day grew closer, I worried about how I could talk about my book without explaining what the story was about. How would fourth graders handle the subject of a mother giving up her child?

I called the principle of the school to tell her what my book was about and ask her advice.

"No," she said. "I would not want you to discuss *that* subject with the children."

She was quite firm about it and, even though I had some trepidation myself I was left feeling a bit tarnished.

On my way to the school the morning of the talk, I believed I would be speaking to students from wealthy families, given the address. So, I was surprised to be greeted at the classroom door by children who were mostly from Mexico. They were clearly excited about my visit.

I took the teacher aside. "Do you know what my book is about?" I asked.

"Yes, I do and I want you to talk about it," she answered without hesitation.

"But your principal specifically requested that I not touch the subject."

"This is my decision to make, and I want you to be honest," she insisted. "Trust me."

I took a deep breath and entered the classroom, as the children scrambled to sit down in a big circle. Somehow I was able to find the right words. After my talk, I asked if there were any

230

questions and received a flood of compassionate responses instead. The teacher saw my shock and explained in front of the class that most of the children were separated from at least one of their parents, who out of necessity had to remain behind in Mexico in order to give their children a better life. One after another, the children spoke of their longing to see their parent, about their nightmares, and how they were trying to be strong. They asked questions about how Jack was doing now, how I was doing. I was moved to tears.

They asked me to stay an extra hour, and I suggested they spend the time writing their stories. Instinctively I knew they were old souls, and so I asked them to be silent for a few minutes and either pay attention to what feeling came up first for them or else a part of their story that needed to be told, the same exercise I used, and then begin writing. A few shared their stories after, and even the teacher was surprised at their depth. Then it was lunchtime and time to say goodbye. I regretted having to leave, since I felt so close to all of the children and would never see them again.

A week later, a big package arrived in the mail, full of drawings the children had made thanking me for my visit. As I read each one, I couldn't help wondering, despite never wanting them to have suffered as they had, if they were better off than many privileged children and that their young wisdom might someday begin to change the world.

As my first Christmas in my new apartment approached, I found myself thinking about the little red stocking ornament from the home for unwed mothers my mother had offered to send years before. Why not make myself miserable and ask her to finally send it! Actually I had grown tired of the specter the little ornament held over me. Why did I give it so much power? The only conscious memory I had of the little stocking was the scene in the movie where a very pregnant "Carol" hung it on the tree at Seton

House, and then caught a glimpse of the tragic face of one of the girls returning after leaving her baby behind in the hospital. And, of course the scene at the kitchen sink with my mother when she pulled the ornament out of a tin can.

I had yet to return to Richmond, Virginia, where Jack was born, and walk through my past. The idea still unnerved me, despite reports from mothers, who had dared to return to the places that had caused so much pain and trauma, that seeing the homes again shrunk them down to size. The homes were no longer mythological in their minds, their memory not so potent.

"Mom, if you still have that ornament, could you send it?"

"Of course."

We didn't discuss why I wanted it now.

A few days later, the package arrived. I observed myself circling around it, until I finally told myself this is silly and opened the envelope. The red felt stocking ornament was much smaller than I expected. As much as it stirred me to hold it, no memories were evoked about why I had thought it so important to pack along with my few belongings, as I naively prepared to return to my former life. Was it that I felt I had to have some tangible object to prove I'd had a son? The sorrow I felt for the young woman I was back then suddenly overwhelmed me, as I hung the ornament on the tree.

Over the next days, I'd hoped the little stocking would lose its power and instead purge me of the past. That didn't happen. In fact, I found myself mystified over the waves of fresh grief that would wash over me – after all this time, after so much effort at healing. It was common for mothers who had lost their children to adoption to have anniversary reactions, often taking the form of deep depression, around the time of their child's birth, and mine was always around Christmas. But since finding Jack, the underlying depression had begun fading. Now, it was full blown again.

One night, as I was wrapping presents to send to Jack and his family, it came to me what to do with the stocking ornament. I put a small quartz crystal in the toe and tucked in a note to Jack: "I am eternally grateful every day that you are part of my life."

When I called them on Christmas, the package hadn't arrived. A severe ice storm had delayed mail deliveries.

The next morning, the phone rang. It was Anna. "Carol, the package arrived today and I can't tell you how much your note meant to Jack, to both of us."

Apparently, Jack and Ray had had an argument over their being late for Christmas dinner. They were left feeling devastated, that their move had been a huge mistake. I tried to reassure them that the conflict was probably all due to stresses of the holiday, and not to worry. But I could finally see beyond Jack's easy going nature to how vulnerable he was, as we all tried to forge again our natural bonds.

I sat for a long time after hanging up the phone, feeling tremendous relief that I had followed my impulse to send that note in the little stocking. Little did I know then that that tiny ornament was to have an even sweeter role in the future.

A few months later, I was finally able to visit Jack and Anna at their new home. After the first nineteen years of not knowing where he was, I felt at loose ends, until I could actually see where they were living. Upon returning home I felt more at peace again.

However, my visit had created another layer of tension with Ray and Jean. Because I was there, they didn't want to come to Dylan's soccer game. I was sad that my presence was so disturbing and began to suspect that the tensions were undermining my relationship, at least with Anna, who because of her great love of Jack still seemed to hold some resentments toward me for having given him up.

We had been sitting on a blanket by the soccer field with a couple hoping to adopt a newborn, when Anna brought up the fact that I seemed to be against adoption. I had learned over the years that, in order to get someone to listen to my side of the adoption story, I had to learn to walk in the shoes of adopting parents as well, and I did feel their longing for a child and all the pain of not having one of their own.

At one point, after giving up Jack, I had fantasized myself about adopting a child. Perhaps from all the fairytales I'd loved as a young girl, a part of me felt it was a romantic idea to rescue a child. But when I allowed myself to follow the path of my feelings, I realized it was my own lost baby I was looking to adopt and, since that was an impossible fantasy, at least I could understand all he was experiencing through another child. Then, after the therapy with Toni, I was able to follow the path further to a need to rescue a part of myself.

As I sat on the picnic blanket with Anna and her friends, I struggled with the same feelings that came up for me every time I'd been asked for my stance on infant adoptions, which happened often, ever since I'd become a public figure on the subject. While I didn't want to negate another's reality, I couldn't reconcile the desperation of many prospective adoptive parents with a mother in a desperate situation being taken advantage of. Listening to adoptive parents, who shut out the reality that their child had another family - all in the name of love - left me feeling like I didn't have a right to exist. One of the strange results of having lost a child to adoption was a feeling of being invisible. So many of the mothers used that term to describe themselves. We had been forced to "vanish" at the most powerfully creative time in our lives, such an essential part of ourselves never to be acknowledged again.

"So, you don't believe in adoption, Carol?"

The question was always asked couched in anger, whenever anyone asked me, as if I were violating a great social ideal.

"I didn't say that," I would always respond, angry with myself for feeling defensive. "I am only saying that, for the mother adoption is a permanent solution to a temporary problem. A vulnerable expectant mother should be given all options and be thoroughly educated about the long-term impact on both herself and her child, as well as family issues healed before an adoption is made. How could adoptive parents feel good about raising another's child otherwise?"

With such views I was seen as a radical.

Hoping to enlighten prospective adoptive parents, I had accepted a couple of invitations to speak before them, but I found the effort draining, as they weren't ready to hear what I had to say. So, I declined further offers, until an adoptive mother friend, Ellen Roseman, a real proponent of true open adoptions, asked me to speak on a "birth mother" panel at a conference for adoptive parents.

When I had entered the classroom used for the panel discussion, the children's seats were filled with prospective adoptive parents, which was encouraging. Five mothers of all ages were to speak. I was surprised to see Betsy from our workshop, the woman whom had been raped, was one of them. The glaring fluorescent lights illuminated all of us. I had a sick feeling in the pit of my stomach.

The mothers who spoke before me, all in some form of open adoption, took a reassuring stance, as they told their stories. Open adoption was different from the old closed system they said.

As I listened to their stories, I wondered at how disconnected from any feelings they were. To me they sounded brainwashed, but in a different way than we had been. The mothers of my generation had been told we were giving a gift to atone for our "mistake," but few of us bought that notion. Now I was hearing these young women on the panel proudly talk about the gift they were giving, as if their needs or their baby's didn't matter. I would have believed them when they said how happy they were, if they also expressed natural feelings of grief and ambivalent feelings about their decision. But they seemed afraid of closing down access to information about their children by speaking or even knowing their own truth.

The level of brainwashing was difficult for me to comprehend. What would happen if they ever woke up from their trance? Were they really at peace, or would they be even more traumatized than we had been when they realized the deception? Would they ever be able to naturally question their decision?

As I waited my turn as the last to speak, a young pregnant woman I'd met in the corridors of the California Assembly kept popping into my mind. A group of us, spearheaded by the tireless efforts of Kate Burke, were fighting for a bill to unseal adoption records and allow adopted persons access to their original birth certificates - the key to their ancestry and their story and what should have been considered a basic human right. The young pregnant woman was there to oppose the bill, which had passed through all the Assembly and Senate committees, only needing this day to pass the Senate Appropriation Committee, the final step before sending the landmark bill to the Governor to sign.

I'd been there the first time the bill was presented, when the prospects of it passing through the Legislative Committee were looking bleak. The committee members were about to rule against the bill, when one mother spoke up about the fact that none of us had ever had any legal representation. As if one, the entire committee turned toward her in shock. That reason was enough to get the bill through to this last committee.

Now what looked to be certain victory was headed toward certain defeat, because of the efforts of the infamous Bill Pierce, head of the National Council of Adoption, who at the last minute organized a massive fear campaign through letters to the committee, mostly elicited through the Children's Home Society. Bill Pierce was our enemy and to me the vilest of men, when I never thought like that about anyone. I'd encountered him personally on CNN, when Betty Jean Lifton, Joe Soll, Jack and I were on *Sonia Live*, debating his opposition to open records. His condescending, dismissive attitude was meant to demean us and keep the business of adoption flourishing.

The young woman was about seven months along and kept insisting, as she pointed fiercely at her belly, that this was *not* her baby, it never was meant to be her baby. This baby was meant for the adoptive parents. I was horrified by her vehemence, and worried for her baby. The level of brainwashing she had been subjected to could only be imagined. The level of rejection being imprinted on her baby's soul had been difficult to contemplate.

When it was my turn to speak before the prospective adoptive families, I told my truth as clearly and honestly as I ever had, without emotion but with strength that couldn't be denied. I also told the story of Phyllis, a mother of twins who had the most open adoption I'd ever heard of. Phyllis saw her sons several times a week for nearly five years, even had them for weekends sometimes. When she first came to the group, she was proud of her choice to have her babies placed with a family that was so open to including her. Their relationship had become a model for open adoption, and Phyllis often spoke to groups as an advocate for open adoption.

Then, after five years, she was suddenly cut off from any contact, unfortunately a common occurrence in open adoptions. The boys were becoming aware that Phyllis was their mother, too, and the adoptive mother felt threatened. Like many of the even older mothers from the closed system in the group, Phyllis had chosen adoption for her boys to protect them from her own dysfunctional family. If she had known the adoption would be closed, she would never have placed them. There wasn't (and still isn't) a law in the land that absolutely protected her agreement with the adoptive parents, and now she was completely derailed emotionally.

After my honesty I was sure I would never be asked to speak before adopting parents again.

A young woman in the front row raised her hand first. "Carol, I am so grateful to you. Listening to your talk I can come to only one conclusion, that the only right thing to do would be to adopt both the mother and the child, so that they can stay together. I could never feel right otherwise."

"Thank you for understanding" was all I could say. But I knew she could feel our connection with each other at that moment. I wondered what she would end up doing.

Other adoptive mothers spoke about wanting to keep the adoption open but the mothers of their children had stopped all contact. They felt terrible for their children that their other mother was rejecting them, which was hard for the adoptive mothers to take. "Please try to see that their pain is too great to face right now, but by continuing to be there for them you are helping them heal," I responded. "Remember, they aren't rejecting the child you share, only the painful feelings."

By the time our session was over, I was drained but encouraged. At least they were open to facing some painful truths.

I was glad I'd scheduled an appointment for a massage the next day, as a lot of emotions had come up during the conference. Over time I'd become convinced that releasing emotionally charged energy held in the body, both from past and present wounds, was essential to healing. Understanding issues with the mind or delving into traumatic feelings without purifying the body at the same time keeps us stuck in our stories, replaying the same tapes over and over without resolution as if the charged energy in our bodies were magnets, drawing our stories back to us. I'd found that nature was a great healer, as well as massage work and long baths in sea salt. Others in our group were finding the same results.

Paula, a birth mother and adoptee, was a Touch for Health practitioner, a method that combined acupressure with massage. She was also clairvoyant and a gifted healer. Despite all the issues Paula had to deal with, she was one of the most positive people I knew. So, when I opened her screen door on the morning of our appointment, I was alarmed to find her sitting in a chair completely despondent.

By then she'd met her son, whom she'd given birth to at fifteen after living with her adoptive mother in a motel room for months, in order to keep the pregnancy a secret. The preacher's son had raped her, though at the time Paula, like so many of our generation, didn't know to call what happened to her "rape."

Her son, Cole, had spent a week with Paula after they first connected again, which became a catalyst for her to search for her original family. The searcher had recently found her father's side of the family, but Paula felt she had to wait to get in touch with her newly discovered five half siblings until she met her older full-blooded sister, whom had been raised by their mother, so they could meet their siblings together. She'd learned about her older sister from non-identifying information the agency had sent. However, the searcher was unable to find even a trace of her mother and it had been many months.

I sat worried on a chair beside Paula, listening to her deep despair. She wasn't even sure she wanted to go on, which frightened me. Why did any adopted person have to go through such pain for simply wanting to know their original family? There was nothing I could say to console her that wouldn't come out sounding hollow.

Then the phone rang, startling us both. I watched Paula's face change in an instant from sorrow to joy, as she listened to the caller on the other end. The searcher had found her mother! The news was so unexpected we both felt spun around.

There was sad news, too. The searcher had found the name of a younger brother to contact from her mother's death certificate. But the news that her mother was dead didn't surprise Paula.

One night fifteen years before, Paula had awakened from a deep sleep feeling a huge loss and a strange mixture of sadness and anger from the depths of her being, and knew without question her original mother had just died. For days after she'd felt depressed, from being kept from knowing her mother and being powerless to do anything about it. But then the spirit of her mother came to her and healed much of her depression. Paula was excited to "see" her and experienced her mother's spirit as soothing and mellow.

Her original father had also passed away years before, but Paula hadn't sensed his death. Instead, she always felt she was more like him than her mother. Since she first tore her bike apart when she was seven, she'd been driven to be mechanical. She loved working on her cars and even took apart some. But when she learned from the non-identifying information she'd been given that her father had been a mechanic, she found she no longer needed to fix her own cars and her interest in mechanics faded, to be replaced by a desire to be a healer and fine-tune her psychic abilities.

The week after the searcher's call, Paula drove down to the cemetery where her mother was buried. When she inquired at the mortuary, she learned her mother had indeed died at the time that she had awakened with the terrible sense of loss fifteen years before.

Soon after, she finally spoke with her full-blooded sister and, despite the fact that they were very different from each other,

Paula found her sister's voice soothed her in exactly the same unique way as her mother's spirit had. If, as has been proven, babies recognize their mother's voice, then Paula must have carried the soothing feeling of her mother's voice with her for her whole life.

That summer, a year after Kip and DeAnna's wedding, Brett and Jessica were married in Las Vegas, where he'd become a firefighter and paramedic. Brett had wanted so much for Jack to be in his wedding, like he had been for Kip's, but Jack and Anna were still struggling financially and couldn't make it, and I had no means of helping them get there. Even understanding the situation, Brett was hurt. Jack was his older brother and he wasn't there.

I had been reading the work of Bert Hellinger, a German psychotherapist, because his work with family constellations directly dealt with adoption, where so often the subject was ignored in psychoanalytic literature. Hellinger's theory, that each family is its own energy system within which each family member holds a unique and important position not to be duplicated by any other member, was the basis for his healing work.

Within that energy field is held the entire family history, including powerful events that had impacted the lives of ancestors, the effects of which still reverberated through the field and which the current family members may or may not be aware of. To the extent that family members are unaware of past secrets and traumas is the degree to which they are removed from their own personal destiny and instead likely to play out unconsciously a family member's secret trauma. According to Hellinger, at least one family member will manifest the family secrets through depression, suicide, childlessness, unwed pregnancy, mental or physical illness or addictions, without any conscious awareness of the cause.

When Hellinger spoke about family members, he especially included aborted or stillborn babies, children who'd died that were not mourned or remembered, and children who were given away for adoption and never talked about. He also spoke about adoptive families who refused to acknowledge the natural parents of their children. Counted, too, as necessary to be honored were previous partners or significant relationships of any of the adults, including grandparents. All are a part of the family's energy field whether acknowledged or not. Hellinger maintained that only when the secrets are mined and lost family members acknowledged was the inherent love within the family's energy field able to flow, what he called *Love's Hidden Symmetry*, the title of his best-known book. To think society still prefers secrets remain intact, effectively blocking any chance for families to heal.

Since secrecy is usually an integral part of adoption trauma, I found Hellinger's work compelling. I'd also heard enough stories over the years to qualify my own research validating his theory. One remarkable observation I'd made was how adoptees seemed to know, even before finding the truth, that they had a brother or sister or huge family that they'd always longed for. Their longing was actually for something they already had.

So, according to Hellinger's work, Brett's soul would have known before being born that he was not my first child, even if he didn't consciously know, so that, until he heard the truth, something about his place in the family didn't feel quite right. I was glad that I had told Brett and Kip about their older brother while they were young and able to accept the truth so readily and easily. Finding out late, after the secret had more chance to erode the fabric of the family, may account for some sibling's negative reactions at the time of reunion.

Even though they hadn't grown up together, battled it out as siblings do, and so didn't have the same relationship Brett and Kip had with each other, Jack's absence at Brett's wedding was deeply felt. For Jack's part, not having known us for long most likely kept him from realizing his true importance to us. In the near future, I was to learn the impact on Jack's other brothers upon discovering Jack was adopted.

As it turned out, working at the flower shop proved not to be a sidetrack after all. My weakness as a writer was dialog, so I began to listen more intently to the rhythm of speech of the customers and especially the young women with whom I worked, who also proved to be an inspiration for the characters I was developing for my play.

Over and over I was struck by the great contrast between generations. As much as my generation had attempted to rebel against the norms of the fifties, we were still a product of those times, still tenuous about the ground we were breaking, still reacting to our upbringing, where these young women were simply free spirits. I would tell them about how embarrassed and shamed we would feel if our slip or bra strap showed, as they listened shocked - with everything showing. I began to appreciate how liberating the singer Madonna had been. Because of her rebellion what had been so taboo for us, keeping us in little boxes, was no longer even a concern. So I decided to have the same actors play both the unwed mothers of the sixties and the young women of the nineties to make the contrast more striking.

We weren't a FTD type of flower shop and the arrangements we made were always creative, sometimes works of art. I'd also become close friends with Joe, a master of flower arranging, who was from Australia. Once Joe and I were arranging thousands of dollars worth of flowers for an Indian mogul, whose family was moving into a huge mansion he'd built in the hills of Sausalito. As original works of art by the likes of Ruben and Rembrandt were being uncrated, all anyone could talk about was the beauty of Joe's creations.

Of course, the reason for giving or getting flowers ran the gamut of human emotions. Though not part of the job description, we listened to stories and sometimes gave advice about a whole range of relationship issues and often consoled stories of deep grief. But for those who came into the shop and spoke about how they'd always wanted to work in a flower shop, we always told them they were lucky they didn't. They had no idea what hard work was involved.

Nancy and her then husband Bruce knew from the beginning about my work in adoption. At first Nancy had little interest in searching for her original parents. But reading *The Other Mother* softened her to the idea and she watched the movie a couple of times. Before then, she had no idea that her mother might have felt grief about giving her up. Finally, after I'd worked there for two years, she came in one morning and said she had found her mother.

Ever since living in New York City in the late sixties, I'd wanted to move back. The city was still in my system. Kip and DeAnna had moved to the city, where Kip took a job with Bear Sterns. Each time I went to visit them there, I wanted to return home, pack and move back to the Big Apple. But as soon as I would get home I fell in love with the beauty of San Francisco all over again and couldn't imagine leaving. The ambivalence continued for almost three years. I got closer to making the move when I realized I would regret not giving New York one more chance, while Kip was still there.

One day I was talking with my friend, Kay, who pointed out that I seemed to be at a stalemate in my life the past three years, nothing much was going on and I couldn't make anything happen. "Follow the energy," she suggested. She was right. So many of my close friends had already moved away. The Bay Area had changed dramatically from a cutting edge area of new thought, where environmental concerns were a high priority, to a place where wealth took over as technology companies moved in. From the vantage point of the flower shop on Bridgeway Road in Sausalito, Humvees were the norm in the now congested traffic. And the customers were changing, acting much more entitled.

Finally, San Francisco gave me a shove out, or at least I decided to take it that way. My landlady raised my rent four hundred dollars, beginning the next month. There had been a leak in the bathroom from an upstairs apartment and mold had developed. Her solution was to paint over the problem, which she knew I wouldn't tolerate, and so she drove me out in order to fool the next person. I really had to thank her for being the last straw. As it turned out, a writing job was already awaiting me in New York City.

Adoptee and therapist, Maryann Koenig had recently approached me about editing her photo essay book on adoption, *Sacred Connections: Twenty-Four Stories of Adoption*. We were excited about working together, but her concern was that I lived on the West Coast and she was in Philadelphia. When I told her I was moving to New York City in a month, we cemented our deal.

One month to wind up thirty years was not enough time. Not knowing how long I would be staying, I arranged storage for all the furniture - mostly antiques, my favorite things that I felt I could never sell. My recent moves had forced me to downsize considerably, until all that was left were the things that meant the most to me. Saying goodbye to friends was the worst part, but I told myself I wouldn't be gone long. Little did I know.

Maryann wanted to show the spectrum of adoption stories in her book. As it turned out, Jack was going to be in New York the same weekend I was arriving there to attend the wedding of one of his adoptive cousins. His two brothers, Mark and David, would be there, too, and so I suggested to Maryann that we fly Brett in from Las Vegas, since Kip was already in New York, and get all four of Jack's brothers together for an interview. "Great idea," she said.

My plan was to stay with my former sister-in-law, Barbara, until I found my own place. But, Carol, how do you think you can afford New York City when living in San Francisco is so difficult was everyone's question. I wasn't as worried; somehow everything was going to work out.

The morning I was to leave was harrowing. I had one more trip to make to storage before catching the plane, which seemed doable, until I got there and found out the building wouldn't be open for another hour. Panic set in.

When I got back from the second trip to storage, having shoved as much stuff in there as I could and barely managing to close and lock the door, Phyllis arrived to take me to the airport, and there was still much to be done. Now my biggest concern was how my cockatiel, Magic, and Foxy, my cat, were going to get through the trip cross-country. Foxy was twenty-years-old and near death. Her brother, Blackie, had died in my arms in the middle of the night only a few months before. I had never shared my bed with anyone for so long as with Foxy and Blackie. When I took Foxy to the vet two days before making the trip, he told me that no one would blame me for putting her down. Was I being cruel taking her in her condition? But I'd looked into her eyes and could see she wasn't quite ready to go.

After taking the stuff I couldn't fit in storage to the garbage area, we packed the car and took off, with thirty minutes left to make the forty-five minute trip to the airport.

"Phyllis, we're never going to make it in time," I howled.

"Didn't I tell you I was once a racecar driver?" Phyllis asked, as she sped down the freeway, expertly weaving in and out of traffic. "Sit back, we'll get there in time."

She was right, we did get there just when the plane was about to depart, but how would we get Magic and Foxy on board? Fortunately, the fog had rolled in thick and the flight had been delayed just long enough for us all to make the flight.

Chapter Fourteen

Kip and DeAnna met me at the airport. It was August 1999. We'd been waiting a long time for Foxy and Magic to be taken from the hold of the plane, when the first animal was brought out - a huge black dog, whose bark was so loud I was certain we'd find Foxy dead in her carrier from fright. We heard Magic's whistle before we spotted the attendant carrying his cage. Everyone in the baggage claim area turned to see where the tune was coming from. Foxy's carrier was right behind. When I peaked in, I was relieved to see she was fine.

Barbara lived in a huge artist loft space in a building that had formerly been a warehouse. And the amenities were pretty crude. Kip and DeAnna cast a worried look over their shoulders as they left me behind. But I was excited, at fifty-three primed for new experiences.

The next day, we all met at the photographer, Niki Berg's home on the Upper West Side, where Maryann would be doing the interview for *Sacred Connections*. The brownstone had been the residence at the turn of the century for the pope, whenever he visited New York, and was beautiful. When Niki and her husband, Peter, first moved there, the neighborhood was so dangerous that

Niki had to carry a stick with her when she walked her kids down the block to get the school bus. Now the area was posh.

Jack's two sets of brothers had not seen each other for fourteen years, not since we all first met. Now they were young men. Jack had told me once that he felt somewhat in limbo between his two sets of brothers after the reunion, not feeling he truly belonged to either family. Jack had always asked Rosemary if he could have a brother or sister, but it wasn't until he was ten, when Mark came along and then David a little over a year later, that his wish was fulfilled. The pregnancies were a huge surprise to Rosemary, having never believed she could become pregnant. Not being related by blood to his two brothers was never a concern for Jack. Mark and David were his brothers. But learning he had two brothers related by blood, that he hadn't grown up with, had changed his perspective somewhat. He felt loss at not being a biological child in his adoptive family and loss at not having been raised by the family he was related to by blood.

There wasn't much time for the interview, as Jack and everyone had to get back, so Maryann asked that they get started right away. Niki took them out to the garden for the photo session. The guys were happy and relaxed, quite comfortable with each other, as they pulled their chairs into a circle.

Anna had brought the kids and DeAnna had come with Kip, so we decided to walk up the block to Central Park and get out of their way, not wanting the guys to feel intimidated about being honest during the interview with our presence there. I was a little distracted, wondering what they would say. But I would find out soon enough, when I transcribed Maryann's tape and shaped the story. I hoped I could handle it.

When we got back an hour later, the interview was over and the guys were laughing, so all must have gone well.

As we rushed to leave, Maryann handed me the tape. "It was a good interview," she said. "Just too bad we didn't have more time."

Jack and his gang headed back to Queens, and Brett and I went with Kip and DeAnna to their apartment in Hartsdale, where DeAnna was studying to become a physical therapist. Brett was staying with them, as were Foxy and Magic, until I found my own place.

That evening as we sat around the floor, Foxy on Brett's lap, I knew why I couldn't put her down before leaving. She seemed to want to be with Brett, Kip and me one more time, all of us together.

Before listening to the tape, I had to finish the first story Maryann had given me to work on, the test of whether or not we could work together. I'd actually thought our deal had already been sealed before I left California, but it made sense that she needed concrete proof. I had such a good feeling about the project and tried not to let myself worry.

I found myself wishing I had not deliberately sabotaged the typing class my boss at the advertising company had sent me to when I first began working there. Besides the fact that I didn't enjoy typing, my gut told me that if I became a proficient typist I would be doomed to a career as a secretary, so I only did well enough to not let him think he'd wasted his investment. Typing for Will was torture because he wouldn't allow us to use white out. Even the tiniest mistake meant the whole document would have to be retyped. Sometimes I worked late into the night, trying to type a perfect letter with three carbon copies. One day, Will called me into his office and declared the only thing he could do with me was make me a copywriter, since my typing was too bad to be a secretary, I had no aptitude for details that a producer needs, and no artistic skills. My instincts had served me well.

But now transcribing Maryann's tapes was laborious. However, my work as a journalist came back to me, as I shaped the story of Susan Cox, a Korean adoptee, who was adopted from an orphanage at age four by an American couple from Oregon. Susan had memories of her mother and of having her hair dyed black at the orphanage to make her appear pure Korean, and thus more desirable. Her birth father had been an American soldier. For me, the most touching part of the story was when she met her two brothers, who took her to see her mother's grave and, while enacting the traditional Korean gravesite ritual, tried hard to teach her how to correctly pronounce her mother's name. Susan was never sure whether she finally got it right, or if they gave up on her.

The sadness at the gravesite was burned into my heart, and I couldn't work on the story any more that day. So, I went up to the roof of Barbara's building to sit in the warm summer evening and look out at the stunning view of Manhattan across the East River. As I watched the lights of the city slowly come on, I recalled Steve's advice to me as he encouraged my move, despite all apparent obstacles.

"When I first came to New York and was looking for a place to live," he'd said, "I would gaze at the millions of lights in the city and tell myself there's one light there waiting for me. And there was."

I decided there was one light for me, too, and vowed to begin looking the next day.

The next morning, I woke up eager to get started but wondering where in the world to begin. Rental agencies required first and last, security deposit and a broker's fee, which was impossible to come up with. I'd had a strong urge to stop by the Open Center, a metaphysical bookstore on Prince Street in SoHo, so I decided to finally go into the city and check it out. Maybe they had a bulletin board there.

I was finding the city reminiscent of the late sixties, an exciting place again, so alive after years of deterioration. SoHo was especially fun, and I had wondered why I never ventured downtown when I lived here before, until I remembered how dangerous it had been back then.

After browsing through the books at the Open Center and finding nothing drawing me to read, I asked if they had a bulletin board. Yes, over in the corner. Only a few notices were posted and only one for a sublet, which was in Manhattan, a studio and almost affordable. The person's name was Susan and the number to call had a Philadelphia area code. Well, I was born in Philadelphia and the publisher for *Sacred Connections* was located there – maybe this was a sign.

I raced back to Barbara's, still unsure of the subway connection I had to make and more uncertain as I listened to the train operator's unintelligible announcements. But I found my way, and dialed the number as soon as I walked in the door.

A young woman answered. I explained how I got her number and told her I just moved to the city and had a job working on a book by a publisher in Philadelphia, trying to convince myself as well as her that I could afford the rent.

"I only know one editor in Philadelphia," she said, and she told me his name.

"Oh, my God, that's my editor!"

"Oh, wow, I sat next to Jason for two years when I worked in New York."

We were both speechless at the coincidence.

"I just moved here from California," I told her.

"Wow, I'm from California. Where?"

As it turned out, Susan had grown up in Mill Valley, a town where I had lived in Marin County. Now, we were both speechless. How could two strangers have so many coincidences? We made an appointment the next day to meet at the studio.

The apartment building was on 16th Street and Seventh Avenue, cattycorner from Loehmann's, my favorite place to shop. How cool. I took the elevator up to the fifteenth floor and pushed the buzzer. Susan let me in. She was an attractive woman in her early thirties, with an air still of California but now very much a New Yorker, too.

The large square-shaped studio apartment was full of light and had a nice view. She would be leaving the couch and the Murphy bed. Murphy bed! I'd only seen those in the movies. The building didn't allow sublets, Susan explained, so we had to be discreet. I could do that. My problem, I told her, was coming up with the deposit. Did she mind if I paid that in installments? She was understanding but said one other person was coming to see the place, and she'd let me know later on in the day. I doubted I had a chance, given my request.

I went back to Barbara's to await Susan's call. Those were the days without cell phones. Early evening the phone finally rang.

"Despite the lack of deposit, I've decided you should be the one to have the place," Susan said. "You called first, and how can I ignore all the coincidences?"

She was a true California girl! I couldn't believe my good fortune. I figured New York must have wanted me there to get the first place I looked at in a city where affordable and decent apartments were nearly impossible to find. I could move in October first.

Kip and DeAnna were relieved. Their apartment didn't allow pets. The next Sunday, I took the train to Hartsdale to visit them.

When Kip opened the door, he said Foxy had stopped eating and drinking that morning. She was lying on a towel on the couch and there was nothing left of her.

DeAnna was away studying. I picked Foxy up and cradled her in my arms, while Kip and I sat on the floor watching football games. We knew she had little time left, and then she began to breathe hard the same way her brother, Blackie, had the night he died. Three huge breaths and she was gone. We wrapped her in a blanket and put her in the pet carrier. I had an overwhelming feeling that we meant as much to Foxy as she had meant to us. I was so glad Kip was there with me.

Just down the street was the Hartsdale Pet Cemetery, "America's First and Most Prestigious Pet Burial Grounds" founded in 1896, the sign bragged. We always joked when passing it about how a pet cemetery could call itself "prestigious." Kip and DeAnna had already had their iguana cremated there, the ashes scattered in the cemetery garden, which is what we planned for Foxy.

The next morning, with Kip at work and DeAnna at school, I walked with Foxy's body over to the pet cemetery. The sun was shining brightly, as I followed the sidewalk and passed through the ornate gates. My heart was heavy, but I also couldn't help being amused at the whole situation. Inside the gates were rows of old, weatherworn tombstones with barely readable carvings describing beloved pets.

I found the office and made arrangements.

"Would you like me to show you the garden where Foxy's ashes will be scattered?" the kind older woman asked.

"No thanks." I had an idea where the spot was already, and my heart was getting too heavy to handle any more.

I caught the next train back to Manhattan. I'd be moving in a few days.

When the buzzer to the new apartment sounded, I had to find my glasses to see which button to push to let Barbara in downstairs. After only one day there, I was still getting my bearings in the new place. The night before had been my own private comedy routine, as I tried to figure out how to set up the Murphy bed, and then how to sleep in something so uncomfortable. The pre-war building had not had hot water for four days - something I learned was a periodic problem. Still, I was so happy.

Before going out to dinner, Barbara and I sat by the window, having a glass of wine and looking out at the view of the Hudson River in the distance. Just as the sun went down, fireworks began going off down by the river and a certainty came over me that it had been the right decision to move away from San Francisco and risk a new life in New York City.

The building elevator was packed when we got in on our way to dinner. Someone mentioned the lack of hot water and I wisecracked that it was like living in a third world country.

"You have no idea what it's like to live in a third world country," a man's voice calmly responded. I turned to see who had put me in my place, suddenly horribly ashamed at myself for sounding like a spoiled chick from California.

"You're right, I'm sorry. That was a stupid thing to say," I apologized. Something about the man's soulful eyes struck me as familiar, but I couldn't think why.

The next day, while I was setting up my writing space in the oversized closet, the door buzzer went off. There stood the man who had chastised me in the elevator the night before. Now, in the light of day, I could see he was quite handsome.

"I apologize for speaking up in the elevator last night," he said, in an accent that I couldn't quite place.

"No," I reassured him, "I deserved it."

"Can I show you a few of my photographs?" he asked.

"Come in! I'd love to see your work." How could I worry about letting a stranger in, even if this was New York City, who was obviously much more sensitive than me?

255

He introduced himself as Arturo, the name he'd gone by since emigrating from Moscow in 1991, because people found it easier to say than his given name, Artur. The black and white images he showed me were beautiful, but one really struck me with its originality and I thought to myself then I should pay attention to this man.

"Can I call you Art?" I asked. Calling a Russian "Arturo" seemed incongruous.

"Of course, Art is the name my family calls me by," he said.

As it turned out, Art was living across the hall and two doors down from me. Before leaving, he asked if I would like to go with him to the Cloisters on Saturday. That would be great.

After he left, I went back to organizing my writing space, but a nagging tug from my unconscious kept me distracted. Why did Art seem so familiar?

That night, before tackling the Murphy bed again, I sat by the window, gazing out over the Hudson River, and it came to me. Before moving to New York, I'd had a vivid dream about a man whose face was very distinctive. In the dream, I was walking alone on a desolate dirt path, when two men on horseback appeared. One took the fork away from me, but the other rode his horse up to me and stopped. Both the man's eyes and the horse's looked straight into mine for the longest time, and then I woke up. The man in the dream was Art.

I was aware that I came to New York with relationship issues I had yet to work through. Though I had dated some really wonderful men, I'd been afraid of becoming too close, of having a real relationship. After Ron and I divorced, I'd told myself that I wanted to search for my son while on my own, so that nothing interfered with the process. Then, when I began writing the book, I didn't want to be distracted by becoming too involved with someone. Those excuses served me for a while, but now were irrelevant and had been for some time.

Intellectually I was well aware of how the loss of Jack, loss of Ray and loss of myself, how grief, shame and rejection caused me to avoid deep connections for fear of reliving the horrible feelings of being abandoned all over again. But understanding intellectually did nothing to heal the wound. As if I had an internal monitor, I found myself pulling away, creating distance, as soon as I reached a certain threshold where trust would be essential. I simply couldn't trust anyone, let alone myself.

Nancy Ann's husband, Bruce, used to tease me that the guys coming to the shop would have to dump a bucket of water over my head for me to realize they were interested. What? I'd never been that way, but his joking made me look back and pay attention to how different I'd been before and after entering the home for unwed mothers. Before Bruce's comment, I'd had my excuses, but now I could see how I also still carried some level of shame that kept me from intimacy. Why would anyone be interested in me? We were told we were "damaged goods," after all. Sometimes issues take years and years to surface. But I was to find that with Art I'd met my match, and no longer would be able to avoid my fears.

We took the subway up to the northern edge of Manhattan. When we got out at our stop, a Chinese man was playing a haunting melody on a guqin, the ancient instrument of sages said to enrich the heart and elevate the human spirit. I was transported.

The medieval gardens and architecture of the Cloisters was further transporting, as if we'd stepped into another time. Despite the chill fall day, we spent hours in the gardens talking. We both found what we'd been missing – someone who understood us at our depths. Art was a twin, but tragically his brother died in infancy. So when I told him my story, he knew exactly what I meant when I described the emptiness before finding Jack. In addition, his twin son and daughter lived in Moscow. He wasn't able to see them as much as he would like, and he missed much of their growing up years. But he really stole my heart when he told me about having married a friend of his when he was young, whose boyfriend ditched her after finding out she was pregnant, just so that she could keep her baby.

When we checked the time, we realized that if we didn't hurry we wouldn't get to see the museum and bookstore. On the way, I told him about my trip to Italy and how I'd fallen in love with Sienna, so we were both astonished when we randomly picked a thick book about European cathedrals and the first page we turned to was about the cathedral in Sienna. Never would we have guessed that was a sign of the future photographic work we would be doing together.

That week, I heard from Maryann. She loved my work on the story of the Korean adoptee. She would be sending the tapes from interviews she'd already done for me to work on. Meanwhile, I could get started on Jack's story. But I hadn't screwed up enough courage to hear what the guys had to say, and decided instead to explore the neighborhood.

I wanted to stop by and see Laura to tell her of my move. Soho's office was nearby on Broadway near Union Square. The doorman pointed me in the right direction and off I went. It was a sunny day and I was having fun walking "side by side" with the young, naïve woman I'd been when I'd first come to New York. I found myself crossing Fifth Avenue, puzzled at how I could have walked right by Broadway and not notice. So, I retraced my steps, crossed Fifth again and walked down 13th Street, hoping to find Broadway. Since I'd never ventured far past 42nd Street in my early days, I didn't know that the two streets crisscrossed at some point further up town.

Halfway down 13th Street, I saw an adorable little theater, like from another era. At first I hesitated, but then decided to be brave and go in. Two women, one older and one my age were sitting together in the lobby. I introduced myself, told them about *The Other Mother*, both the book and the movie, and that I'd written a play. Would they be interested in reading it?

"Sure, bring it by," Sandra, the managing director replied.

I floated on air the whole way home, never finding Broadway. In fact, I began to feel like a puppet on a string the way so many things were happening for me so fast. Little did I know what a huge seed had just been planted.

A few days later, I stopped by the theater to see if Sandra had the chance to read the play. She had. They wanted to give it a full staged reading. Oh, my. They would let me know when they found a director, which would be soon.

I'd been circling around the tape from Maryann's session with Jack and his brothers too long, finding everything else to do, but couldn't put off listening any longer. I wanted to know their truth but was afraid of it at the same time. With so many possible variables, such as birth order, the unique personality of each sibling and their complicated family relationships both with the adoptive family and family of birth, sibling reunions can be complex. What was the aftermath for Jack's brothers?

As a writer, I thought "Great line!" when I heard Brett say on the tape how strange it was to think his mother was like the people on talk shows, who discussed having children at a young age. But as a mother his comparison was difficult to take in. When Brett, Kip and I drove down to meet Jack for the first time, Brett was thirteen, Kip nine and Mark and David were nine and eight respectively. The contrast was huge between the experiences of Jack's two sets of brothers. Where Brett and Kip were excited about the prospect of gaining another brother, Mark and David were terribly fearful of losing to strangers the brother they'd known all their lives. "Was she going to take Jack away, and we'll never see him again?" I listened to Mark recall.

When Rosemary first told me about their fears, I'd had a difficult time understanding why they might feel so insecure, and wondered if Rosemary's own trepidation might have been mixed in with theirs. But no, that hadn't been the case at all. In fact, though David had always known Jack was adopted, Mark had been shocked to learn Jack wasn't his "real" brother.

"That's pretty heavy," Jack said, learning of Mark's experience for the first time during the interview.

"Where the rest of the family was nonchalant," Mark continued, "finding out about Jack's adoption was a big deal to me. I felt the relationship was now "tainted."

Had I harmed Mark? What a terrible thought. Why hadn't I realized the potential problems I could create by coming into their lives? Of course I had thought through all ramifications beforehand, but I'd concluded the reunion would only be beneficial to everyone. I didn't think I was blinded by my own needs, or had I been? As a product of the sixties, I still believed in the line of a Beatles' song, "Love is all there is."

However, Brett and Kip were much more practical than me at the time, I realized, listening to the tape. Brett revealed he had worried about Jack's mom. Kip had wondered if we had the right to barge in on Jack's adoptive family, misgivings they'd kept to themselves.

"So, you thought about everyone's feelings, too?" Jack asked them. "I tried to protect everyone for too long by not letting anyone know how I felt," he went on to explain. "Now I figure everyone has to deal with how it is for them, but it took until I was thirty to come to that understanding."

I listened to Jack say how Rosemary was curious about meeting us, but that she thought that would be the end of it.

"I was talking to Mom recently," Mark said. "She said the exact same thing. She'd expected to meet just once. When Carol said, 'I want to have a relationship', my Mom said, 'What?'"

260

At the time, I'd suspected she felt that way, which was my worst fear, but hearing spoken out loud how close I'd come to never seeing Jack again pierced me like a knife, and that she might still wish it had gone that way made me sad. Jack's next words pulled the knife back out. "But, once you open that door, you might as well try to work together."

"If Mom had it her way," Kip said, "Jack would be there for Christmas and all the holidays." He was right. For himself, Kip wished he didn't have the added pressure of thinking about the adoptive family. "I wanted to get close to Jack and be his brother. There was a natural bond, but I was tentative because I knew it wasn't necessarily our place." Kip reflected that there was no perfect solution, and that he knew there was some feeling for us on Jack's part but also hesitation, so he put the brakes on.

At the end of their interview, they all agreed that they would get along well, if they had the opportunity to hang out together, and Jack affirmed his relationship with each of them would be life-long.

As I sat down to write the story, I was forced to confront my reluctance to reveal the hard truths of what Jack and his brothers had had to deal with. Why did I have an impulse to sugarcoat the truth? I stared at my computer as if it were a crystal ball, waiting for an answer. But my mind remained blank, a reliable sign that I was hiding something from myself. I got up from my desk, fed Magic and let him out of his cage. Then it came to me.

When I had walked down the church aisle, maid of honor at my cousin Joanie's wedding, four and a half months pregnant and wearing the three girdles my mother had insisted on, I had felt such shame at defiling her ceremony with the sin of my unwed pregnancy. But, halfway down the aisle, I stared up at the golden light streaming through the stained glass window above the altar and suddenly knew in the deepest part of myself that God was not judging me, that I was blessed to be carrying a child. Only days before I had felt the quickening.

But then there were still all those people filling the church, who would be horrified if they knew and were the reason why I would soon be entering a unwed mothers home. Their opinion, not God's, would prevail.

One of the most important lessons I had learned from writing *The Other Mother* was how essential it is to be authentic. Despite my fears of losing everyone I loved by telling my truth in the book, I told it anyway, and in the process of allowing myself to be so vulnerable became more real to myself and the opposite from what I expected happened. All my relationships were enriched and closer now that I no longer needed to keep a major part of myself closeted away. But the real surprise was the deeper connection not only with those I loved but also with strangers who read the book and trusted they could be as real themselves – many for the first time ever. The closer I came to my own truth the closer others came to theirs.

The image of myself walking down the aisle at Joanie's wedding was like fire in my brain. Whether God had actually let me know His feelings or I had simply caught a glimpse of my own, I didn't know then to value what was revealed and trust that drawing strength from such an inner knowing would open the way to a different outcome from where I was heading. As a result, my firstborn was thrown into a life full of losses and Brett and Kip and Mark and David had to deal with pain and confusion. The truth of it all was too hard to take in, but the least I could do was tell their raw unvarnished truth. I sat back down at my desk, now able to tell their story.

"Readings are for the benefit of the playwright," Sandra explained as we waited for the director to arrive in the theater's lobby, furnished with an odd assortment of sofas, chairs and tables, nearly all found on the street. The mish-mash of styles and colors worked, creating a unique welcoming charm. Because the play wove past and present and the staging was complicated, Sandra said she and Edith wanted to have a staged reading, meaning the actors would be reading from the script while moving around on stage, as opposed to a straight reading while seated.

When the director arrived, she was all business right away. She had notes all over the script, and we went through each one. Much rewriting needed to be done. I became worried as we talked that the director didn't really have a strong feeling for the play, which surprised me since she was from the era when much of the play took place. Even if spared becoming an unwed mother, my generation's sexuality had been controlled by the implicit punishment for an unwed pregnancy. Not once did she mention knowing a girl who was sent away or having much sympathy for the play's premise. Her interest was in making it work. I went home with a lot of work to do and a slight sense of unease.

But, over the next few weeks, I came to appreciate the director's concerns, although I stood my ground on some of her suggestions. I knew from my work with Laura that being edited was a struggle, but essential. No way can a writer be completely objective about his or her own work. When my friend, Lynn, had seen the shadows cast by the venetian blinds as prison bars, I'd learned how much more a reader can bring to my writing with interpretations I had never thought of. Then to have actors interpret not only my story but also me in the film version of *The Other Mother* - if I ever had any control issues they were obliterated.

But I was unprepared for the fascinating experience of hearing lines I'd written with one idea in mind being read in a different and often more powerful and profound way by each actor who auditioned for the play. Writing and reading are such solitary acts and, even when a book is published, there's no way to really get into a readers head for their impressions. For my writing to suddenly come alive in so many variations through the actors was a revelation. How could I have ever known that my thwarted acting career would reemerge in such a rich and complex manner?

I'd invited everyone I knew, especially those from the adoption community, and the seventy-seat theater was packed for the staged reading. As I anticipated the audience reaction, I found I was detached in a way that I couldn't be with *The Other Mother*, since *The Sacred Virgin* was so opposite from my own story. The heroine, a birth mother, didn't want to be found. Even so, I was heavily invested in hoping the play rang true and opened eyes.

By the time the audience took their seats my nerves were shot, and for a little while I forgot that I was supposed to be paying attention. Even though the reading was awkward to follow, as the actors worked from scripts and it was hard to visualize the real action, the audience hung in there and afterward offered great suggestions and much encouragement.

Both Edith and Sandra were pleased with the response and told me afterward that they wanted the play to have one or two more readings before they put on a production.

No way then would I have imagined or been prepared for the intense emotional reaction the actual production would evoke not just for those whose lives were impacted by adoption but also for so many others, who had no connection to adoption.

Chapter Fifteen

Be careful what you ask for, as the saying goes. Since arriving in New York my creative opportunities had exploded, to the point where I could barely manage all I was doing. But I wasn't complaining.

The stories I was helping Maryann write were greatly expanding my compassion for the struggles and the complexity of relationships all sides of the triad dealt with. Granted the subjects were hand-selected for their courage to face and explore their daunting issues and their stories were intended to inspire others to face their fears and forge lifelong relationships, but the diversity of stories were adding up to a far more complex portrait than even I, with all the stories I'd heard over the years, could imagine.

One day, I called Maryann with a story idea I felt was missing and was perfect for describing the intimate connection we all have as we weave our birth and adoptive families. Sherwood Cummins, an old friend of mine, and his wife, Jan, had adopted a little girl from an orphanage in Romania, after being horrified at the plight of the 13,000 children left housed in orphanages after the end of Ceausescu's regime. For me though, as fascinating as their process had been, that wasn't the story.

A year after they brought Katarina, now two and a half, to their home, she began telling Sherwood and Jan that she wanted her baby sister. Did she want a baby sister or did she actually have a baby sister, they wondered? Sherwood's intuition told him to follow up with the orphanage to see if Katarina actually had a real baby sister. As it turned out, five months after Katarina left the orphanage, her mother had indeed given birth to a baby girl and placed her in the same orphanage, as the family of nine were simply too poor to feed another. Somehow Katarina knew. Now that was my kind of story!

Katarina traveled with Jan and Sherwood to meet her baby sister, Gabriella, as soon as the second adoption was finalized. While they were in Romania, Sherwood and Jan tried to find a way to directly contact the girls' original family, but found it impossible. Sherwood's dream was that, when the girls married, their two fathers would walk them down the aisle.

A few years later, they were able to connect and brought the girls back to Romania to see their other family, what Sherwood and Jan said was a remarkable experience. When they arrived at the village where the family lived, they discovered all the people there had adopted *them*.

"Would you mind flying to California to do the interview yourself?" Maryann asked. She was swamped with work.

Would I mind? It would be the first time I'd had a chance to go back to Marin after leaving six months before.

Before I left, I dropped by the theater to tell Edith and Sandra I would be gone for five days. When I told Edith I would also be seeing Tennessee William's biographer, Lyle Leverich, who'd become a friend, she told me a story that made my world shrink in an instant.

I had met Lyle through Paul, an adoptee friend I'd made after he called me at four in the morning, not being able to wait any longer after finishing *The Other Mother*. A huge fan of Tennessee Williams, Paul had befriended Lyle, in his words "like a heat-seeking missile." I was a huge fan, too, so Paul arranged for me to meet Lyle.

Lyle, in his mid-seventies at the time, was the loveliest of gentlemen. When he told me the story of meeting Tennessee while producing *The Two-Character Play*, also known as *Outcry*, at a small theater in San Francisco, I was astonished and pleased at the coincidence. The monologue I'd selected, but became too frozen to read in the one acting class I had taken, was from *The Two-Character Play*. That failure was the inspiration for the opening scene in *The Sacred Virgin*.

Lyle had become important to Lee as well. After Paul, Lyle and I had attended Lee's play, *Kindertransport*, at the Marin Theater Company, Lyle walked up to Lee, whose directing he greatly admired, congratulated him and then asked Lee if he would like to do "the unproduced play of a young unknown playwright." I could sense Lee's polite hesitation, which I imagine Lyle expected, making Lyle's punch line even better – "Thomas Lanier Williams!" *Spring Storm*, the play Lyle was referring to, was written in college before the playwright was known as Tennessee.

"I'm heartbroken that I will miss Lee's production," I told Edith. The run was ending just before my arrival - such bad timing. Edith asked me to follow her into the theater.

"See this spot right here," she said, patting the edge of the stage. "Tennessee Williams sat right here." I immediately sat right down on the same spot. "He was actually here for a reading of *The Two-Character Play*," she said.

I was glad to be sitting, as I took in the awesomeness of such an unexpected and magical full circle. I must be on the right path was all I could think, as scary as it felt.

As the plane circled above San Francisco and I took in the breathtaking beauty of the city I loved so much, I wondered how I would feel being back. Which city was my true home now?

I was staying with Yvonne, who'd moved to a townhouse overlooking the San Francisco Bay and San Quentin Prison. As we sat having a glass of wine and watching the sunset, I felt nostalgic about no longer living amongst such beauty and about the great friends I'd left behind, as well, friendships that can't develop overnight. At the same time, I remembered Kathy's comment, when she and John moved down to Los Angeles, that friends can hold you back from changing, as they quite naturally keep you in their minds as the person they've always known in your shared history. I wondered if that were true, or if the person themself stays stuck from all the memories. All I knew was that one of the reasons for going to New York was to find out who else I was.

Niki and I met the next morning to go together for Jan and Sherwood's interview and for Niki to take photos. The sun was shining and the sky a beautiful blue.

The first time I met Sherwood, I was surprised to discover I still harbored anxiety around men of the cloth, whom I'd grown up being told were all powerful. Marybeth had set up a doubles game at the tennis club, and I was running late. When I arrived, they were already warming up, and I took my place next to Marybeth who was to be my doubles partner. She introduced Sherwood from across the net as the minister of the local Presbyterian Church. Suddenly, before this handsome man of God I felt exposed. Dormant guilt I was oblivious to, from my violation of the church's teachings, flew up in my face. I felt like a spotlight shown down on me that only Sherwood could see. I was bewildered and exceedingly uncomfortable at my unexpected reaction and kept hitting the ball into the net.

Meanwhile, from the other side of the net, Sherwood was teasing me, pretending to look up my tennis skirt each time I tucked a ball underneath. My discomfort disappeared with his kidding. As Sherwood and I got to know each other and our friendship grew, I told him of my initial certainty that he, as a minister of God, could tell I was a "wanton hussy." At least I could now joke about my bizarre reaction. We had a good laugh over it.

Sherwood and Jan greeted us warmly, and their interview was open and honest. They didn't try to portray a fairytale about the girls' first meeting and their adjustment. For eight months before they were able to pick up her baby sister, Katarina was in a state of high expectation, promising to share Gabriella with Jan and wondering if her other mother would be at the orphanage, too. But their initial meeting was a disaster. When Katarina bolted out of the car and ran to her sister, throwing her arms around her, Gabriella reacted with fright and began screaming. Katarina sat down on the orphanage steps, head in her hands, and sobbed. But soon they were playing and exploring the orphanage together. When they returned home, though, Katarina was extremely possessive of Gabriella, which created difficulties when children tried to make friends with her baby sister. At the time of the interview, they'd been together for five months, and the initial problems were fading away.

The remainder of the trip was spent catching up with friends. The day before the flight back to New York, I visited Lyle in the hospital. He wasn't doing well at all, and three days after I returned to the city Paul called to tell me the sad news that Lyle had passed away.

"Mom, DeAnna and I are going down to the Outer Banks for Christmas at her parents' house. What do you think about asking Jack and Anna if we could spend Christmas Eve with them?" Kip asked.

269

This would be the first Christmas we'd spend together, since we met fourteen years before. I was over the moon at the prospect.

When I called Anna to ask if our coming would be all right, she was excited but said there was one complication. Ray and Jean had already been invited, and she doubted they would want to come if I were going to be there, too.

"I'll just tell them that you are the priority, since we've never spent Christmas together, and, if they want to come, they just have to get over whatever is bothering them."

I was so grateful to her for sticking up for me.

It was dark by the time we pulled into their driveway. The house was festive with Christmas lights, and Jack greeted us at the door. I had assumed, since I hadn't heard otherwise, that Ray and Jean had decided to stay home, so I was a bit unprepared to see them when we walked in.

They were nervous, as they stood up to greet us, and introduced their son by her first marriage, Jimmy, and his wife. This was the first time Jean and I met, and I liked her right away. All problems melted away with the first introductions. Instead of being seen as a threat, I could tell I became a normal, life-size person in Jean's eyes right away. She'd had so much to deal with. Not only was I the mother of her husband's son but I had also intruded on their lives with the book and the movie. We all quickly became absorbed in the kids' excitement about Christmas and relaxed, as if we'd known each other forever.

At one point in the evening, Ray was sitting by the tree with Asia on his lap, as happy as anyone could be. Jack caught my eye and pointed to the little red stocking ornament from Seton House hanging in the center of the tree right above Ray's head. "Did you notice?" he asked with a big smile.

Ray looked up at me and our eyes met for a moment and deeply conveyed all the evening meant to both of us. Both Jack

270

and Kip had noticed and looked over at me un. everything. I was so grateful that in that moment Jack wa. see his original parents had really cared for each other an Kip could see his mother's story in a different light. Much healed for me, too. Sometimes all we need is a moment.

Christmas morning we awoke to an inch of snow on the ground, the first time the kids had experienced a white Christmas. Such a fitting end to a magical journey for one little red felt Christmas stocking.

Publication date for *Sacred Connections* was set for February 27, 2001. Much work needed to be done before then, work I never wanted to end. I loved the stories and the challenge of crafting them. At the same time, I was revising the script for *The Sacred Virgin* in preparation for another staged reading.

I still took photographs, but my eye was changing. After a while, I realized the photographs I was drawn to make reflected my need to find solitude in the midst of the chaos of New York City. I missed my long hikes in nature that always replenished me, and couldn't find the same nourishment anywhere in the city. As beautiful as the parks were, I was always aware of the city, even when shaded by a huge oak or willow in Central Park, the buildings hidden from view, traffic sounds muffled. Even in my own apartment it was difficult to find real peace.

Once, while Art and I were walking in a rundown area of the city on our way from the Hudson River, I complained of missing the beauty of California.

"You just have to look for the beauty here," he said. "But you'll find it. It's just different."

So I tried to retrain my vision and retune myself, but it was a challenge.

One January night, as I walked home nearly frost bitten in below zero temperatures, with wind chills even greater blowing

gan sobbing and talking out loud to
ther slightly deranged person on New

o yourself deliberately! How could you have
What were you thinking?" And, on and on – all
ot caring whether or not anyone was watching. It
J.

ck away from home, I ran into Art coming from the opposite direction.

"Would you like a strawberry?" he asked, offering one from the clear plastic package.

Strawberries in the middle of a snowstorm? Under the street lamp, the bright red berries set against the white snow were the most beautiful things I'd seen in a long time.

Every chance I got, I'd walk through Central Park, but this particular evening I simply had to in order to stay calm, as I headed toward a meeting at the Spence Chapin Adoption Agency. Not since I'd sat side by side with my mother across the desk from Sister Dominic had I been inside an adoption agency. One minefield left.

Lynn Franklin, who'd invited me to the meeting, believed that our voices were important in changing the system, and I agreed wholeheartedly. I'd met Lynn, while still living in San Francisco, when she interviewed me for her memoir, *May the Circle Be Unbroken*. We also both agreed that diplomacy was the only way to make inroads, and angry voices, though justified, only put people on the defensive, unable to hear our truth. I had come to believe that minds could never be changed unless the heart is changed first.

But, as I stood in front of the beautiful townhouse that was the agency's offices, I froze. I was entering enemy territory. Of course I knew I wasn't, but at the same time memories of my helplessness before Sister Dominic flooded in.

Since coming to New York, I'd met mothers who had gone through Spence Chapin and I knew their painful stories. I knew of the two elevators: one for the mothers and a different one for the adoptive parents. How different was that from the separate water fountains and restrooms, one for "whites only" and one for "coloreds," that I witnessed after moving down to North Carolina in ninth grade? Hadn't I been forced to sit in the "back of the bus" since becoming an unwed mother?

Finally, I pushed open the door. A pleasant woman directed me to the meeting room. On the way, I tried to guess which elevator was which.

Everyone greeted me warmly and I was put somewhat at ease, as they tried to assure me that they were a modern agency that promoted open adoptions. I already knew that they were on our side fighting for open records, though, until the law passed they would not take it upon themselves to break the existing one by facilitating reunions. At one point, they proudly handed Lynn and me their new brochure, which did discuss their belief that open adoptions were much healthier for both mothers and the adoptive parents.

As I looked through the information, I noticed they referred to expectant mothers as birth mothers. "A woman isn't a birth mother until she signs papers," I pointed out. "She isn't even a mother, yet, while she's still pregnant. She's an expectant mother. Language is powerful and you all could be sending a vulnerable expectant mother down a path just using that word."

Lynn backed me up. The idea had never occurred to them, they said, and quickly promised to remove the word right away, which they did. Finally, I was glad to be there.

The remainder of the meeting dealt with plans for the upcoming Birth Mothers' Day Commemoration to coincide with

Mothers Day, which the agency was going to sponsor. In the past few years, such celebrations were springing up around the country. Finally, at least privately, we were acknowledging ourselves for who we were – mothers, whether or not anyone else agreed. However, out of the blue, one event became hugely public.

Two years before, in 1998, Mary Fay phoned to inform me that there was to be a healing Mass said at Our Lady of Victory Basilica in Buffalo, to acknowledge the loss and grief of unwed mothers, who, like her, were forced by the church and society to surrender their infants for adoption. Mary had been hidden away in the maternity home affiliated with the church. She said she had cried continuously for five years after losing her son, and then could cry no more. Instead she felt dead inside from then on.

"In the past, the church had offered healing Masses for mothers who had lost a child through abortion, miscarriage and stillbirth but had never considered one for us," Mary said.

When Mary approached the priests about the need for a Mass to acknowledge adoption losses, they readily agreed. "I hope some people will attend," she told me. "But most likely it will be only the four of us who are planning the event."

After hanging up the phone, the significance of the Church's acknowledgment of our grief, the first of its kind from any authority responsible for creating our loss, began to sink in. The acknowledgment felt almost like an apology. So, I got on the Internet and wrote an email about it with the heading "Historic Healing Mass," and sent the email to as many people as I could. I knew from my advertising days that the words "free" and "new" were great attention getters, but the word "historic"?

Mary phoned a few days later in shock. CNN and the major networks all wanted to cover the historic healing Mass. After talking it over, we concluded that, despite the need for greater public awareness of adoption issues, the media should be kept from the event. Mothers needed to feel safe and not suddenly exposed.

As it turned out, over six hundred people - mothers, adoptees and adoptive parents - attended the Mass. People had flown in from all around the country. Hundreds, who were unable to attend, sent roses and letters to be placed on the altar. Newspapers called the Mass pioneering, historic, needed. When we talked after, Mary said the Mass was an overwhelmingly emotional experience. At the end of the service, nearly everyone there walked down the aisle in tears and placed a rose on a blanket on the altar.

"But there were a few women, wearing sunglasses and scarves to disguise themselves, who remained seated in the back pews," she said. "It must have taken so much for them to risk coming. I was glad we kept the media away for their sakes."

As I absorbed the significance of the healing Mass, I realized that any attempts at personal healing from our losses could only go so far, and that public acknowledgment of the role society and the churches played was essential. Without their banishment of us as sinners for being unwed mothers, there would be no need to heal in the first place. And, without public acknowledgment of the wrongs we endured, many would still feel we deserved to be treated with disdain. Acknowledging our pain and suffering and our role as legitimate mothers could only serve to open hearts and minds to our need and right to be a part of our children's lives.

Walking home from the meeting at Spence Chapin along Fifth Avenue on my way to the subway, the bare branches of the great trees lining Central Park hanging over me like dark, menacing shadows, I let myself feel the full weight of our collective grief and wondered if it would be possible for us all to ever become whole again.

Work on *Sacred Connections* completed and with the publisher, I had to scramble to find another source of income right away. I'd begun supplementing my income doing headshots for actors and working for an events planner whenever they needed flowers for big events, but the work was sporadic.

One day, while walking through Chelsea Markets, I checked out their bulletin board and saw a posting: "Writers wanted for spiritual biography series."

When I got home, I called the number right away. The editor of the series, Barbara Ellis of Scribes Editorial and Literary Agency, answered. She explained the idea behind the series was to match the author's story with the subject's. We made an appointment to meet, and I was to consider whom I wanted to write about.

Mary Queen of Scots was the only person to come to mind, as I'd always felt a mysterious connection to her.

One early spring evening in 1977, during a brief vacation alone to London, I visited Westminster Abbey. Only a handful of tourists were there, and it felt like I had the great cathedral all to myself, as I allowed myself to wander randomly wherever I felt drawn. When I unexpectedly came upon the queen of Scots majestic tomb, a strange feeling came over me, and I felt my footsteps had been guided. When I touched her tomb, startling tears came to my eyes. Were the tears from deep within me, or were they hers? It was as if Mary Queen of Scots had reached through time and touched me at my core.

Years later, my father had researched our roots to help Brett with a school project. We had suspected we were of Scotch/Irish descent, but had no idea that our roots reached through all of Scottish history, including shared ancestors with Mary, and we were also descended from others, including her enemies, who were an integral part of her life.

But, after reading about her life, I realized a blood connection wouldn't account for my sudden tears. Mary must have reached through time to me because we shared a similar grief. She, too, had not been able to raise her firstborn son.

The publisher agreed to my choice after much deliberation. Another author, with better credentials than me, had also selected Mary. Somehow I convinced them I was the better choice. The deadline for turning in the manuscript was six months away. My job was to capture her essence in a short book.

My first trip to the New York Public Library on 42nd Street proved how daunting such a task would be. Hundreds of books had already been written about her, the most famous by Lady Antonia Fraser. What could I write that would be different?

Every morning for months, I walked to the library and researched her life in the majestic Rose Main Reading Room, which I imagined looked very much like the splendid palaces Mary had lived in. As I delved into books written hundreds of years before, I discovered a woman way ahead of her times and completely misunderstood by the men who wrote about her. Much of her lore had been passed down from their limited and narrow perspective. Each morning, as I set out for the library, I felt her spirit with me.

Meanwhile, in March of 2001, *Sacred Connections* was published to wonderful reviews, including one from *People Magazine*. That month, too, the theater had its final reading of *The Sacred Virgin* and decided to give it a full production the first three months of 2002. None of us could have anticipated how cathartic the play would be, not only for those whose lives were impacted by adoption but for many New Yorkers as well, who were about to live through hell.

The morning of September 11, I had turned off the *Today Show* early when a friend called. We were so involved in our conversation that all the sirens outside only subliminally registered. St. Vincent's Hospital was two blocks away, so, though the number of sirens did seem excessive, I didn't think anything of it. As soon as I got off the phone, it rang again. It was Barbara.

"You don't know what just happened?" she asked.

I couldn't believe what she was saying and turned on my little black and white television. From then on, everything became surreal.

I ran across the hall to Art's friend's apartment and pounded on the door, waking him up. By then, Art had moved to an apartment in Jersey City and I was unable to get a hold of him. Michael thought I was joking when I told him one of the twin towers had been struck by a plane, but turned on his big screen television anyway to indulge me. Before our eyes the second tower was hit and the buildings were collapsing.

When I ran back to my apartment to check on Kip and DeAnna, the phone was ringing. DeAnna was coming over to my place right away. She'd seen the second tower collapse through the window of her physical therapy office. All I could think was thank God I moved to New York. To have to watch such horror and be three thousand miles away and unable to help them would have made me crazy.

A colleague of DeAnna's had walked her over, and we stood in the middle of my apartment unsure what to do next. DeAnna hadn't been able to reach Kip, so we decided to walk the seventy blocks up to their place on the Upper West Side, where they'd moved the year before. Already all traffic had been banned from the streets.

The scene on Seventh Avenue was eerie. Thousands of people were walking north in a daze, not knowing whether or not we were under attack. Stealth bombers were flying overhead in the now incongruously garish bright blue sky, providing some reassurance. I never thought I'd be relieved at the sight of a stealth bomber.

A clear message, a voice inside my head but not my own, kept repeating, "Don't give into the fear." The only other time that I had such an experience was when I returned home from the unwed mothers home. I was sitting in a cloud of pain in my bedroom, when somehow a message was given to me that I knew with certainty to be true. "You will never go through such a difficult experience again in your life."

At one point, we stopped to get ice cream in order to feel normal. "I might be pregnant," DeAnna said.

Now I felt an even greater responsibility to get her safely back to Kip.

DeAnna didn't want to walk through Times Square but I thought it might be the least dangerous route, given the police would have to be in full force there of all places in the city.

When we reached the center of Times Square, a television news reporter from somewhere in South America was standing on a traffic island, beckoning us to say a few words. "What do you think, should we go to war?" he asked.

We both agreed that war wasn't the answer to anything, especially since we didn't have a clue about what had happened. Then I found myself rambling on about how no city in our country had been decimated like this since Atlanta during the Civil War. All I could imagine was the scene in *Gone With the Wind*, where Scarlett O'Hara walked through the streets filled with injured soldiers lying from end to end on the ground.

"I can't believe I just said that," I told DeAnna, as we headed toward Central Park. It was strange to feel hyper alert and in a trance at the same time. The only way I could think to get back to myself was to walk among the beautiful old trees, the majestic guardians of the park and its people. As soon as we entered the park, I felt calmer. Somehow everything was going to be all right. I sought out the dirt path, instead of using the sidewalks, needing to feel the Earth under my feet. There in the park it was hard to imagine what had just happened.

By the time we got to their apartment, DeAnna had heard from Kip. He was making his way home. DeAnna suggested we take their dog Maddy, a little Boston Terrier, to the dog park to gain some sense of normalcy in the meantime.

When we arrived, only one other person was there, and we sat down on the bench next to her. From that day on, New Yorkers would no longer feel the need to be isolated from one another. The importance of feeling connected became indelible the instant the first plane had hit the first tower.

When I told the woman about being stopped by the television reporter and my analogy to *Gone With the Wind*, mostly as a joke but also to reassure myself that I hadn't been a complete idiot, she looked at me horrified.

"That's what we need right now," she said, "a blonde, blue-eyed WASP talking about the Civil War and the South." Now I felt even worse.

After meeting Kip at the apartment, we stayed glued to the television coverage for the rest of the day, still finding the magnitude of the horror incomprehensible, still uncertain what could happen next.

A few days later, John flew in from California, and we went down to the site. The early evening sky was a grim gray, as we inched our way through the crowd, past storefronts with merchandise covered in white dust. When we spotted the piece of structure still left standing, I was struck with how much it looked like the ruins of the Roman Coliseum. Another burnt metal piece looked like a twisted cross. When I stared up into the now exposed sky, it felt like a hole was blown through the ethers and the twin towers still stood there, filled with people going about their daily routines, as if they were too shocked to even know they were gone.

No one was allowed to linger. Besides it was impossible to take in the enormity of the tragedy or stay long in such a well of grief. So, John, who loved good food and fine restaurants almost more than anything, suggested we see if a couple of famous restaurants nearby, with a usual minimum six months wait for reservations, might be open. They were and they were practically empty.

To shake off the shocking images of the smoldering destruction, we drank a couple of martinis each at the first place and one more where we decided to have dinner. By the time we were back on the deserted streets, we had shaken off everything, including good sense. All phone booths in the city had been declared free of charge, even for long distance calls, and so John made a drunken call to Kathy and then I called a few friends pretending to sound normal, which I was far from. I just needed to connect with the outside world beyond the city to hold onto any sense of normalcy.

All along the walk home, burning candles flickered below pictures of missing loved ones – inside bus stops, on street corners, by phone booths. One wall of St Vincent's Hospital had become a shrine with hundreds of candles and photographs of faces from all nationalities. How was it possible to still hope a loved one would turn up? Still, I understood what the families were feeling from all the years that Jack had been missing from us.

The focus on the grieving process after 9/11 was naturally on the families of the victims, but I was to soon find that there was much stirred up in New Yorkers in general.

Chapter Sixteen

I had no illusions that *The Sacred Virgin* was getting a major production. The theater was an Off Off Broadway seventy-seat, non-profit repertory company that provided actors, writers and directors a safe opportunity to develop their talents. In order to offer the chance to act to as many in the company as possible, the play would have two alternating casts, which meant twice the number auditions and rehearsals – a lot for the new director to handle. I was present for all the auditions and rehearsals, not wanting to miss one minute, as the process was fascinating and I was learning so much. With writing such a solitary occupation, being part of a collaborative effort was exciting.

To be able to fulfill my unrealized dream of being involved with the theater in such a rewarding and unexpected way made me wonder if everything had turned out the way it was meant to, when, after returning from the home for unwed mothers I decided to let go of any aspirations for a life in the theater, believing I had used up my quota of rebellion. Or had it simply taken all this long time to finally reclaim myself and fulfill my creative potential? Probably the latter was truer. In some inexplicable way, my feelings about not being able to keep my firstborn were bound thereafter with an inability to believe in my creative work, and I hadn't found the key to untangling the two. Perhaps it was because I was told I would be the worst mother for my child that I believed anything else I created afterward would be judged the same way. Maybe the reasons really did run that deep.

But who would I have become had Ray and I married and kept our baby? Would I have poured all my energy into being president of the PTA, instead of exploring my creative talents? The sand in the oyster analogy seemed too costly a price for everyone involved to have to pay for my inner journey.

Beating the odds, where one out of five people in this country are somehow impacted by adoption, surprisingly only one cast member, an adoptee, out of fourteen (seven for each production) had any connection to adoption. Most members of the young cast had never heard of such a thing as unwed mothers homes and were appalled. Still, many of the women in the cast said times hadn't changed completely, that they still felt a great deal of pressure to hide an unplanned pregnancy.

In the play, the lead character, Bridget, has just received a letter out of the blue from the son she gave up for adoption nineteen years before. She doesn't want to open it. The pressure of taking the class and a Christmas tree and decorations left on the stage from a partly broken down production trigger a flood of memories, and she's back in the home for unwed mothers. The same actors that play the girls in the home also play the acting students in her class, to show just had much the times had changed. At one point in the class, Bridget tries to explain to one young disbelieving girl, with everything hanging out, how having a bra strap or slip show was once the greatest crime against the civilized world.

When Bridget finally decides to open the letter, she has one of the male students read it to her. Night after night during rehearsal the actors would break down during that scene. In the tenderly written letter, Bridget's son reveals why he was committing suicide. I had to give a voice to those adoptees, who had taken their own life, given that their rate of suicide attempts was four times greater than for the normal population.

I had asked Jack if I could use an image he'd created years before for a friend's baby shower for the poster, and he agreed. It was a simple line drawing of a faceless mother tenderly holding her faceless child.

As opening night approached, I grew increasingly nervous. Would anyone come? How would the play be received? What would it be like to actually be able to watch people react to something I'd written?

The show opened on January tenth, the day after Jack's birthday, to a packed house. Seats had to be added. Dad came with his wife, Lucy, all the way from South Carolina, and my cousin Joanie and brother, Bob, traveled to be there, too, as did Kip and DeAnna. Many in the audience were from the adoption community, but not everyone.

As the play progressed, there was hardly a dry eye in the house, which of course any writer would be thrilled about, except me. As much as I loved tragedies, I felt horrible that I was making everyone cry instead of laugh. When I confided my regrets to a writer friend after the show ended, she assured me that tragedy was an important part of theater, that people love to be able to cry and I should feel happy that I could make them feel deeply. But I wasn't consoled.

I attended every performance of the three-month run, because I usually knew someone who was coming, but also because every night was different and so the process deepened for me. Night after night, even for audiences that knew little about adoption, which was surprisingly the majority of audiences, people wept during the play. One night a woman had to leave to throw up in the bathroom. Something else was going on.

After a few nights of talking with audience members following the play, I understood. Living through the grief of 9/11, still so fresh in everyone's minds, had opened up people's psyches to their personal losses, and the play was all about loss and secrets to which no one is immune. So, the play was a cathartic experience for many. After 9/11, the focus for grieving had naturally been the families of the victims, but New Yorkers had also lost much in the aftermath. Yet their grief had not been recognized with any formal ritual. I felt it necessary to be there to listen to their stories, since I understood too well the effects of unresolved grief.

One night, a busload of people from Adoption Forum, an adoption group in Philadelphia, came to see the play. When their bus pulled up in front of the theater, I ran out to greet them. I'd come to know them and all their stories from speaking at two of their conferences. That evening's performance was the first time I got to experience an audience who understood everything, even the little jokes.

Midway through the run, Karen Vedder, then president of CUB (Concerned United Birthparents), flew in from California with a few friends to see the play. Karen had been forced to give up her second child, a daughter, after her divorce left her unable to afford to raise another. It's natural to wonder how a woman who already was a mother could ever give up a child, just like we found it impossible to understand how our mothers could have ever asked that of us. But, in reality, no one can possibly imagine the profound pain involved, until they have the experience themselves. Until then, what is in the best interests of the child, the mother and society can seem of greater importance. Karen's great grief over the loss of her daughter had propelled her to become one of the major activists for adoption reform.

Karen's first child, Eddie, the lead singer for Pearl Jam, was a good friend of the actor Tim Robbins, and had wanted Tim to meet his mother for a long time. Karen arranged for Tim to come to the play, and I was both thrilled, as he was one of my favorite actors, and nervous that someone with such achievements would be seeing my humble play. We didn't want to create a big scene that he'd have to deal with, so only a few people knew he'd be there. Still, word had spread.

The play was about to start, and Karen and I were still waiting in the lobby for Tim, afraid he wouldn't show up after all. But suddenly he appeared, his tall frame ducking down to accommodate the small entrance, a big apologetic grin on his face, and Karen showed him to his seat as the theater darkened and the play began. As always, I stood in the back, taking it all in, relieved it was a sold out performance.

When the play ended, my friends from California were the first out of the theater. "Tim Robbins had tears in his eyes!" they told me, excited. "We're going to have to see the play again, we were too busy watching Tim watch the play to take it all in."

Then Tim came out with Karen, who introduced us.

"Congratulations!" he said, shaking my hand and looking directly into my eyes. He was such a humble person for someone with such a powerful presence.

One word, "Congratulations," sent me over the moon.

My guess was that Tim was hoping to escape, but suddenly someone appeared with a candlelit cake and the crowd in the lobby began singing "Happy Birthday" to Edith, who turned eighty-five. He was trapped. But he was gracious about it, and I was happy to talk a little longer and introduce him to Kip and DeAnna.

As the last month of the run began, I noticed something had shifted for both casts; their performances were raised to a new level and the play flowed effortlessly. When I told them, they were surprised. They were no longer drawing on their own pain to fuel their performances and so felt ineffective, they said. Interesting that the opposite was true, that releasing their emotions created more powerful performances.

But for me, by the time the play's run was over, I was burned out. As much as I missed the cast and the whole experience, I was emotionally drained from carrying the load of pain I'd uprooted in so many of the audiences night after night.

Fortunately, I was spared a huge letdown, as *Mary Queen of Scots* was being published in April. Not that I expected much to come from the publication, as it was one in a series of books from a relatively unknown publishing house, but I was proud of the job I'd done. I had loved my time spent with Mary. It had felt like her presence was with me as I wrote, but then sadly was gone.

After two huge projects, I was creatively spent and unable to think of a new project for myself. Fortunately, I was able to edit two books on adoption back to back: *The Same Smile* by Susan Mella Souza and then *Finding Me in a Paper Bag* by Sally Howard. Susan's was a devastating story of losing two daughters, one to adoption and the other to leukemia. It wasn't the tragedy of her story that appealed but instead her immense courage that allowed her to immerge heart and spirit stronger. Sally was literally left on someone's front porch in a paper bag, and despite searching for most of her life never discovered the mystery of her origins. If that wasn't enough, she also surrendered a baby daughter for adoption after being raped.

Both women were great examples of not becoming a victim of one's life but instead triumphing over all adversity. It seemed to some degree or another all stories of adoption had the mythical quality of a hero's journey to them.

On the morning of November 5 that year, my brother, Bob, called with shocking news. My mother had been found dead in her apartment. The women in her apartment complex had made a compact to check each other's doorstep first thing each morning to make sure the newspaper had been picked up. That morning, my mother's newspaper was still on her doormat.

My mother had been in good health, except for a minor stroke from which she'd fully recovered. Six months before, Bob, Janice, Elena and I received a surprise in the mail – Mom's Last Will and Testament. But, she assured us then, she had no plans of leaving any time soon. I had not called her for a couple of weeks, not since returning from speaking at a CUB conference in San Diego. For us not to talk for so long was unusual, but for some reason each time I considered calling I couldn't dial her number. Finally, the night before I did call, but got no answer. Janice had spoken to her earlier. The landlord found her on the ground by the phone, which was off the hook, and I wondered if she'd been trying to answer my call. As much as I wished we'd talked one more time, I had no regrets. Thankfully, nothing felt unfinished between us.

As soon as I got off the phone with Bob, I called Paula. I'd come to trust her ability to see "the other side," and I wanted to know if she could tell me anything about my mother's passing.

"I'll bet her real mother, who died when my mother was five, was the one to meet her," I said, being biased in my expectations.

"No, I don't see that," Paula responded. "I see it was her father and she was thrilled to see him, despite being disoriented by the suddenness of her death."

"Wow, that makes perfect sense, she worshipped her father," I told Paula, who would never have known that fact.

"Wait," Paula said, "your mother's short!"

"Yes," I affirmed.

"But I thought she was tall; you're tall and the woman who played her in the movie was tall. I expected her to be tall, too."

As much as I always intellectually believed gifted psychics could "see" the spirits of souls that had passed, I was completely unnerved by Paula's vision of my mother. After hanging up the

288

phone, I sat down on the couch and stared out the window for a long time, completely spun around, before I began making calls.

When I called Jack to see if he would come to the funeral, that I would pay for his airfare, he agreed. I was so happy he said yes. He would finally meet Janice, and I wanted him to see his Grandmother's home, as I felt he would sense a familiarity there.

Somehow I'd been spared having to deal with death. My Nana's was the first wake I'd ever attended, and that was a couple of years after losing Jack. She'd been staying at our house and it was the Fourth of July.

Her last words to me were a request: "I want to say a novena for you. Tell me what you want me to pray for."

All I could think of was please say a novena for the welfare of my baby, but she didn't know about him, so I thanked her and said I was fine, that I didn't need any prayers, as I rushed out the door to meet my date. As much as I believed that others could have their prayers answered, in my case mine never were.

Dad had met me as I came home from my date and told me through the screen door that Nana had died during the fireworks of an asthma attack. My first impulse was to stop my date's car before it pulled out of the driveway and be with him. We hadn't known each other long, but I felt close to him. Instead, I stayed watching a moth circling the yellow bug light, and finally let myself inside.

At the wake, I watched everyone approach the casket to kiss Nana, my mother's step-mother, goodbye, but I couldn't make myself do the same. Tortured by my indecision, I finally forced myself to approach the casket. That's when I understood death for what it is. That wasn't my grandmother in there, and they'd even parted her hair on the wrong side. But then my eyes fell on the worn rosary beads entwined in her folded hands, the rosary that was used countless hours in prayer for us all, and I lost it. I ran outside sobbing. Dad found me, and for the first time since I was a little girl I let him see me cry.

So, as I approached my mother's casket at the wake, I wasn't afraid. Just as Paula had seen, her spirit was no longer in her body. But when I looked in I was horrified. Mom would have been appalled. Instead of the still attractive woman she'd always been, she looked nothing like herself - more like an old Chinese woman. Not wanting anyone remembering her that way, I grabbed the card for her memorial with a great picture of her on it and propped it up on the casket. I had a feeling her old boyfriend, Gordon, would be coming and she'd hate for him to see her that way. He'd married someone else, and we all felt that was why Mom suffered her small stroke a few years before.

Sure enough, Gordon walked in the next moment. I was still standing by the casket. Knowing how my mother kept all her feelings to herself, I was sure Gordon never knew just how much she'd cared for him. So I decided to tell him, be real with him in a way my mother never could. I could feel his depth of caring for her, while we spoke. In the back of my mind, however, I was wondering if Mom was standing with us and if she was upset with me or grateful that I'd been so honest with Gordon.

The morning of the funeral, we all met in the church parking lot. Right next to the church entrance was a gravestone carved with the words: "For all the souls lost to abortion." Inside the foyer were pamphlets about choosing adoption. How such propaganda must impact vulnerable young women even before they consider having sex, I thought cringing.

We followed Elena's husband, Claude, an Episcopalian minister, to the rectory to meet the priest and decide on the readings for the service and who would read what and in what order. Jack was selected to read first. There was no time to prepare.

When the service began, it became obvious pretty fast how we had all fallen away from the church. We'd be sitting when the rest were kneeling, kneeling when we were supposed to be standing, finally turning around to see what the others were doing so we wouldn't make more mistakes, embarrassing Mom any further.

Jack took his clue and walked up to the pedestal to read his passage from the Bible. We watched, barely able to suppress our giggles, as his eyes grew wide with dismay while reading the frightening words, more a warning for the living than a consolation for our loss. No doubt Jack was one of us. My passage wasn't any better. Kip was the last of us to read, and did a great job considering he'd never been to church.

After the service, the priest approached us in an unwelcoming manner and, with a recriminating tone, told of how Mom would often come to him tormented about her sins and the fact none of her children practiced the faith. Her divorce weighed heavily on her mind, he said, and she knew she could never remarry, as long as her first husband was still alive. Ah, Gordon, that explained a few things. I felt badly that she must have died believing she had failed God and worried she would be spending a good bit of time in Purgatory. How tormented I could have been hearing this priest's words, if I didn't know better. I had the feeling Mom figured things out pretty fast, once she got on the other side.

She was to be laid to rest in the newer part of the cemetery. Close by were ancient graves of slaves in the once "colored only" section. Even though I knew her spirit was free, I still felt sad that Mom would always be buried alone there.

Back at the house, friends gathered. At one point, I happily noticed that Jack and Janice were involved in a deep conversation. Jack had always meant so much to Janice, and they appeared to be talking like old friends. I just hoped Janice didn't go too far into the family stories.

Mom's friends, the women who watched over each others' doormats, kept stressing how they always prayed that they would go just as Mom had, suddenly and without suffering. Knowing I would be staying for a while after to deal with all of Mom's belongings, they asked me to come to tea before I returned to New York.

After a week of going through everything, Elena had to leave and I was by myself, so I took the women up on their offer to have tea. As we sat together in the sunny apartment of one of them, it didn't take long for the women to get right to the point.

"Carol, Anne never told us anything. We had no idea until her funeral that you had another son and there was a book and a movie, too."

They were so accepting and tender in their understanding, and I felt badly that Mom hadn't leaned on them for support, instead of dealing with everything all by her self.

On the flight back home, I had no clue that my mother's death would mark the beginning of a bleak period in my life, where everything that could go wrong did.

Two weeks after I returned to New York, the landlord of the building phoned to let me know he was not going to give me a lease. He was purging the building of all sublets and no one subletting would be given mercy. His news came as a big blow, and the timing couldn't have been worse. DeAnna was sitting by me on my couch, in the midst of a miscarriage. We were waiting for the doctor's call letting us know when to go to the hospital for a DNC. This was her second miscarriage. She had indeed been pregnant during 9/11, but had miscarried soon after, as had a much higher number of women right after that traumatic event.

Somehow I was able to hide my distress over the landlord's demand, so that DeAnna didn't have more to worry about. After what felt like hours waiting, she got the call and we walked over to

292

St. Vincent's Hospital. Kip met us there. We were allowed to be in the room with her during the procedure, and she couldn't have had more love and support from the doctors and nurses through her ordeal. At one point, I found myself nearly in a trance as I was pulled into the memories of the cruel way I'd been treated during Jack's birth, such a contrast to the compassion DeAnna was being given. In the midst of her ordeal, DeAnna's eyes caught mine and I knew she understood all I was going through.

The next day, I sought out the landlord.

"My mother just died," I told him, "and it's a difficult time. Can you please reconsider?" I tried to be brave, but I burst into tears.

He practically snickered. "How dare you cry," he said.

In the elevator on the way back up to my apartment, my tears turned to anger. Dante had made a mistake in his *Inferno*. He should have added a special circle in Hell just for landlords.

As it turned out, the week I was searching for an apartment *The Other Mother* was airing again on the Lifetime Channel. Wherever I went to check a place, the people would say, "Your name sounds so familiar" and then we'd figure out they'd seen the commercials for the movie.

The film had first aired on Lifetime Mothers' Day, 2000, which was so gratifying. We were finally being acknowledged nationally as mothers, too. The film would air many times on Lifetime over the next eight years. The incongruity of being anonymous on one hand and having my life public knowledge on the other never went away. Whenever I knew it was airing, I still always imagined the story rolling over the country like a big wave and worried for the mothers, still in the closet, being confronted with their story all at once.

With Kip's help, I was able to get a new apartment just three blocks away from my old place. Steve Loring had come with me to see it the first time, and said I should take it. Though it was much more rent than I had been paying, it was still cheaper than most apartments I'd seen. Besides, it was a garden apartment – a rare find.

Finally finished cleaning the old apartment, I was sure I looked like a bag lady as I walked the three blocks to the new place at two in the morning, with all the random loose end leftovers from the move stuffed in a cart. Little did I know then how close I would come to my comical sight becoming reality.

Art stopped by the next day to see the place. Though we'd remained close, we didn't see as much of each other anymore. When I took him out to the garden, which had once been a little park for the old church next door built in the eighteen hundreds, I pointed out four pieces of old stone that were about to be thrown out. In less than a minute, he'd put the pieces together and we discovered the image of a Madonna and Child, worn from age, which must have once belonged to the church. Art carried the stones to a spot in the garden under a fir tree and reassembled them. I felt then that I was meant to be there.

Four studio apartments shared the garden. The two to the right of mine were empty when I moved in. A woman in her forties, who lived to the left of me, was rarely there. Then two weeks later Rachel moved into the apartment next to me. We became great friends right away. She loved having the garden as much as I did, so we set about making it beautiful. I never could have imagined living in New York City and being able to dig into soil and plant a garden. I wouldn't have thought after years of home ownership that I would even want to do that again.

I had been able to see Jack and Anna and the kids fairly often, since Kip and DeAnna often visited her parents in the Outer Banks and would drop me off in Virginia Beach on their way. I was Grandma to the kids, but in the back of my mind I remembered Jack's desire for me to be called something different.

Every time when I visited I would bring videos for the kids, mostly Disney movies, and on one trip I brought the movie *Anastasia* for them. As we watched, huddled together on the couch, Anastasia found her Grandmother and exclaimed, "Grandmama!"

"That's it," I told them. "You guys can call me Grandmama," I said, dramatically rolling the "r" like in the movie.

After the movie was over, we practiced saying the word with an exaggerated "r" but Tess couldn't get it right, as hard as she tried. On the next visit, months later, they all greeted us at the door.

With a big grin on her face, Tess exclaimed, "Grandmama!" rolling the "r" perfectly, obviously proud of her accomplishment. That sweet moment meant the world to me.

On one trip, when the kids were a few years older, Anna had made mojitos for the first time and, not knowing their effect, Jack and Anna and I got toasted pretty fast. Sensing the opportunity like bloodhounds, the kids began asking a million pointed questions about the adoption, questions they'd obviously stored up for a long time. In our state, we answered them all, which was great, since so much had still been left unsaid between us. Much like my mother and Ray, Jack continued to deal with his feelings privately and in his own way.

At one in the morning of December 13, 2003, Kip called. DeAnna was in labor Could I come to the hospital right away? I was out the door in five minutes, wide-awake. This would be the first time I'd be there for the birth of a grandchild – grandchild number seven. Brett and Jessica already had two little boys, Cole and Reed.

The hospital lobby was magical as I entered, all decorated for Christmas. When I found them, I learned that DeAnna wasn't being admitted yet, as she wasn't far enough along, and they'd been advised to go back home and wait. But DeAnna couldn't bear the thought of another bumpy cab ride adding more pain to her already painful contractions. So Kip and I walked her around the hospital for hours among the colored lights and Christmas trees. Each time we went back to the nurses' station to have her checked, DeAnna was still not far enough along to be admitted. So we'd walk her some more, until it was impossible and we decided to stay in the waiting room. At one point, DeAnna was on her hands and knees on the floor from the pain, and we had her examined again. They quickly checked her in.

Her parents had left the Outer Banks as soon as they got word, the trunk of the car having been packed for days. Early in the afternoon, Bud called from the Holland Tunnel. Brenda was swearing like a sailor at the slow moving traffic.

After they arrived, DeAnna debated about whether or not to let her Mom and I stay in the room for the delivery, but she was leaning against the idea. However, in the evening, when she was getting close to the end, she relented, as long as Brenda and I sat over on the windowsill and didn't move from that spot. If we got up even once, we'd have to leave the room.

Suddenly the doctor was concerned. The baby was sunny side up and there was a chance DeAnna might have to have a c-section, if the baby didn't turn in time.

Kip began talking to her belly, encouraging the baby, "You can do it!" At one point, he asked DeAnna if he could play his tape of the theme song from *Rocky* he'd brought. Tears came to my eyes, as years of Kip playing that music to get pumped up for each game flashed through my mind.

"No way!" DeAnna responded.

The effort to move the baby's position was heroic, and slowly he was turning. A nurse came into the room and called the doctor away for another patient. Brenda, who was wound up like a top from worry, jumped up from the windowsill to go to her daughter's side.

I grabbed her sweater in the knick of time and pulled her back down. "We're going to get kicked out of here!"

The doctor returned and then suddenly the baby was born – a boy, Hudson David Schaefer. I took pictures as DeAnna held him and Kip cut the cord, tears streaming down all our faces.

I'd beheld the miracle of birth, one of the most profound moments of my life. I sat back down on the windowsill, while the nurses tended to the baby, in awe and wondering how in the world anyone witnessing a birth could ever separate an infant from its mother.

Chapter Seventeen

Ever since moving to the new apartment, I'd struggled to keep up with rent and expenses, landing odd jobs editing and ghostwriting, but never able to get far enough ahead to develop my own project, which was frustrating. DeAnna was going back to work part-time as a physical therapist and I was to take care of Hudson, which lightened the load somewhat.

But everything changed one beautiful evening in June of 2004, when I attended a women's gathering for a talk about a council that was being formed of indigenous women elders from around the world. The gathering was held in a penthouse on the Upper West Side, and there must have been seventy women there. As the talk was about to begin, I sat down on the floor to listen - the only space left in the packed room. Carole Hart, who owned the penthouse, asked that we all introduce ourselves first before the program began. She looked to me to start.

When I gave my name and said I was the author of *The Other Mother*, the woman sitting on the floor right next to me gasped, "Oh, my God! I've watched your movie so many times and cry each time! I can't believe it's you!"

When I turned to her, it was like I was meeting an old friend. When Bonnie and I talked later, she said she'd never had children of her own, never had been pregnant, but that she was blessed with the ability to see past lives, both hers and for others, and the movie connected her to the pain and grief of losing a child in another life. Wow.

When we finally made it all around the room with the introductions, Carole introduced Jyoti (Jeneane Prevatt), Spiritual Director of the Center for Sacred Studies, who told of a vision she'd first received in 1995 from the Divine Mother, foretelling the time of the Grandmothers. Jyoti committed to following the vision and her mission was culminating in a gathering of thirteen indigenous Grandmothers in October. Carole and her husband, Bruce, were to make a film about the historical event. As I sat listening to Jyoti, I thought to myself that they needed a book.

When I got home, I couldn't shake the idea of writing the book for a week, there seemed to be too much energy behind it. But who was I to approach them? I hadn't had a vision, only a great interest in the wisdom of indigenous cultures and this unexplained power behind the idea of writing it. So, I consulted with Lynn Franklin, who suggested I write a book proposal. Then, I consulted with Jyoti to see if they would mind and got the go ahead.

All that summer, I struggled with the proposal. Self-doubt fueled some of my inability to pull the proposal together, but the lack of knowledge about what to expect was the greater obstacle. When I was about to give up all together, the ideas finally began to gel and the writing flowed. I was able to get the proposal to Lynn in September, hardly enough time for her to sell the idea before the conference in October.

I was to learn that in native traditions, one is always tested before being granted permission by Spirit to take on an important task. The week before the conference was to begin, Lynn had interest but no book deal. Without attending the conference there would be no book. So, I had to decide whether or not to risk spending money I didn't have to attend. Deep down I knew I had to go.

The bus dropped me off by the side of the road in the tiny village of Phoenicia, New York, nestled in the foothills of the Catskill Mountains. I'd been in the city way too long, I realized, as I waited for my ride to the Menla Retreat Center nearby, site of the conference, afraid to venture too far from my suitcase. I probably could have left it there all day and no one would have bothered it.

I'd been given permission to attend the private council, when the Grandmothers would first meet and decide whether or not they would work together in the future and, if so, what their mission would be. I knew I had to somehow prove myself to the Grandmothers and the Center for Sacred Studies, as I doubted I'd been a part of any of the visions that had brought them together, and I wasn't a part of their community. I'd come to them out of the blue.

Jyoti had taken a lot of time explaining to me how I needed to carefully approach the Grandmothers, that the Native American Grandmothers especially would be suspicious of my motives. Would I be yet another white person there to exploit them? Fortunately, I understood their trauma. If ever a nun or a priest would approach me to write my story, I'd find myself instinctively freezing up with a complete lack of trust. Strict limits, as well, had been set on my ability to speak with the Grandmothers, as many demands were already placed on them. I could follow the filmmaker, Carole Hart, around but couldn't ask any questions of the Grandmothers myself. How was I going to write this book then?

A half hour later, my ride arrived and we traveled through the beautiful countryside up to the retreat center, where the driver showed me to the room I would be sharing.

"There will be a ceremony this evening," she said, "the lighting of the sacred fire that will burn for the full week."

At dusk, I walked through the golden woods down to the area where the ceremony was to take place and stood at the outer edge of the circle. The fire had not yet been lit. Fire is one of the four sacred elements to native peoples, along with earth, air and water. I had always loved a roaring fire and felt changed by being near one, but had little understanding about why. This fire would be burning for seven days, until the conference was over. Two men were designated the fire keepers and would sleep by the fire to make sure it never went out. Three times a day, in the early morning, at noon and then each evening, the Grandmothers would come to the fire to pray.

Chief Shenandoah of the Iroquois Nation had created the original spark that would light this fire by rubbing two sticks together at the steps of the United Nations building in 1986, fulfilling a thousand-year-old Hopi prophesy. The flame then traveled around the world and was seen by hundreds of thousands of people before being placed on the altar of the holy Santuario de Chimayo in New Mexico, the oldest church in the United States, where it remained until now, when it was brought to initiate the unprecedented gathering of Grandmothers from the four directions. Indigenous peoples rarely share their rituals, prophecy and wisdom, even with each other, which was what made this gathering so meaningful. After the fire was lit, each of the Grandmothers performed their own ritual around it. I watched it all fascinated. Little did I know then how this fire would work on me over the coming week, how I would come to realize the profound difference between intellectual understanding and true knowing.

Lynn phoned the next morning. Two excellent publishers were interested. The one with the larger offer required a sample chapter before commitment. Lynn advised me to go with the other lower offer.

"A bird in the hand," she advised. "Think it over."

But I had grown intimidated by the project. Who was I to write this book? How could I ever convey the Grandmothers' ancient wisdom, being from the white culture?

I'd discovered a beautiful walk through the woods that circled the retreat. A lake and a river were alongside part of the path, and I was beginning to tune into the magic of the valley and the towering Catskill Mountains that surrounded it. After finishing the walk and before going into the dining hall for lunch, I sat for a long time in an Adirondack chair under a huge fir tree, seeking an answer. As I stared up into the sky, I felt a certainty settle over me that would carry me through all my doubts and the difficulties I would encounter in the process of writing the book. After lunch, I called Lynn and told her to accept the solid offer.

The week was remarkable and the work of gathering as much information as I could was intense. I was also taking lots of pictures to be included in the book. Though never able to interview the Grandmothers myself, I was able to sit in the room where they were being interviewed for the film. Every one of the Grandmothers had overcome great struggles in their lives, and I found their stories inspirational and their wisdom essential. Over the days, I was gaining an increasing appreciation for the power of the feminine, as I witnessed it for the first time expressed in its greatest possibilities. And, over the week I was gaining the Grandmothers' confidence.

One of their common teachings was respect for the land and all living things and for the Spirit World, an idea I naturally embraced. But it wasn't until the second to last day, after attending every prayer ceremony by the fire, when I experienced the oneness of all life that the Grandmothers had talked about all week. During the morning-prayer ceremony, I looked up and saw with my own vision the towering ancient spirits of the surrounding mountains watching us. The fire had worked its magic on me.

When I returned to the city, I was still in some sort of altered state and found the bustle of the city overwhelming. Missing the power of nature, I walked down to the Hudson River and for the first time, after many trips there, I was able to "see" the spirit of the river. That ability lasted one day, as the effects of my immersion in nature quickly faded in the hustle and bustle of city life. At least I had the memories.

Despite the advance, I had to face the reality that, given I had only a year to write the book, I had to find a cheaper place to live. My first thought, to call Sandra at the theater, proved fortunate. The theater was housed in a brownstone built in the seventeen hundreds, and was owned by Edith. Everyone knew that Edith was like the Old Woman Who Lived in a Shoe. She could never turn anyone in need away. At one point, actors and writers were stuffed everywhere: the rehearsal room, the lighting booth, backstage. One fellow, a talented costume designer, who lived in the storage loft, had sawed the legs off a sofa and table to accommodate the low ceiling and hung a sign saying, "Home Sweet Home."

Until coming to New York, I thought badly of myself for hanging in there with my writing and photography, despite the financial sacrifices. Art was the first person I'd met who would rather buy a roll of film than eat. But I was soon to find many other kindred souls, artists and writers willing to sacrifice what most people felt essential in order to do their work, and I felt less alien.

I had grown to admire Edith, after hearing story after story of how she, despite being under constant siege because of the value of her property, held strong and refused huge offers in order to preserve what had become a lost ideal – maintaining a place for artists to have a chance to do their work.

The enclosed patio room, with windows along one wall and access to the roof, was available immediately. Someone was watching over me. As I climbed the steps of the brownstone with my first round of boxes to be moved, Liche, a gifted actor and writer, who once lived in the lighting booth but now had his own apartment in the building, greeted me. "Welcome to the asylum!" he said.

Uh, oh. What was I getting myself into? This was a far cry from my home so many years before in Marin with a swimming pool on one side and a redwood grove on the other. Since then, my homes had been gradually diminishing in size, until now this.

Only days after moving in, Art and I began living together.

For the first six months, I was buried in paper from notes and transcribed tapes, as I pieced together the book like an intricate puzzle, a passage from this page, a quote from another, where the heck is that sentence I just read somewhere. All the while, the Grandmothers' wisdom grew inside me. From all my years in adoption reform, I'd seen how we carry our stories of pain, loss and grief with us as if it is the truth of who we are. Trauma expert, Dr. Peter Levine has said that, "trauma is not what happened to us, but what we hold inside in the absence of an empathic witness." We were becoming our own empathic witnesses, but still defined ourselves by our pain. Not the Grandmothers.

Most of the Grandmothers had lived through incredible hardships, including the loss of children. What was it that allowed them to transcend their stories, see themselves beyond their pain, in fact grow in wisdom as a result of their sufferings? Yes, they were deeply spiritual, but that wasn't what set them apart. All were from an ancient lineage of basic teachings that had evolved a way of living in this world in peace. With such a perspective, they were able to draw strength from their ancestors and their history and, therefore, deeply understand the importance of their actions for the future, up to seven generations away.

From such an expansive point of view, so different from the culture of today, their personal stories of loss were held in a far greater and healing context that included humility before all of Life. I wanted so much to know what it meant to see all of Creation as they did, but I had not been taught the teachings from birth, and so had to be content being awakened to a true knowing of the Oneness of All little by little.

One of the Native American Grandmothers told of how, if they needed a part of a plant for a specific purpose, for food or medicine, the gatherer would pray over it, asking the plant's consent and only when given permission would then take only what was needed, using great care to ensure the plant's survival into the future for the future. That even one small plant against the backdrop of all of Creation was treated with such tenderness, respect and gratitude to me was one of their most striking and at the same time tragic revelations – tragic in that we are so far from that basic understanding that by following would turn the whole world upside down.

But the one story that stood out from all others for me came not from the Grandmothers but from one of the attendees. The woman told of how she had been beaten and raped nearly to death in a Chicago hotel room. As she peered into the mirror through eyes that were now mere pinpoints, while waiting for the police to arrive, she was unrecognizable to herself. After staring at herself for many moments, she began to see beyond the horror, pain and trauma and discovered "the face she had before she was born." In that moment, she felt a joy beyond anything she ever could have imagined.

One month before the one-year deadline to get the manuscript to the publisher in December, my computer died. Fortunately, my brother was able to get me a new one, and I was able to finish on time. Then came the process of selecting and printing the pictures to be included in the book and choosing a cover image. A big dream of combining both my writing and photography was being fulfilled.

The Grandmothers had been telling me that my work was done, that the book was theirs now. Of course it was. There was no way that I could claim their wisdom, or even desire to. Still, their words cut me to the core, until I understood why. Again I had given birth, and again it felt like my creation was given to someone else to nurture and enjoy, and I was being cut off from any connection to my work. At least I was finally able to recognize the cause of my irrational emotional response, untangle my story from theirs and let the book go.

Ten years after my fiftieth birthday, when Ray and I had met at the Norfolk Airport for the first time in forty years, I was traveling the same road again, this time with my Dad and Kip. We were on our way to Dylan's high school graduation. I sat nervously in the passenger seat, waiting until we were halfway there before telling Dad that Ray would be at the ceremony, too, certain that before then he would ask that we turn around and drop him back off at the beach house.

Kip and Brett had rented a beautiful beach house on the ocean in the Outer Banks for my sixtieth birthday and to celebrate Kip and DeAnna's tenth wedding anniversary. Kip and DeAnna now had two boys, Hudson and Quinn. Bud and Brenda were with us, too, and Bob had brought Dad to come stay with us as well. It had been a special week.

As the familiar scenes swept by, I was waiting for my favorite, the old white clapboard houses with gravestones in their front yard, and growing more anxious about deceiving Dad. Ten minutes past the gravestones, I finally turned around to Dad, sitting behind me in the back seat, and told him he would be seeing Ray.

"Carol, turn the car around right now," he said, as agitated as I had ever seen him.

"Too late, Dad, we'll miss the graduation. Don't worry everything will be fine."

But I wasn't sure. Ray had no idea Dad was going to be there. Both were Southern gentlemen to the core, so the worst I could expect would be superficial politeness. Neither one would ever dream of making a scene. If only they would take the opportunity – Ray to express regrets and Dad to forgive.

Jack met us and showed us to our seats in the packed gymnasium. I could tell he was pleased that we made the effort to be there for Dylan. All week I'd hoped the kids would come down to the beach to see us, but that didn't happen. It had been a few years since I'd gone down to Virginia Beach to see them, so I was probably more like a stranger again. Anytime I thought about going, I felt blocked for some unknown reason. In the future, I would understand why and the reason was nothing I could have guessed.

Ray and Jean were sitting in the seats in front of us and turned to greet us. If Ray was surprised to see Dad, he didn't let on. After the ceremony, we all gathered outside in the parking lot, where we finally had a chance to talk. The girls were turning into beautiful young women, and I felt sad about not seeing them for so long. Ray shook Dad's hand, looking a little shell shocked, and I introduced Dad to Jean, who immediately took his arm and was by his side the rest of the time. Her warmth toward Dad surprised me, and I found myself wondering if she was trying to make up for everything in a way for Ray's sake, since he obviously couldn't even find his tongue. I understood how he felt.

Kip's quiet but strong presence was easy to read. He felt obviously proud to be there as a brother and uncle. After getting directions to the restaurant in case we got lost, we followed behind Ray and Jean's car.

"That wasn't so bad, Dad, now was it?"

"I don't know."

"Jean is so nice, isn't she?"

"Yes, very, very nice."

The dinner was fun. Jack and Anna always had a way of making everything fun and festive, and their kids had acquired the same gift. But, sadly, Dad and Ray kept a safe distance from each other the whole time. Without the tragic circumstances of the past, they would have enjoyed each other's company. In many ways, they were a lot alike. When we were saying our goodbyes, they politely shook hands. That was it. I couldn't help feeling let down.

Grandmothers Council the World was published November 14, 2006. I was involved in a couple of book signings and radio shows, but for the most part the Grandmothers handled all the publicity, a strange feeling after all the excitement of promoting *The Other Mother*, both the book and the movie, when I found I loved connecting with the readers. The Barnes & Noble bookstore a few blocks away hosted a reading and had made a huge display in one window of all my books. That was a thrill.

I continued to take on editing and ghostwriting jobs, but I needed my own project. I wasn't able yet financially or emotionally to mount a production of *The Sacred Virgin*, though it was always in the back of my mind. What I did find, though, was that I missed Mary queen of Scots, and so I got the crazy idea of writing a screenplay about her and enlisted Steve's mentorship.

What followed was a great deal of frustration. Whenever I met with Steve, he would pull everything apart, as my writing was more like for a book than a screenplay. As much as I had wanted to give up, I felt compelled to continue. One day, in total frustration, I decided to add dialog, even though I hadn't finished the requisite outline, and it was then that I grasped the difference in genres and the screenplay took off. Characters were coming to life in a way

308

they never could in a book, and the screenplay was practically writing itself.

The next year and a half was spent alternating between writing the screenplay and scrambling to make a living. Then, in April of 2008, I was thrown by two unexpected events.

Jack called. He was in town to work on a film and wanted to come by to see us. Jack had become successful as a production designer for television and films – all of his prior odd jobs combining to make him great at what he did.

As soon as he walked in, I knew something serious was up.

As he sat down in the chair, Jack looked like he was going to jump out of his skin. Art had come to know Jack well over the last few years, as he visited us whenever he was in the area working on a film. To try to help Jack relax, Art decided to tell him a funny story about a conversation he had with his son, Rudolf, that morning. Both Rudolf and his twin sister Beata were law students, so serious about their studies that they never dated.

"So, I found out my son's not gay," Art joked. "He does like girls." Art had lots of gay friends, since coming to the United States and working as a fitness trainer in Chelsea, but his concern was for his son being gay in Russia, a country with little tolerance for alternate lifestyles.

"Well, that's what I came to tell you," Jack said quietly. "I'm gay."

A flood of emotions ran through me in an instant. Thankfully I was able to say, "Wow, I'm so happy that you felt comfortable enough to tell us."

Jack relaxed immediately, but Art began falling all over himself trying to make up for his ill-timed story. The last thing he wanted was for Jack to feel anything but proud of the fact he was gay. As I took in the news, I understood one of the reasons Art and I were together. Through him, I'd come to understand the gay community quite well. My only concern for Jack was the prejudice he might now encounter. And, I knew from my friends who were both gay and adopted how doubly difficult it was to feel like they could fit in society.

"How are Anna and the kids taking the news?" I asked him.

"The kids are fine with it," Jack said. "They're from a different generation, more open about everything. In fact everyone seems to be pretty accepting. But Anna is taking it very hard. I understand that."

I'd known for a long time that their marriage was rocky, but attributed their difficulties to having four kids right away and always struggling financially. Jack said he'd had a few experiences when he was young but that he might never have explored that side of himself if they hadn't had so many struggles in their marriage.

By the time Jack left a few hours later, Art and I had made certain that he felt even more loved and supported than ever before. Afterwards, Art, sensing I was still shocked, reassured me over and over that Jack would be fine. If there were complete societal acceptance for being gay, I would never have allowed my mind to entertain some of the questions that kept popping into my head. Being gay was no longer believed to be a choice. A person was born with their sexual orientation and being gay ran in families. But I couldn't come up with a genetic connection in our family, though I didn't know about Ray's side. So, I found myself wondering if the constant painful losses and separations he'd experienced, the direct result of my having given him up, weren't the main reason for him taking up a gay lifestyle. Until I worked through another layer of guilt for not being able to keep him, I couldn't see clearly that my theory just didn't ring true or was even fair to Jack's choice.

The next day, I called my siblings without any worries about their reaction. Bob and Elena were completely accepting and happy that Jack could finally be him self. Only Janice, despite being non judgmental, was confused. So I called her two days later to talk some more. Right away I could tell she was "out of it" and not making much sense, so different from her clarity two days before. In her state, there was no way to make conversation, so I quickly got off the phone feeling heartbroken. Janice was in failing health, the result of her lifelong battle with addiction. She'd probably had too many beers.

The next day, her husband called. Janice was dead. She'd fallen asleep in her chair that afternoon and never woke up. As much as I would miss her and her great sense of humor, I was relieved for her that her suffering was ended. She'd had a hard life.

That our last conversation was about Jack was fitting. It was hard to imagine the cost to her of knowing her big sister was sent away to a maternity home and have to pretend to know nothing. She was only fifteen at the time. When I returned home without the baby and with a case of the "flu," she had to go along with the charade, even though she knew ever since overhearing the "Battle of the Girdles." How my situation impacted her life could only be imagined.

A few years later, when she was in college, she was afraid she was pregnant and called home. Dad and Mom insisted she have an abortion, which shocked her, but revealed how deeply affected they had been by losing their first grandchild. Even though abortion was against their beliefs, there was no way they could live through such a nightmare again. Fortunately, her missed period was a false alarm. She wasn't pregnant after all.

While holding a constant vigil in the hospital for Janice, who was at death's door the summer I was searching for Jack, I had learned his name. Despite the fact she was still in a coma and hooked up to life support, I wanted to tell her first. When Elena and I entered the ICU unit for the once an hour five-minute visit, we found Janice bathed in sunlight from a nearby window.

"Janice, I know my son's name. It's John Aloysius Ryan III."

Janice's smile was beatific, her first response to anything in a week and a half. That's when I knew just how deep her feelings for my firstborn ran.

Somehow I had not been able to bring myself to tell Brett and Kip about Jack, not because I was worried that they would love Jack any less but because I felt they might have a lot to process upon hearing the news. Kip was going through a tumultuous year. His company, Bear Stearns, collapsed along with the stock market crash, and he would be out of a job in June and looking for a new one. His apartment in New York had sold, and they were now living in their weekend home in the Catskills, which entailed a long commute during his remaining months at Bear Stearns. On top of that, he and DeAnna were expecting their third child. I wasn't sure I should add one more thing to his plate, and I couldn't tell Brett without telling Kip.

"Mom, are there any more skeletons in the closet you haven't told us about?" Brett was with Kip, and they were driving to the Atlanta airport after their annual fall football weekend outing together. They'd stayed with Bob.

My mind drew a blank.

"Come on, Mom, try to remember. There must be something."

I couldn't conjure what in the world he could be talking about.

"Well, it seems now I have two gay brothers," he joked, ribbing Kip who was sitting in the passenger seat.

"Oh, yes, well ..."

"Why didn't you tell us?" Brett was rarely angry, but they were both upset with me for not telling them sooner.

My explanation about finding the right time and then actually not having the fact of Jack being gay on my mind any more didn't go over. They were insulted that I didn't seem able to trust them with the news.

"Bob told us. He said he was sick of the way our family kept secrets."

I felt awful.

"Before Bob told us, Kip and I were going to sleep in the king size bed in the guest room, but after that I told Kip he had to sleep on the couch." Typical Brett - making a joke, especially in heavy situations. "But, seriously, Mom."

I felt relieved and upset with myself at the same time for not trusting my sons. When he got home, Kip said he wrote Jack a loving letter. Though they never said it, I had to wonder how angry they were with me for their not being able to grow up with their brother. Sometimes there were places in my heart that I didn't want to look at.

The phone rang just as I finished cleaning the dust-blanketed shelves, a major project I'd been putting off for months. But Jack was stopping by and that was incentive enough to get the job done in a couple of hours, instead of dragging the chore out for an entire day.

"We're a block away."

We? We could only mean Jack's partner, Dan. I wasn't even dressed yet, let alone prepared emotionally. Jack was so much like Bob in the way they both rarely gave any warning of their plans.

My first impression when they walked in was how much Dan and Jack looked like each other, only Dan was taller. The words flew out of my mouth before I had a chance to censor myself: "Wow, I didn't remember giving away two sons!" Oh, God, how insensitive could I be? But, they both laughed, and we all were immediately at ease.

I could tell right away that Dan was a great guy and perfect for Jack. He was so easy to get to know and quite interesting. He was

313

vice president of PETA (People for the Ethical Treatment of Animals) and was responsible for their sometimes outrageous and always provocative advertising. An activist! He'd written a book, too, *Committed: A Rabble-Rouser's Memoir*, so we had much in common.

When I asked him how he got involved with PETA, Dan told a story that became burned in my brain. When he was young, he was always teased because he was obviously different and one day found himself flat on his back in the playground, helplessly looking up at a group of bullies surrounding him. A few years later, he was watching a circle of people on a fishing boat, laughing their heads off at a large flounder desperately flopping around on the deck, gasping for life, and felt an instant identification with the fish and its plight. From that moment on, he was an animal rights activist.

As we talked, I could see that Jack was obviously happy and more relaxed than I'd ever known him to be. Dan was good for Jack. He was a rare person, completely authentic, where Jack had always been more of a people pleaser, losing much of himself in the process. I was sure Dan would never let him get away with that.

Too soon they had to leave for an appointment. After seeing them out, Art turned to me and said, "Looks like you have a new son-in-law!"

So much shifted in our relationship now that Jack could be more open. He was much happier and far more himself. His work as a production designer in the film industry was flourishing and he was coming to New York every few months. His only concern was how hard the separation was on Anna.

Right after Jack had told me he was gay and that their marriage was over, I called Anna to express my sympathies and offer any support I could give. I told her she'd always be my daughter-in-law. But all this I said on her voicemail and never heard back. I understood. More than ever, she needed Oprah's arms around her, but this time, rather than consoling her about having three mothers-in-law, she needed to hear Oprah say, "Hey Girlfriend, what's it like learning, after years of marriage and four kids, that your husband is gay?"

But, Anna was strong. That Christmas she invited Jack to bring Dan with him for their family celebration, despite her still raw feelings. Still, I knew I couldn't go down to visit until she healed, which would take a long time and finally a remarkable gathering of all of us who had been a part of Jack's life.

Chapter Eighteen

One morning the following April, I could not make myself work on a ghostwriting project I'd begun after finishing the Grandmothers' book. Something was on my mind. As I sat before the computer screen, willing myself to get to work and resisting with all my might, a sufficiently distracting thought came to me. I could easily find Jack's first adoptive mother, now that searching techniques had become so refined. Why hadn't I thought of that before?

Those lost first eight months of Jack's life still weighed heavily, despite the fact I had talked with the adoptive father's mother early in our reunion and been reassured "the baby" had been greatly loved and well taken care of. Learning from Rosemary about the previous adoption had been a blow, especially when I had consoled myself with the nuns' reassurance that he would be placed with a good family and have a better life without me. My hopes were to be able to give Jack knowledge and pictures of those early months of his life, something every human being should have. That the social worker didn't even think it important to gather such information for him and for Rosemary was appallingly inhumane to me.

Knowing her name and that she was Catholic and from Charlotte, I checked out the local Catholic high schools. When she would have attended, there was only one possibility, and so I called the alumni office. Bingo! I explained that we had been friends and I'd lost contact with her. Could they give me her contact information? No, but they would call her and give her mine. That was fine.

The next morning, the phone rang. It was Annilu.

"I received a call from the alumni association that you wanted to be in touch with me. Whom am I speaking with," she asked?

When I explained, she was shocked and overjoyed. She'd always wondered how Dennis, the name she had given my baby, was doing. Right away, I found her easy to talk with and honest.

Annilu revealed that the circumstances around giving the baby back were different from what Rosemary had been told or what over time had remembered. True, Annilu and her husband were getting a divorce at the time, but the nuns hadn't taken the baby from her as a result. She herself made the decision to give him back, based on a lot of thoughts about me.

"What thoughts about me," I asked?

Memories of all my fantasies about the adoptive mother being unable to keep my baby during the months after his birth kept intruding as we talked. The magical thinking part of me worried, as I listened to Annilu's story, that my intense wishing might have actually caused harm to everyone, even though I knew better.

Annilu explained that she believed I had hoped for my son to have two parents, and now she couldn't provide that for him.

Prevailing social attitudes had a great deal to do with her marriage falling apart, as her husband was constantly being teased about not being "man enough" to produce his own children.

"Oh, my God, I forgot how stupid and unkind people could be," I consoled.

317

Her husband had been in a car accident and had fallen in love with the nurse who took care of him, in an effort probably to salvage his manhood. They had only been a year or two older than Ray and I at the time of adopting our baby.

My anger with the nuns for not being asked if my circumstances had changed before finding another adoptive family for my son flared up, but I kept that to myself. Instead, I had to be honest and say I would not have wanted another traumatic separation for Jack, or for her to go through the pain of giving him back – father or no father. He was already eight months old.

Then, I told her about Jack's memory of standing in a crib and looking at a woman with long black hair to her waist during hypnosis years before.

"Well, you won't believe it," she said. "I will send you a picture to prove it, but back then I had long black hair to my waist."

We were both astonished.

"Jack was always standing in his crib," she explained. "He would never sit in it. He must have been remembering those last days we spent together. The nuns had asked me if I could keep him a few more days, as the new parents weren't ready. They'd been expecting an infant, not an eight-month-old. Those last two heartbreaking days, Dennis would stand in his crib, looking at me with such understanding eyes, as if he knew what I was going through."

During our conversation, I ironically found myself sympathizing with how Rosemary must have felt when she first heard from me. Annilu kept referring to Jack as our son, meaning hers and mine. As much as I understood that she'd known him as her son for those eight months, I was startled at how difficult it was to digest her feelings of still being his mother, too. In her mind, she may have even felt more entitled than me to call herself his mother, since I'd only given birth to him and she'd known him for the first eight months of his life. I found myself appreciating Rosemary's graciousness in accepting me into their lives even more than ever before - given the turmoil I was unexpectedly feeling now.

Unfortunately, Hurricane Andrew had destroyed all the baby pictures, save one or two which Annilu promised to look for. She had never heard of my book or the movie. She was going to get the book, and I promised to send her a copy of the movie. I told her I would tell Jack about our conversation and see if he minded being in touch with her. We would talk again soon.

As soon as I got off the phone, I called Jack. He was fascinated with what I'd learned and said he'd be happy to talk with Annilu. I decided, like Rosemary had with me, to leave the rest in his hands.

Annilu called back a week later. She was thrilled that she had talked with Jack, but upset with her wrong portrayal in the book. Giving him back had been her idea, not the nuns, she reemphasized. They had actually been upset with her decision, she said. So strange that all three of Jack's mothers had faced single parenthood: me, Annilu and Rosemary, when her first husband died in Vietnam and she feared the nuns would take him from her now that she didn't have a husband. She once told me how she wanted to hide, so that I wouldn't find out and take Jack back before the adoption was final. He had been her only reason for living after her husband's death.

I was fortunate that both women were able to be so honest with me. The majority of adoptive mothers, at least before the era of open adoptions, simply wiped their child's original mother from their minds as if she never existed. What part of their good sense was buried in order to be so inhumane, if explored, might be the key to opening their hearts not only to their child's other mother but also to their child in a more complete way.

Over the years I'd come to understand that adoptive mothers were told the same sort of soul killing lie as us, when we were promised we could go on with out lives and pretend "it" never happened – soul killing in the sense that such adamant advice destroyed our ability to trust in our own primal instincts and see such an unnatural counsel for the lie it was.

This is your child now, a tabula rosa - blank slate, on which you can pin all your own hopes, dreams and aspirations and mold the child to your desires. If you are a good mother and love them enough, you can trust they will have no questions and no need to search for their roots. You are their roots now, they were told.

When I received Jack's illicitly obtained amended birth certificate, I had stared at it in disbelief that the date, time, hospital and even the doctor's name were accurate but, instead of my name as the mother who gave birth, there was another woman's name, instead of Ray being the father, another man was named. How was it that the adopting parents didn't find such a blatantly false document an appalling insult to them?

Without working through their deepest insecurities about being unable to bring life into this world, and for some perhaps their fear that God was somehow punishing them, for many adopting mothers salvation became another woman's child. Any normal questions from their child or desire to search threatened to expose the lies they'd been told, that now there was no other mother, and perhaps unveil long buried feelings of deficiency. Like us, their deepest knowing was overruled by authority figures we believed we could trust. The healing journey to release themselves from the deception and embrace the truth could only strengthen their relationship with the child they adopted. Sadly, such a journey was one too few adoptive mothers wanted to take.

But I had seen first hand from adoptive mothers who read *The Other Mother* how understanding our story had profoundly changed them. One adoptive mother told me how she had thrown the book against the wall several times while reading it, because she'd been so angry at having to face our reality and could no longer remain in denial. Deep down, she'd always known her joy was at the expense of another woman's suffering. Ironically, when she finally faced the truth, she no longer felt threatened by her child's other mother.

Though I'd written the book to help others understand our story and why we could never forget our children, I hadn't anticipated how Rosemary's courage would be so inspirational. If the two mothers who shared the same child could acknowledge their unique relationship, adoptees could be free to be themselves, instead of being held prisoner by the insecurities of those who love them. They wouldn't feel split in two between the nurture versus nature debate, having to deny half of who they are from a demand to declare one mother more real to them than the other. Is the real mother the one who changed the diapers, nursed them to health, took them to school and helped them grow up, or the one who gave her child life? The debate forces an adopted person to struggle with which half of them is valid, instead of embracing both and becoming whole. Even with all my opinions on the matter, I could empathize more with their reluctance to go there after talking with Annilu.

On my way to our artist studio building, I looked up and saw enormous black clouds bearing down. By the time I reached the building and ran up the stairs, the wind was howling and pounding rain was blowing sidewise. Our studio would be drenched. Mark, an artist whose studio was close by ours, met me in the hall, carrying sheets of plastic, nails and a hammer. He was heading to our unfinished studio, as worried for us as he would have been for himself. We'd only recently met. As we struggled to nail the plastic sheet onto the exposed window, I felt I was living through the movie *The Perfect Storm*.

After knowing each other for eight years, Art and I first began seriously working together only a year before, when the opportunity came up for a studio in Manhattan. The once beautiful old building on the Hudson River had become derelict, used only by the homeless, when friends of the owner suggested they could use some of the space for artist studios. Our friend, Marcus, had had a huge space there for the past three years, but was not using it enough now that he was living out of the country. When Art lost his studio in New Jersey, Marcus suggested we share his, on the condition we not let anyone know. For the handful of artists there, the rent was free. The landlord paid for electricity and water, but there was no heat in the building.

Our first day in the studio, Art and I huddled together in the enormous space trying to get warm in the November cold and find our bearings, after being so used to living together in our small converted patio. We were figuring out how to lay low so that we wouldn't be asked to leave, when suddenly someone was knocking on the door. Uh, oh.

"Dinner is at six," John announced, poking his head inside the door and then abruptly leaving.

Art and I looked at each other in amazement. We knew John through Marcus, but only barely. Dinner?

At six o'clock, we ascended the steep stairway up to the third floor and found ourselves in a large room, nearly the length of the building, filled with an eclectic assortment of furniture found on the streets and a long table that could easily seat fifty. At the other end of the great room was a big kitchen. A few of the artists had erected the walls from salvaged wood and old molded tin used for ceilings in the early part of the century, giving the whole place a true bohemian atmosphere. John was cooking and the others were drinking wine and keeping him company.

One of the artists started setting the table, when John stopped her. "The plates have to be heated!" he insisted, handing her cloth napkins for the table.

Someone else was lighting candles. As we sat down to as good a meal as could be found in any five star restaurant in the City, all of us wearing winter jackets, scarfs and hats, vapor from our breath filled the cold air. Art and I had no idea then what an incredible experience our time in this last of its kind artist building would be, which we learned that night was fondly called the Cold Castle.

The near impossibility of working through the entire winter with no heat took most of us to a new level in our work and forged a special bond among us. Up on the top floor, one of the artists, forced to accommodate not just the terrible cold but also the lack of electricity, began to incorporate light into his work to stunning effect. For all of us the choice to brace ourselves for another day's work served to deepen the process.

Art's photography was intense and conceptual - he was Russian after all. He often used me as a model, and, since he understood my story so well, he was somehow able to translate all the emotions in his black and white images. My challenge as an artist was to get out of his powerful shadow and trust my own vision. Our work was opposite from each other in most ways.

By spring, the owner decided to make the whole building artist studios and charge rent. Danakah, who managed the building, deliberately set about bringing in artists who would be compatible with the core group who already were there. His Irish instincts were right on. We all became like family.

But, now that we had to pay rent, Art and I went from having the largest space in the building to the smallest, which was all we really needed. We'd actually shown Danakah where they could build a studio for us, and he and the owner, Alf, agreed. All that was left to complete was our window, when the storm came along.

Years before, when Brett and Kip were still young and we lived the typical comfortable suburban lifestyle, I remember telling a friend I wanted a bohemian life, not having a clue about what I was asking for.

Annilu called. She and her husband, also named Jack, would be coming to New York in the spring. Would I like to get together? Sounds great! A few days later, Jack called to say he was coming to town, as it turned out on the same weekend as Annilu's visit. The odds of such a coincidence were so slim, I had to believe it was meant to be that the three of us meet together. When I asked Jack if he would be willing, he agreed.

Annilu and her husband were staying at the Waldorf Astoria, and the plan was for us to meet by the famous clock in the lobby and have a drink at the bar in the early afternoon on Saturday.

The morning of our meeting, I asked Jack if he'd like to meet me there or go together. From the sound of his voice, he was feeling nervous. "No, let's go together."

For the first time, I felt needed, like I could be there for him as his mother.

When we found the clock, only one woman was standing there. Annilu spotted us right away and came right up to us with a warm hug. Her husband had decided to stay up in the room, she said, to give us time alone together. Later, he'd come down.

We followed her to the bar.

"I don't drink much," she explained, "but this occasion calls for one."

Jack and I couldn't have agreed more, and in fact we couldn't wait for our order to arrive. Pleasant small talk masked our tension, as we waited for the drinks to arrive. Annilu kept staring at Jack, coming to terms with the baby she had mourned and the handsome man before her. She promised to keep from getting too emotional, but it was obviously a battle.

As it must have been for him when hearing my story, yet having no conscious memories of his own, Jack listened with curiosity as Annilu, in effect a stranger as I had been (though our blood connection did make us in some ways feel like we'd always known each other), explained how she'd never forgotten him and always wondered how he was. She told the story again, that we already knew, about how she had come to the decision to give him back, reassuring him that he was well loved and cared for.

She also wanted to set the record straight, after reading in the book that Rosemary wondered if he'd ever been outside much since when she got him he was so pale, that she used to take him for long walks in the stroller. She talked about what a good baby Jack had been, how he hardly ever cried, and how everyone loved him.

After the second round of drinks, more of the story came out. Not only had her husband been teased about his inability to father a child of his own, Annilu's mother, with whom she had a stormy relationship, refused to acknowledge Jack as her grandchild, since he was adopted. Jack and I both took a big gulp of our drinks at the same time, trying hard not to look shocked. By now, my mind was racing as I tried to imagine him growing up being shunned. My family hadn't rejected him when they insisted I give him up for adoption; they were more worried we both would be ostracized by society's sanctions against unwed motherhood. That Annilu's mother held the same scorn hit me hard. I felt badly for Annilu.

I tried to lighten the conversation by bringing up Jack's memory of standing in the crib and looking at a woman with long dark hair.

"Yes," she said. "Jack would never sit down in his crib. In fact, I had to finally put pillows around him so that, when his hands got sweaty enough and he finally let go of the railing and fell back, he wouldn't hurt himself."

Only part of me could listen to her story. The other part would have gone crazy thinking about what I had asked of my baby – to learn to survive in this world without me.

She told the story of how once, while she was very ill, he had to stay in the crib all day because she was too weak to lift him out. I imagined, as I listened, that that must have been after her husband left her and she was alone with no one to call for help, certainly not her mother. No wonder she didn't feel it was fair to the baby to bring him up alone.

She said she hadn't expected the nuns to ask her to keep the baby for a couple of extra days and had steeled herself for what she felt she had to do, but those extra days all she could do was cry.

"You just kept looking at me with such compassion, as if you understood everything," she told Jack.

That was Jack, and must have been a part of his soul. I'd often seen that same look of caring concern in his eyes.

By now, I was drained. I was sure Annilu was in some emotional turmoil as well. How deeply was Jack being affected, I wondered. But at least I could be there for him now.

"Why don't you have your husband come down," I suggested. "I'd love to meet him."

Annilu was so happy in her marriage and that must have made up for the difficult times. Soon, her husband joined us and I could see why. He was a kind and caring man, as open and honest as she was.

Finally, we said our goodbyes. As Jack and I walked out of the sumptuous lobby and out onto the busy street, I came to the conclusion that human beings were not wired to deal with such immensely complicated emotions. I felt like I was drowning.

"How are you?" I asked Jack.

"How are you?" he asked back.

"She's very nice."

"Yes."

But he looked shell-shocked, most disturbed by the fact that Annilu's mother wouldn't accept him. Rosemary's mother had been his rock and had always made him feel he was the most special of all her grandchildren. She'd meant everything to him.

Art was waiting for us at home. I was glad Jack had agreed to come for dinner. We needed time to process everything.

I woke up the next morning in the blackest hole, wondering how I could go on or if I even wanted to. Only twice before had I ever felt this way. The first time was sometime during the next night after my baby was born. I'd been able to feed him that day, and that evening Ray had snuck in to see us. I'd awakened then, already sitting bolt upright, wracked in sobs that had begun while I was still sleeping. I'd never felt so alone, so helpless, so unable to ask for help. The second time was after the Los Angeles morning show, when Jack and everyone left in one direction and I walked away by myself. Then I believed I would never have the relationship I'd hoped for, and that nobody really cared. This morning, I faced all that Jack had to go through at such a young age and couldn't bear it.

It wasn't that he was neglected. Annilu had obviously cared deeply for him. But, a month before, during the support group I facilitated, an adoptee had told of finding out how he'd had a hernia operation before he was a year old. He'd been in one foster care home, where he had thrived, and then was taken from that one to another, where notes said he'd stand in his crib for hours and cry. James had concluded the naval hernia was the result.

I had been devastated by James' story. Now, my mind was insanely connecting dots that weren't there. Jack had had a hernia operation when he was ten months. How could I live with myself after what I had done to him? My slim thread to sanity was the memory of having pulled myself out of the other two episodes.

I called Jack. "Jack, I am so sorry for all I have put you through."

"That's okay," he said.

Still, I could tell my words meant a lot to him. The dark cloud began to lift, and I found myself grateful for the fact that the cloud had come to show me what I had not wanted to face. As difficult and painful to unravel as my story had been, the complexity of Jack's path to reconciling his life was daunting.

I was holding onto one last secret. I hadn't told Dad about Jack's being gay. Where, with Brett and Kip, I had only worried about when would be the right time to tell them, with Dad I wasn't sure what his reaction would be. All I knew was that I could no longer keep such a vital part of who Jack was from him.

As I thought about what to say, the image of Jack's obvious physical discomfort before telling us kept popping into my mind, reminding me of something similar but I couldn't put my finger on it. Then it came to me.

One afternoon, while the boys were still little, I was talking with a neighbor about nothing really, when I became aware of an extreme discomfort I was holding in my body and vaporous feelings of shame seemed to be escaping into the air around us as we talked. Some part of me kept trying to beat back down the unnamed embarrassment, as if I were pushing back down a skirt that was billowing in the wind, revealing everything. I cut our conversation short when the feelings became uncontrollable and, when she left, sat down on the lawn chair by the pool completely dismantled.

Ron and I were living in an upscale neighborhood at the time, filled with successful people that had done everything right. As I sat in the sunshine, I couldn't come up with any reason for my sudden discomfort, though I was seeing that I'd often felt that way, only the severity this time made me aware of how unnatural the feeling was. The subliminal distress had disappeared after I went public with my story, so I hadn't thought of it until remembering Jack's obvious discomfort. Thinking of the immensity of the physical effort it takes to keep a secret and the soul destruction that ensues until we can own our truths was a revelation and a release.

I dialed Dad's number. I had underestimated him, only remembering who he had been - a product of his times while I was growing up. But he had allowed himself to change over the years.

"I wondered if he might be," he said. "Lots of people in the film industry seem to be."

That was it. His feelings for Jack hadn't changed at all. I hung up wishing they could somehow get to know each other better.

In August, I received a surprise phone call from Dylan. Except for his high school graduation, I hadn't seen him or the girls for a few years, while Jack and Anna worked things out. I'd reached out to Anna several times over the years but still got no response, so going down there didn't seem possible. I wondered if Anna was angry with me, maybe blaming me for all that had happened.

Not seeing the kids had been torture, but I also knew they were young adults now with busy lives. Most likely they didn't miss not seeing me. Now three years had passed by so quickly and Dylan was about to begin his senior year at James Madison University.

"Grandma, I have exciting news! Gina and I are engaged. Before we firm up the date of the wedding, I want to make sure you can be there. Would you be able to come August 24th next year?"

"No way would I miss your wedding, Dylan. Congratulations, and thank you so much for wanting me to be there. I love you."

"Love you, too, Grandma."

Searching ...

It was like no time had passed.

Chapter Nineteen

Most family functions have some dysfunctional element to them, but Dylan's wedding was loaded with possible uncomfortable scenarios. My main worry for myself was how Anna was going to receive my being there, having no idea where we stood with each other but suspecting the worst. I'd had several conversations with both Brett and Kip, who were particularly worried about how Anna's family would treat Jack since they had to be angry that Anna had been so hurt. I told them not to worry.

'Yeah right, Mom."

Ray and Jean would be there. They'd learned about the divorce and Jack coming out through Anna, when they ran into each other at a local bar. Jack hadn't found a way to be able to tell them. The wedding would be the first time Ray and Jean would see Jack, since learning everything, and they hadn't met Dan. Would Dan be at the wedding? Jean and I had long since made peace with each other, so that wouldn't be an issue. Rosemary had met Ray and Jean a couple of years before, when they all had dinner together. I hadn't seen Rosemary since leaving California. She was coming with her longtime partner, Marty, but would Jack's stepfather be there, too? Jack's brother, Mark, was coming but

David couldn't make it. All in all, Dylan's side of the family was quite complicated, to say the least.

Art and I had sat a little too long under the trees of Kip and DeAnna's home in Philadelphia, enjoying morning coffee in the fresh air, such a change from New York City. The tumultuous time after Bear Sterns had collapsed resulted in a great opportunity for Kip to do work in Philadelphia that he felt was worthwhile.

Their third child, a daughter they named Avery and my ninth grandchild, had been born two years before in Poughkeepsie, New York, while they were still living in the Catskills. I'd taken the train that ran along the Hudson River after getting an early morning call from Kip, and saw her an hour after she was born.

They were already down in the Outer Banks staying with Bud and Brenda, and would be coming just for the wedding, missing the rehearsal dinner. Brett and Jessica would miss it, too. Their plane was getting in too late. Cole and Reed were coming with them. It was incredible to contemplate that my whole family would be gathered under one roof for the first time ever.

Art and I were in Philadelphia to pick up one of Kip's cars for the drive down. Poor Art. He'd grown up on the Black Sea and in Moscow where few people drove, and now he had to be my co-pilot when he'd never driven a car. It had been ages since I'd taken a long road trip, since moving from San Francisco eleven years before, and I was nervous at first. The rehearsal dinner was at seven and we could make it if everything went well.

But everything didn't. I missed one major turnoff that took us pretty far out of the way. Now we were in trouble. But Art was a calming presence and kept my panic at bay, until we reached Virginia Beach – my personal Bermuda Triangle - at eight o'clock. I never could figure out what they were thinking naming the highways 64 and 264. Was I the only one who confused 264 with "to 64," when trying to follow directions?

We finally arrived at the restaurant at nine, a little frazzled. As soon as I walked in, Anna got up from her seat and rushed to greet me, giving me a huge hug and whispering in my ear how sorry she was that she never returned my calls. She'd been through a lot the past few years, she said. The pain had been overwhelming at times, but she was doing better now. I told her I completely understood. We stood by the door talking for ten minutes.

"You will always be my daughter-in-law," I promised her again.

When I finally turned toward the room, I was surprised to see such a large crowd for a rehearsal dinner. Anna was from a family of nine children and nearly everyone was there, sitting at one long table by the window, waving at me to come over. It had been so long since I'd seen any of them and I'd forgotten how much they meant to me from the days they'd grown to accept me as part of their lives. Her mother got up from her chair and gave me a big hug. So many memories of struggling to gain acceptance came flooding back all at once.

Dylan and Gina were sitting at another long table filled with friends and came over to see me.

"Grandma, you missed dinner. Do you want us to order anything for you?"

"That's sweet. No, we'll be fine, but we would sure like a drink!" As hungry as I should have been, I was too wound up to have an appetite.

Jack had been standing back, waiting for me to say hello to everyone before coming over. Art had already found him, the one person he knew in the room. When I asked Jack how he was doing, he admitted to some tension from Anna's family, but he was sure that wouldn't last. No, Dylan had invited Dan but he and Dan had decided the focus could potentially be on the two of them, instead of Dylan and Gina, so Dan was staying home.

However, Dan was going to come by the hotel, where everyone was staying, after the wedding reception. I thought that was brave.

I scanned the room for Ray and Jean but they had already left. Rosemary and her partner were seated at a long table in the center along with Mark, Mia, Asia and Tess. I introduced Art to everyone then took the seat next to Rosemary. I was curious about her reaction to Jack's coming out. After a few minutes of small talk, I asked.

"I just don't know why he felt he couldn't confide in me," she said. "One of my closest friends was gay and Jack knew him, so he had to know I'd be accepting."

But she had never suspected he might be gay. "The girls loved Jack," she said. "He had lots of girlfriends calling him all the time."

I wanted to tell her about meeting Annilu, but I knew from Jack that she wasn't interested, so we went on to more small talk, catching up on all we'd been doing over the years.

The room was emptying, as it was getting late. Art and I were staying at Jack's place and Jack was staying at Dan's.

"Just follow me," he said, as Asia got into the car with him.

Oh, great. Memories of trying to follow him on the LA freeways, heading to one birthday party or another as he weaved through traffic, didn't give me any confidence as we headed back into the vortex of Virginia Beach. With Art's help keeping me calm, I stuck to Jack's bumper like glue and we made it without any traumas.

We pulled up under the trees in front of a sprawling house, where Jack was renting a room.

"You're going to love it," he said, as he led the way down a path around the side of the house. "There's a marsh in the back that's so peaceful."

In the darkness, I could barely make out the marsh, but I could feel its calming presence. When he switched on the light, I could see that the same feeling he'd created in all his other homes, that was so similar to my homes, was here, too. I felt right at home.

Completely done in by the day, Art stretched out on the bed, while Jack, Asia and I sat together in the soft glow of the lamp and talked. How had the little girl, who could quietly imitate all the Disney characters and felt like everything spoke to her, including her cough drops, grown up so fast? Though I knew nothing could have been done differently, I still found myself wishing for those missing years back and a chance to be a true Grandmother.

After they left, I went outside and sat on the steps of the deck by the edge of the marsh, watching the fireflies and listening to all the night sounds, feeling the magic of the place, feeling so grateful for the long journey toward healing we'd all undertaken, no matter the twists and turns and stumbles along the way.

The marsh was bustling with the activity of its birds, insects and butterflies the next morning, as Art and I drank coffee on the deck. Jack stopped by to see how we were doing. He'd be busy the rest of the day helping Dylan as his best man. Brett called and we made arrangements to get together and explore the Norfolk shipyard. It was a beautiful, sunny day.

As we drove to meet Brett and his family, I realized I actually knew where I was going, as the streets were becoming familiar and the vortex I always accused the area of having seemed to disappear. But I was to soon find that the curse or vortex was merely lying low, waiting until the perfect moment to screw everything up.

After our tour of the shipyard and lunch at Hooters, we went back to Jack's to dress for the five o'clock wedding. Brett, Jessica, Cole, Reed, Art and I, all piled into Kip's car. Brett was driving.

"Mom, how long have you been running on empty?"

What! As it turned out, I'd been looking at the wrong symbol on the dashboard, as I marveled at the great mileage cars were getting these days. While we stopped to get gas, Jessica Googled directions on her IPhone, but I reassured them I knew exactly how to get there. And I did. But, they trusted their phone, instead of me, especially after seeing how I didn't even know the tank was empty, and off we went – back into the vortex with one misspelling of a street name.

Over an hour later we found the church, which had been only fifteen minutes away. Dylan and Gina were in the vestibule talking with guests, when we arrived. "Grandma, you missed the wedding!"

"Dylan, I can't believe it," I said, giving them a big hug. "I'm so sorry."

The photographer appeared and asked that everyone come back in the church for pictures. Kip and DeAnna greeted us, shaking their heads in disbelief that we'd only just arrived, then told us about being discovered changing into their clothes for the wedding in the parking lot, when they thought they were hidden from view. We all had a good laugh and I got all the details of the ceremony.

Opposite from Jack and Anna's wedding twenty-one years before, when I had hung around like a forlorn puppy hoping to be included in a wedding picture, Dylan and Gina wanted every possible combination of family recorded. The most touching for me was the one with the bride and groom standing with Jack, Rosemary, Ray, Jean and me. As we all stood together posing for the picture, I was in awe of all the emotional struggles we each had overcome to be together like this.

Then I noticed Kip watching us from the back of the church with a happy, knowing smile. The significance of the moment was not lost on him.

One last hurdle. The reception was being held at Little Creek Naval Base. Back out into the void. But everyone was making certain we understood the exact directions this time. We found the naval base without incident. When Art realized where we were, he got a bit unnerved, having grown up during the Soviet times. What if they knew a Russian was on their naval base? He couldn't believe that only one female naval guard, wearing heavy eye shadow and a pound of mascara, protected the gate to the base. We joked about being characters in a spy novel, as we made our way to the officers' club for the reception, the sky above us a gorgeous orange in the sunset.

Inside, screens were set up around the room scrolling through hundreds of pictures of both Dylan and Gina's lives, from the time they were babies through the whole time they'd dated since first meeting in eighth grade, when they were never apart again. Some were pictures I'd taken of Dylan when he was little that I loved seeing again. As I kept watching, I began to worry that we weren't included, when suddenly there was a picture of Brett and then Kip and then me. Living so far a part, it had been difficult to keep connected, but I was thrilled we were still considered part of the family after all.

Seeing us absorbed by the photos, Anna came over to our table with Mia and told of the fun they had remembering the old days, as they were selecting the pictures.

"Mia, you wouldn't remember this, but your Uncle Brett never let your feet touch the ground when you were little," Anna told her.

At one point, Jack came over and joked about the time it took to decide who sat where and with whom and at what table, so that everything was politically correct on Dylan's side of the room. He confessed to Art and I that he hadn't decided what to say for his toast as Dylan's best man. He ran a joke about marriage by us, that Rosemary's partner, Marty, had suggested. Rarely had I ever stepped into a parental role with Jack, but I had to tell him the joke might not set the right tone, that he had to do better. He promised to think about it some more.

The dance floor was already packed and all my grandchildren were on it, dancing away. I wanted so much to ask the photographer to take a picture of me with my sons, daughters-in-law and all nine grandchildren. When would such an opportunity ever happen again? But I felt it would be too disruptive to gather all of us together and the commotion would take too much attention away from the bride and groom. Besides, this was a memory I could never forget.

But as I let go of the idea, I watched as Brett and Kip walked up to Jack, standing on either side of him in much the same way they protected Dylan at Jack and Anna's wedding. I knew from a few discussions over the past couple of days that they were concerned for him. That picture I had to have, so I found the photographer and asked that she take that one.

I tried to connect with everyone, not knowing when we would all be together again. I particularly sought out Mark. So many questions about how my coming into their lives had affected him still lingered after his revelations during the interview for *Sacred Connections*. He was a young man with a great deal of depth and planned to be a writer. That time in his life had greatly impacted him, he reiterated, especially the shock of learning that Jack was not his brother by blood and his resulting fears that we might take Jack away to live with us.

"Someday, I will write about it all," he promised. "It will be quite a book."

I floundered in my attempt at finding the magic words that would make it finally all right. "I hope you do write that book," I said. "I want to read it."

We were all asked to take our seats again. After the ritual cutting of the cake, it was time for the toasts. Jack stood up. Art and I looked at each other worried. But Jack made a beautiful speech, full of good wishes for Dylan and Gina. He thanked Gina's family and then turned to Dylan's side of the room and thanked us all, naming all five different surnames that had been a part of his life.

"We are all united," he said, "as one *immediate* family."

I couldn't have been more proud of him for the remarkable grace with which he had dealt with such a complicated life.

The toasts over and as we waited for Gina and Dylan to change for their honeymoon, Art and I walked over to Ray and Jean to say goodbye. Ray was beaming with pride. He and Jack had forged a deeply caring relationship over the years that meant a great deal to both of them.

"Next time ya'll are down here," Jean said, "you be sure to stay with us." She meant it, and I could only marvel at her courage and how far we'd come.

As we stood silently together taking in the whole scene, she turned to Ray and me and remarked, "You know, don't you, none of us would be here if it weren't for the two of you."

Searching …

Appendix

The following organizations help birth parents, adoptees and adoptive parents wishing to search for one another. These are the major organizations, but by no means all. Many more search and support organizations can be found on the Internet.

INTERNATIONAL SOUNDEX REUNION REGISTRY
www.isrr.org

CONCERNED UNITED BIRTH PARENTS
www.cubirthparents.org

AMERICAN ADOPTION CONGRESS
www.americanadoptioncongress.org

ADOPTEES LIBERTY MOVEMENT ASSOCIATION
http://www.almasociety.org

BASTARD NATION
www.bastards.org

ORIGINS CANADA
www.originscanada.org

Searching …

Searching ...

Searching …

Made in the USA
Columbia, SC
20 January 2023

10742915R00192